Understanding
Korean
Literature

NEW STUDIES IN ASIAN CULTURE

Understanding Korean Literature

Kim Hunggyu

Translated by Robert J. Fouser

An East Gate Book

M.E. Sharpe
Armonk, New York
London, England

An East Gate Book

Copyright © 1997 by M. E. Sharpe, Inc.

Library of Congress Cataloging-in-Publication Data

Kim, Hŭnggyu, 1948–
[Han 'guk, munhak ŭi ihae. English]
Understanding Korean literature / Kim Hunggyu /
translated by Robert J. Fouser.
p.   cm.
ISBN 1-56324-773-9 (cloth : alk. paper). — ISBN 1-56324-774-7 (paper : alk. paper)
1. Korean literature—History and criticism.
I. Fouser, Robert.
II. Title.
PL955.K4913   1997
895.7′09—dc21
97-11941
CIP

Printed in the United States of America

The paper used in this publication meets the minimum requirements of the
American National Standard for Information Sciences—
Permanence of Paper for Printed Library Materials,
ANSI Z 39.48-1984.

⊗

BM (c)   10   9   8   7   6   5   4   3   2   1
BM (p)   10   9   8   7   6   5   4   3   2   1

Contents

Translator's Preface

This project began with a conversation I had with Lee Hyeong-dae, one of Professor Kim Hunggyu's Ph.D. students, in Seoul in August of 1993. I mentioned that Professor Kim's *Hanguk munhak ŭi ihae* (Understanding Korean Literature) would be of great help to foreigners interested in learning about Korean literature, as it had helped me gain a clearer understanding of Korean literature. Several weeks later, I met Professor Kim, who kindly agreed to let me translate his book.

Since its publication in 1986, *Understanding Korean Literature* has been reprinted several times, and it is widely used as a textbook in university courses. It appeals as well to general readers because it covers areas typically ignored in such introductory studies: Korean literary criticism and the history of printing and transmission of literary works in the nation. As a scholar of traditional Korean poetry, Professor Kim has also given a great deal of attention to genres of Korean literature that are often mentioned only in passing, and he adds a fifth category, "mixed genres," to the standard four-genre classification of Korean literature, which has caused considerable debate in scholarly circles.

Many important Korean literary works are available in English translations, but no scholarly work of Korean literary criticism has been translated into English. As interest in Korean literature and the number of students learning Korean increase, the dearth of information on Korean literature in English becomes even more glaring. This translation of *Understanding Korean Literature* helps to fill the void. It is, however, only a beginning, and I hope that its publication will stimulate the writing and translation of a variety of reference materials in English and other languages.

I have followed Professor Kim's original closely, omitting and embellishing as little as possible. Where possible, I have added dates to give readers more background information. To make the text easier to follow, I placed all original Korean titles in parentheses after the English translation of titles. I translated most titles into English because romanized Korean is difficult to read and remember. I left titles which make use of a proper noun or which do not have an English equivalent in Korean. Titles of major historical writings in the East Asia tradition were taken from the two-volume *Sourcebook on Korean Civilization,* edited by Peter Lee, and *A New History of Korea* by Ki-baik Lee, translated by Edward Wagner. Taking Professor Kim's love of originality to heart, I decided to provide new translations of the well-known literary examples; many of the literary examples, however, appear in English for the first time. I provided romanization of poems only in sections of the book relating to poetic meter and form, using the slashes to indicate segments of poetic meter, as Professor Kim did in the original.

Romanization of Korean presents any translator with problems. I decided to follow the modified version of the McCune-Reischauer system used in the *Korea Journal,* which provides a more accurate indication of the pronunciation of such words as *shilhak,* romanized awkwardly as *sirhak* in McCune-Reischauer. I have eliminated the apostrophe in *han'gŭl* and the hyphen between the two elements in Korean given names, except in cases where persons write their names with a hyphen; for passages written in older forms of Korean (mainly poems), I used an "ă" for the *arae a,* and romanized the passages as given in the original. I have made these modifications in the interest of accuracy and simplicity. For Chinese, I used pinyin throughout; for Japanese I followed Kenkyusha's *New Japanese–English Dictionary.*

To help readers who are familiar with Chinese characters, I have included a glossary at the end of the book that gives titles of literary works in the original *hangŭl* and Chinese characters, with romanization and English translations. Professor Kim included a long bibliography of Korean works on topics presented in the book; I have replaced this with a select bibliography of germane works in English and other Western languages.

Translating a detailed book like *Understanding Korean Literature* is not an easy task, but it would have been impossible without the many people who helped me. My foremost thanks goes to Professor Kim for trusting me and encouraging me, and to Mr. Lee Hyeong-dae and Mr. Kweon Soon-hoi for sharing their love of Korean literature with me in our many conversations. I would also like to thank Ms. Connie Glavin, Mr. Drayton Hamilton, Ms. Mary Mooney, Mr. Ken Kaliher, and

Mr. Duane Vorhees for their comments and encouragement in the early stages of this project. As the project progressed, Mr. Kim Jun-heon helped a great deal in interpreting difficult literary examples. I would to thank Mr. Seok Sung-gyun for providing the maps. I am deeply indebted to Ms. Jung Eun Kim and Ms. Beth Fouser for their copious corrections and comments on the final draft. Without them, the project would have fallen behind schedule. I am deeply thankful to the Korean Culture and Arts Foundation for awarding me a translation grant for this project. I would also like to thank Mr. Douglas Merwin of M.E. Sharpe, Inc., for his patience, and Mr. Park Maeng-ho, president of Minŭmsa Publishing Company, for granting copyright permission.

In the course of this work, I thought of the many Korean people who instilled in me a passion for Korean culture, which has greatly enriched my life. I hope that this translation stands as a token, however small, of my appreciation.

Robert J. Fouser
Kyoto, August 1996

Author's Preface

As far as possible, this book is a general introduction to Korean literature for a broad readership.

Although there has been rapid progress in the field since the late 1960s, most introductions to Korean literature, have not reflected the results of recent research and have become somewhat out of date; I was motivated to write a new introduction to bridge this gap. I also wanted to write a book that dealt with such issues as the cultural and social context of literature as a linguistic system, the need to distinguish what we know from what we need to know, the relationship between traditional and modern literature, the relationship between past events and contemporary meaning, the need for balance between detail and the big picture that goes beyond textbook descriptions, and the need for a balanced introduction to the entire range of Korean literature. Despite these goals, the manuscript that I sent to the publisher did fulfill my original expectations. I hope, however, that criticism of the weak points of this book will lead to a deeper understanding of Korean literature.

I am indebted to the many researchers from whose hard work this book benefited, but I have chosen not to cite their works in footnotes because I wanted to make the book accessible to the widest possible readership. If I had included such note citations, the length of the book would have been increased by about one third. By dispensing with footnotes, I was able to make the book shorter and cheaper, in keeping with my goal of reaching out to a broad readership. To make up for the lack of citations, I have added an appendix containing a detailed list of references that readers may use to explore particular areas of interest on their own.

Finally, I would like to thank my students and colleagues at Korea University and all of the members of the Minŭmsa Publishing Company for their interest in and support of this project. In the end, this book is as much theirs as it is mine.

Kim Hunggyu
Pukkulli, Seoul, March 1986

Illustrations and Maps

Illustrations

Maps

Understanding
Korean
Literature

1

Introduction

Korea is a country with a rich literary tradition, and literature plays an important role in Korean society. More than 6,000 collections of writings by individual writers from the thirteenth to the nineteenth centuries are extant, despite numerous wars and natural disasters. Korea has a rich oral tradition of legends and folk songs. Despite the growth of film and television in contemporary Korea, most Koreans have a strong interest in literature. For example, Korea leads the world in the per capita publication of books of poetry. An awareness of this is important if we are to have a balanced understanding of the value of Korean literature, as well as of the Korean people and culture.

There are two main reasons for the great body of literary works and the enthusiasm for literature on the part of the Korean people. The first is the original Siberian culture, reflected in geometric patterns on earthenware, that the people who moved from northeast Siberia into Manchuria and the Korean Peninsula brought with them in ancient times. These ethnic groups, who became the Korean people, had a culture distinct from the Chinese culture of the time, as shown by their love of song and dance. According to ancient Chinese records, Koreans gathered together to dance and sing for days on end in ceremonies dedicated to the gods who protected the kingdom and provided good harvests. These same records also show that Chinese visitors were surprised by how much the people of Koguryŏ and Chinhan enjoyed music and dance in everyday life. Although there is no such thing as a permanent national character, the importance of music and dance in the lives of Korean people today can be traced to these ancient traditions.

The second reason is the strong Confucian tradition that prevailed in Korea from the founding of the Koryŏ Dynasty in the tenth century to the end of the Chosŏn Dynasty in the nineteenth century. This tradition valued literary culture over all other forms of cultural activity. Except for the roughly seventy years of military rule from 1170 to the middle of the thirteenth century, Korea was governed for ten centuries by Confucian literati. To train and select literati for public office, educators placed emphasis on literary training based on the study of Confucian classics and especially the composition of prose and poetry. This type of education was particularly dominant during the Chosŏn period, which lasted from the fourteenth to the nineteenth century. Unlike Europe and Japan, which were ruled by knights and samurai, respectively, Korea was ruled by scholars and writers, who used literature to establish and maintain their dominance in society. This tradition continues to exist today, because most Korean writers and poets feel a special sense of duty to uphold social justice, rather than viewing themselves as autonomous artists. The importance of literature and of writers in resisting Japanese imperialism during the first half of the twentieth century and in opposing military dictatorship in the 1970s and 1980s reflects this sense of duty.

These factors not only explain the importance of literature in Korea but also form a useful paradigm for understanding its contrasting aspects.

Korean literature has two main characteristics: emotional exuberance and intellectual self-control. The former comes from the shamanistic energy rooted in Siberia, whereas the latter comes from the tradition of Confucian rationalism. Depending on the times, these characteristics merge or conflict with each other. The overall conflict, compromise, and equilibrium between these two characteristics remains central to Korean literature today.

The unity forged by the spatial and temporal meeting of diverse cultural factors that make up Korean literature is evident in the following example. Contrary to some prevailing foreign views, Korean literature is not an offshoot of Chinese literature, and, of course, it differs from Japanese literature. Korea transmitted many cultural achievements to Japan from ancient times to the nineteenth century. Although it has much in common with China and Japan, Korea has a unique culture that developed through history as an independent state with its own social structure and way of life. This unique culture is also reflected in literature.

As Cho Chihun argued in his *Introduction to the History of Korean Culture* (Hanguk munhwasa sasŏl, Cho Chihun chŏnjip 6, 1973), Korean culture developed from a Siberian cultural base, borrowing its writing system and Confucianism from China, and Buddhism from India. With its Siberian roots, Korean culture has fundamentally different origins from Chinese culture and differs sharply from Japanese

Page from *Correct Sounds to Instruct the People* **(***Hunmin chŏngŭm***)**

culture, which has been influenced by the culture of the Pacific islands. Linguistically, the Korean language, a member of the Altaic family of languages, is totally unrelated to the Chinese language, which belongs to the Sino-Tibetan family. In the first half of the fifteenth century, King Sejong and the scholars he assembled created a phonetic writing system known as *hangŭl*. This system differs greatly from meaning-based Chinese characters. Hangŭl also differs significantly from the Japanese syllabic system of writing known as *kana,* because each hangŭl letter represents a distinct phonetic element rather than a sylla-ble composed of set sounds. How Korean literature interacted with common literary traditions in East Asia while developing its own char-acter is an interesting theme in the study of its history.

Another important topic of research is the influence of Western culture on East Asian traditions in Korean literature. China came into contact with Western culture relatively early, with the Silk Road, and Japan had limited contact with the West through trade with the Netherlands beginning in the seventeenth century. Korea, however, remained closed to the outside world, except for relations with neighboring China and Japan, until the end of the nineteenth century. With the strengthening of the closed-door policy in the late nineteenth century, Korean became known as the "Hermit Kingdom." Thus, when Korea was forced to open itself to the outside world at the end of the nineteenth century, the country experienced a shock far greater than did China or Japan. Although the term "literary revolution" was used in the May 4 Movement in China, the revolutionary change in Korean literature at the beginning of the twentieth century was much more sudden.

In the course of these drastic changes, traditional literary forms, structures, and aesthetic standards collapsed rapidly. New literary stimulation coming from the West, Russia, and Japan contributed to the development of a new literature. However, despite this enthusiasm and interest, Korean literary traditions remained influential. Korean literature in the twentieth century has been dominated by a desire to break away from the past on the one hand and, on the other, the need to establish itself in the face of strong foreign influences as a legitimate national literature rooted in Korean culture.

Amid the interaction between these two conflicting trends, Korean literature since the early years of the twentieth century has been searching for a new balance between literary imagination and sensibility. The historical movement to create a new paradigm in Korean literature based on long tradition and change is another important theme of research on the subject.

The common view that it is possible to understand the folkways, worldview, aesthetic sense, and emotional outlook of a group of people through the literature they create and develop is particularly applicable to Korean literature. The social energy of the literary outpouring that encompasses the ancient tradition of poetry and song, the respect for literature during the Koryŏ and Chosŏn periods, and severe conflicts since the nineteenth century reveal much about the Korean people past and present. Thus, the study of Korean literature becomes a rewarding journey on which we discover the dreams and the fears, the glories and the defeats, and the joys and the sorrows of the Korean people through the ages.

2

The Extent of Korean Literature

Before attempting to understand the unique characteristics and overall outline of Korean literature, we need to define its extent geographically and through time. By "Korean" literature we refer to the entirety of literature written by ethnic Koreans, from ancient times to the present. Contemporary Korea is the present-day result of past periods of expansion and contraction, division and unification; any overall history of Korean literature must take into account this history of evolution and change. In addition, we need to consider the place of the major traditional types of Korean literature, which are rooted in the social structure and cultural background of Korean society before the nineteenth century, and each of which differed in its mode of expression and transmission: oral literature, vernacular literature in hangŭl, the Korean alphabet, and literature in classical Chinese. We also need to have a basic understanding of the defining characteristics of these types of literature, as well as of the relationship among them.

There is little disagreement on the geographical extent of Korean literature: Korean literature can be defined broadly as the entire corpus of literature developed by Koreans in places where they have lived throughout history. This definition does, however, leave us with the issue of how to treat the literature of Koreans living abroad, and the geographical and cultural borders of Korean literature before the rise of the three kingdoms of Koguryŏ, Paekche, and Shilla. Whereas the literature of many nations reflects a mixture of ethnic groups, languages, and cultures, the literature of Korea is closely linked to the history and culture of the Korean people. The first stage in the development of Korean literature is the period from ancient times to the establishment of a proto-Korean state, during which various ethnic groups moved east and south from central Asia into Manchuria and then into the Korean Peninsula. As a Korean people began to emerge from the gradual integration of ethnic groups, the literature of those groups in time became what we could call "Korean literature." It then developed further throughout Korean history: the Three Kingdoms, Koguryŏ (37 B.C. to A.D. 668), Paekche (18 B.C. to A.D. 660), Shilla (57 B.C. to A.D. 668); the era of the Unified Shilla Dynasty in the South (A.D. 668–935) and Palhae in the North (A.D. 698–926); the Koryŏ Dynasty (918–1392); the Chosŏn Dynasty (1392–1910); and the modern and contemporary eras. Ethnic Koreans have also lived outside Korea throughout history; their literature should be included on the fringes of the history of Korean literature, because their cultural roots are in Korea.

In order to map the various types of literature, which are defined by their mode of expression and transmission, in the overall context of Korean literature, we first need to consider the complex cultural history of Korea. Among the three main types—oral literature, vernacular literature in hangŭl, and literature in classical Chinese—oral literature and literature in classical Chinese have been the subject of much controversy in Korean literary criticism and historiography.

Oral Literature

Oral tradition is clearly part of Korean culture; nevertheless, doubts about its legitimacy as "literature" have arisen. The argument that the oral tales and stories that have been passed down to us from the formative eras of Korean culture are not a legitimate literary form is based on the Korean etymology of the word *literature,* which derives from the concepts of "letters," or "that which is recorded in writing." Thus it is argued that literature is basically written text. Accordingly, such tales and stories are excluded from the main body of Korean literature and are classified instead as "protoliterary linguistic structures," or "pseudoliterature."

In the end, however, this argument fails to be persuasive. Just as spoken and written forms of expression are subcategories of language, so literature is an art developed through the use of language, regardless of whether it is written or oral. For this reason, literature in its various forms has continued to develop throughout human history. If it were logical to limit the field of literature to "works of art in writing" throughout all historical eras, then we would simply not be able to classify oral lore as literature. Hence, using the adjective *oral* to qualify *literature* would be impossible. If we were to consider only written literature as such, then we would be asserting that there had been no literature before the development of written language. Furthermore, we would be arguing that the common people in most societies, who remained illiterate well after the development of writing, were not participants in the creation of literature. This argument would also apply to various ethnolinguistic groups that did not develop a written language. Needless to say, this argument fails, because it denies the basic human need for aesthetic expression through "literature." To do so—on the basis of little more than a prejudice for the modern and the contemporary—would be to diminish the vast amount of literary creation that has evolved and gained inspiration from oral transmission since the beginning of human civilization.

Of course, we cannot deny that important differences in the function and characteristics of literature have arisen because of the method of transmission. The difference between oral and written literature is not only limited to the superficial issue of whether it is written down or not; rather, it has a direct bearing on the great diversity of forms of literary creation. Moreover, making a distinction between historical facts and fiction is difficult because of the nature of the transmission of oral literature. We have only scattered fragments of evidence, found in documents or songs and tales that have come down to us from the distant past, as primary sources. For this reason, we cannot, however, conclude that oral literature is not literature, or that it should be treated as supplementary material in the study of written literature. Oral literature is of critical importance in a comprehensive historical study of not only Korean literature but of any literature.

Problems with the Inclusion of Literature in Classical Chinese

The inclusion of literature written in classical Chinese within the body of Korean literature has been a controversial cultural issue, because classical Chinese represents a foreign language. Those who argue against the inclusion of this literature base their arguments on the non-Korean origin of Chinese characters: Korean literature is vernacular literature written in hangŭl that deals with the experiences, sensibilities, and thoughts of the Korean people; therefore, literature that makes use of Chinese characters and Chinese literary forms cannot be considered Korean literature. This argument first appeared in the second decade of the twentieth century and was firmly established as orthodoxy by the end of the 1920s (Yi Kwangsu, *Concepts of Korean Literature* [Chosŏn munhak ŭi kaenyŏm], 1929). This thinking contin-

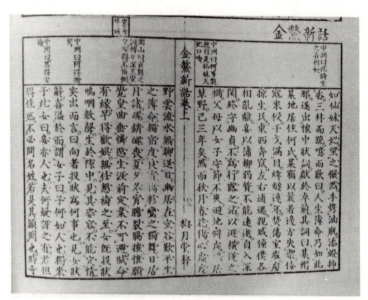

Page from *Tales of Kŭmo* (Kŭmo shinhwa), written in classical Chinese

ued to exert a strong influence on the definition of Korean literature well into the 1950s.

Before discussing the validity of this argument, we need to understand the historical background of the early twentieth century. The Confucian ideology that had served to legitimize the rule of the Chosŏn kings was unable to respond to the upheavals of the late nineteenth and early twentieth centuries, when Korea came under Japanese colonial rule. Confucian heritage was criticized in Korea simply because the Chosŏn Dynasty, which had based its legitimacy on Confucian philosophy, collapsed at the end of the nineteenth century. Under the oppression of Japanese colonial rule, the attempt to assert Korean cultural identity and pride was built on the premise that only literature written in hangŭl should be considered real Korean literature. The traditional belief that literature in classical Chinese was more elegant and prestigious lost its legitimacy amid the dramatic changes in Korean society in the early twentieth century. Thus the argument that literature written in hangŭl should define the extent of Korean literature became the established orthodoxy during this period.

Though we cannot overlook the grave historical circumstances that gave rise to this idea, the elimination of literature written in classical

Chinese reflected a narrow-minded and moralistic analysis of Korean cultural and literary history. Even if we concede that language is the most important aspect of literature, this importance is related to the cultural context of the period and should be understood in this light. In addition, Chinese characters and classical Chinese literary forms are not exclusively "Chinese," as some extremists on this issue have argued.

Here we need to examine the importance of classical Chinese as a common written language in East Asia (China, Korea, Japan, Vietnam, and the Ryūkyū Islands), which lasted well into the nineteenth century. Chinese characters are obviously Chinese in origin, but they do not necessarily reflect the spoken forms of the Chinese language. The term *Chinese characters* refers to the character-based writing system that developed in China from the Qin Dynasty (221–206 B.C.) to the Han Dynasty (206 B.C.–A.D. 250). Classical Chinese was a common written language in East Asia as Latin was in Europe in the Middle Ages, or classical Arabic was in the Arab world. Having become separated from the spoken language in China, classical Chinese spread to Korea, Japan, and Vietnam, where it coexisted with the indigenous languages of each nation. In these three nations, classical Chinese became dominant as the language of the elite. The ruling elite in Korea became highly proficient in classical Chinese because of the strong centralized bureaucracy and the Confucian culture that developed from the Koryŏ Dynasty to the Chosŏn Dynasty. Historical records and official documents as well as private correspondence and written literature activity were all in classical Chinese. A similar phenomenon occurred in Vietnam and Japan, the only difference being the degree to which the social structure in each nation fostered the development of an aristocratic–bureaucratic culture. As a result, literature in classical Chinese functioned as a common language in these two other nations as well. This allowed not only for the expression of diverse experiences and cultures in each nation, but also for the absorption of important indigenous cultural traditions. This wealth of history and literature should not be excluded simply because the orthography and literary forms were borrowed from another language. In the context of common literary languages, and in comparison to the role of Latin as a literary language in Europe, literature in classical Chinese was receptive to local cultural traditions in the various East Asian nations. Thus the development of cultural uniqueness and diversity of literature in classical Chinese should be recognized.

Nobody discussing Europe would argue that Latin literature in each nation was Roman or Italian literature. Despite the strong influence of Latin literature, there is no reason to exclude it from the historical experience and culture of a particular nation simply because it was written in Latin. The difference between Europe and East Asia is that the Roman Empire collapsed and modern Italy is a relatively new political entity, whereas China has a history of relatively unbroken unity and continues to exert a strong influence over the entire East Asian region. Thus, rather than looking at the common culture in East Asia in its historical context, we tend to view things from the vantage point of contemporary cultural and political boundaries. It is not logical, however, to discuss cultural developments that occurred before the creation of the modern nation states from the perspective of these later geographical boundaries.

Another problem with attempting to exclude literature written in classical Chinese from the discussion of Korean literature is that it then becomes impossible to explain the relationship of interior and exterior elements in the development of Korean literature. Furthermore, the vast majority of literature produced up to the end of the nineteenth century would have to be disregarded. The remaining works written in hangŭl would be sufficient to analyze from a literary point of view, but the vast body of works in classical Chinese is a critically important part of the literature that was created in a particular historical era. Throughout Korean history, many people have written literature in classical Chinese, and this literature is closely related to the development of conflict, contact, and influence among the various levels of culture and types of literature. In understanding the "pastoral poetry" of the sixteenth century, for example, we need to investigate the important relationship between poetry in classical Chinese and the neo-Confucian philosophy of the aristocratic *yangban* class of scholar–officials who created most of this genre of poetry. In understanding the development of narrative literature at the end of the Chosŏn dynasty, we need to consider carefully the varied influences among the "gossipy tales" (*yadam*), biographical tales (*chŏn*), and novels in classical Chinese.

Arguments in Favor of Including Literature in Classical Chinese

As research on Korean literature gained strength and direction after the country's liberation from Japanese rule in 1945, the argument in favor

Hyangga, "Song of Tuṣita Heaven" (Tosol ka)

of including literature in classical Chinese became more persuasive. Growing out of the commonly held belief of the 1940s and 1950s that Korean literature was vernacular literature written in hangŭl, the problem of literature in classical Chinese was solved by placing it on the periphery of Korean literature. As a result, literature in hangŭl was described as "true Korean," "pure Korean," or "Korean in the narrow sense," whereas that which included, peripherally, literature in classical Chinese was called "quasi-Korean," "wide Korean," or "Korean in the broadest sense." This analytical framework created a duality in defining Korean literature.

Though this analysis allows the extent of Korean literature to be expanded, it leaves us with the question of which works and genres of literature in classical Chinese can be included. In his *History of Korean Literature* (Kungmunhak sa), published in 1949, Cho Yunje describes literature in hangŭl as "pure Korean literature" and that in classical

Chinese as "part of Korean literature in the broadest sense." Examining major trends in Korean literature, he argued that it was appropriate to include novels and short stories in classical Chinese as "pure Korean literature," because these—which he considered important in the development of "pure Korean literature"—were written in classical Chinese. Yi Pyŏnggi and Paek Ch'ŏl categorized literature in classical Chinese according to content, arguing that it should be used as supplementary material in researching the history of literature in hangŭl. They published a separate history of Korean literature in classical Chinese as an appendix to their *Complete History of Korean Literature* (Kungmunhak chŏnsa) in 1957. Chang Tŏksun argued for greater inclusion of literature in classical Chinese in his *An Introduction to Korean Literature* (Kungmunhak t'ongnon) in 1960. Literature written before the creation of hangŭl was considered Korean literature regardless of whether it was written in *hyangch'al,* a phonetic and semantic system for transcribing vernacular Korean into Chinese characters, or in classical Chinese. Literature written after the creation of hangŭl was considered Korean literature only if it was written in hangŭl, but literature in classical Chinese of "Korean literary value" was placed in the category of "broad Korean literature."

These compromising theories have more to offer than the narrower definition of Korean literature as literature written only in hangŭl, although the basis and legitimacy of these theories remains questionable. First, we have to determine what criteria were used to decide which works or genres of literature in classical Chinese are of "Korean literary value." As is evident from the brief discussion above, various literary scholars define Korean literature in different ways, and there are serious problems in making a practical and theoretical distinction between the various competing theories. In addition, to include only myths and novels written in classical Chinese in Korean literature would reflect a lack of judgment because classical Chinese poetry and philosophy influenced the literary sensibilities of the yangban who produced most of the poetry in hangŭl. A qualitative distinction between literature in classical Chinese written before and after the creation of hangŭl in 1446 is understandable, but conditions for dramatic social and cultural change did not come into existence immediately after the development of hangŭl, and thus this distinction ignores historical evidence and is useful only as a method of classification. Though all research in the humanities is subjective, research on works that have been judged to have "Korean literary value" is narrow; it does not constitute an objective and broad-based approach to researching literature in classical Chinese.

We cannot know the value of something unless we try to understand it, and we cannot embrace something before we know its value. Though it may be possible to overcome the limitations of this circular reasoning, a further problem is whether it is possible to exclude other genres of literature in classical Chinese from Korean literature. Describing the multifaceted relationship among the diverse forms and genres of Korean literature is a further difficulty. Even if we exclude those types of literature that have little literary value, these works are related to the mainstream of traditional Korean literature in meaning and function, and coexisted both in harmony and in confrontation with other types of literature. Disregarding these factors prevents us from developing a full understanding of the other types of Korean literature. In the case of Pak Chiwŏn (1737–1805), for example, it is difficult to discuss works like "Tale of Yangban Hŏ" (Hŏ saeng chŏn), "A Tiger's Rebuke" (Hojil), and "Tale of a Yangban" (Yangban chŏn) in isolation from the *Rehe Diary* (Yŏlha ilgi) or other critical works that discuss the philosophy of literature at that time. In addition, it is possible to dig deeper into Pak's literature by elucidating the complex internal conflicts in Confucian philosophy and in literature in classical Chinese.

From the above discussion, we can conclude that works in classical Chinese written by Koreans should be included in Korean literature on an equal basis with those written in hangŭl. Arguments in favor of including literature in classical Chinese gathered force from the late 1950s as research on Korean literature progressed. The inclusion of literature in classical Chinese had become widely accepted by the 1970s and has become the basis of a growing body of important research in this area.

Outline of Korean Literature

Given the above discussions, Korean literature can be defined as the entire body of literature expressing the experience, thought, and imagination of the ethnic Korean people throughout the development of Korean culture and ways of life. Whatever the means of expression, whether oral or written, in hyangch'al, classical Chinese, or hangŭl, and whatever historical era of the last two thousand years produced it, all of this should be defined as Korean literature. This inclusive definition resolves many of the conflicts inherent in the narrower ones discussed above. Not only can we then broaden the scope of research on traditional and contemporary Korean literature, but we are also able to discuss the interaction and conflict expressed among the literatures of various classes and groups in the process of historical change and the development of Korean literature, without being dependent on makeshift theories. Furthermore, the inclusive definition of Korean literature contributes to a greater understanding of Korean culture in a wider sense.

The following graph shows the relationship between the various types of Korean literature within the inclusive definition:

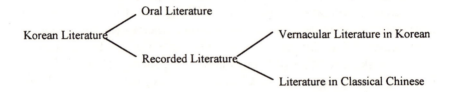

Interaction Among the Three Main Types of Korean Literature

Now that we have divided Korean literature broadly into oral literature, literature in classical Chinese, and vernacular literature in hangŭl, the next step is to arrive at a broad understanding of the defining features of and historical relationship among these three main types. While each has unique characteristics resulting from differences in the method of expression and transmission and in the social background that produced it, these types have continued to interact with each other in the overall context of Korean culture. This interaction has also differed in each historical era. We can discern six stages of historical development:

Stage 1. Oral literature exists exclusively.

Stage 2. Oral literature is dominant, with some oral literature being written in Chinese characters after their introduction to Korean-speaking peoples. Literature in classical Chinese makes its first appearance.

Stage 3. Oral literature exists alongside literature in classical Chinese. Literature written in the hyangch'al transcription system appears, and literature in classical Chinese begins to be adopted by the aristocracy.

Stage 4. Classical Chinese is used as the common written language of the literate classes in society. Literature in classical Chinese is dominant in the yangban class and other literate groups in society, with oral literature dominant among the illiterate lower classes.

Stage 5. Hangŭl is invented in 1446 [King Sejong ordered the development of hangŭl in 1443; it was promulgated in 1446. —Trans.]. Literature in classical Chinese, vernacular literature in hangŭl, and oral literature coexist and interact closely with one another among the various social classes.

Stage 6. Traditional aristocratic–bureaucratic society collapses and literature in classical Chinese loses its legitimacy. Oral literary traditions are weakened by the spread of the printed word. Literature in hangŭl achieves near-total domination.

Oral literature existed from stage one through stage five and can thus be considered the origin and basis of Korean literature. As with other literatures, Korean literature emerged from an exclusively oral tradition. This oral literature changed and evolved throughout the development of written literature and provided a source of inspiration for themes and forms of the latter. *Hyangga,* lyrics in song that expressed the sensibilities of people during the Shilla Dynasty in a beautiful and rich language, emerged from this oral tradition. In addition, novels based on *p'ansori,* tales sung by a traveling *kwangdae,* or bard, were an important genre in the late Chosŏn Dynasty. P'ansorĭ draws on the close relationship between basic Korean oral literary forms and other arts, such as music and drama.

Despite the continued importance of the oral tradition, its position in the history of Korean literature has been in flux. The Korean language did not have a written form in ancient times, and oral literature gradually lost its dominant position as the importance of literacy grew. This can be seen in the changing role of oral literature from stages one, two, and three to stages four and five in the above list. In the first three stages, oral literature was a literary form that had a strong social base of support. In the following two stages, the literate Koreans used Chinese characters, and literature in classical Chinese became dominant in the upper classes of society. Oral literature became the preserve of the illiterate and lower classes. In general, oral literature remained dominant in all classes of society during the formative eras of Korean culture, but declined among the literate upper classes as literature was divided into oral and written forms based on the aristocratic order of society that developed from the early Koryŏ Dynasty onward. This does not mean that the literate and upper classes ignored oral literature entirely after the early Koryŏ period—they would have enjoyed oral tales and songs in childhood and they made use of oral literature to express their deepest feelings in song in adulthood. In spite of this, however, the ruling class, which was in the position to impose written literary culture on society, was more interested in literature in classical Chinese, whereas the illiterate and lower classes had to satisfy their literary needs almost completely with oral literature. Thus, oral literature survived as the basis of a national Korean literature, rooted in the language of the common people.

The basis of a national literature consists of the distinguishing themes, rhythms, motifs, ways of expression, and underlying thoughts that develop in the literature of a particular ethnic group, or as the outcome of an active revival campaign. In Korea, oral literature developed in this basic way during its period of dominance from the beginnings of Korean civilization to the third stage, despite the introduction of literature in classical Chinese. This dichotomy between oral literature and literature in classical Chinese became sharper as the latter developed among the literate and upper classes during the Koryŏ and Chosŏn dynasties. The literate and upper classes used Chinese characters, the common literary language of the ruling elite throughout East Asia, as their language of literary expression. Compared with the pannational and universalistic concepts and aesthetics of the elite, the vast majority of the common people expressed their experiences, thoughts, and aesthetic values through oral literature based on spoken vernacular Korean. Thus, the language of the common people retained and developed a lively vernacular literary quality. Furthermore, in contrast to the literature in classical Chinese of the ruling elite during the Koryŏ and Chosŏn dynasties, with its focus on aestheticism and abstract thought distant from the concerns of real life, oral literature expressed the suffering of a life of hardship and a reality that was closely connected to the everyday lives of the common people.

Because culture develops depth and breadth through exchange and contact with other cultures, we need to recognize the contribution made to Korean literature by literature in classical Chinese. The above two characteristics of oral literature are definitely important in examining the underlying currents of Korean literature.

After the formation of a proto-Korean state and the transmission of Chinese characters from China, literature in classical Chinese created by a minority of the aristocracy developed greatly during the era of Unified Shilla in the South and Palhae in the North. A closer look at the significant primary sources from the Unified Shilla Dynasty reveals that knowledge of classical Chinese at this period was confined to *yuktup'um* writers and scholars who had studied in China during the Tang Dynasty (A.D. 613–907). Korean literature in classical Chinese expanded greatly as the bureaucratic system, dominated by the yangban, developed on Confucian principles after the founding of the Koryŏ Dynasty. In the interest of consolidating their power through a strong centralized bureaucracy, and inspired by the system that developed under Mongol domination of Korea from 1270 to the middle of the fourteenth century, the Koryŏ kings built Confucian schools and established a national civil service examination. As a result, hyangga literature went into decline and literature in classical Chinese became the common medium for written and literary expression among the ruling class. This trend gained momentum in the yangban-dominated bureaucracy in the Chosŏn Dynasty, and literature in classical Chinese became a required subject in yangban education. Many writers produced profound works in classical Chinese during this period.

Literature in classical Chinese was not only the preserve of the ruling yangban elite, it was also an exclusive literature because of the difficulty of mastering the Chinese characters in which it was written. Furthermore, it was also deeply influenced by Sinocentric literature and the universalism of the Koryŏ and Chosŏn dynasties, which idealized the Dao of the ancient Chinese emperors Yao and Shun and of the philosophy of Confucius and Mencius that was the core of Confucianism. This should not suggest, however, a denial of the significance of literature in classical Chinese, and of the historical development behind it as literature in classical Chinese was appropriated by Koreans over time. Diverse development, conflict, division, and change arose as philosophical shifts occurred among those who wrote in classical Chinese. Each Chinese character was given a Korean sound that differed

from the original Chinese pronunciation, and a special method of reading in Korean literature written in classical Chinese was developed. In
addition to these basic linguistic changes, the forms, themes, and topics
chosen by those writing in classical Chinese inevitably reflected their
problems and their concerns about the world in which they were living.
The increased distinctiveness in literature, as reflected in works such as
Korean Poetry (Chosŏn shi), *Korean-Style Poetry* (Chosŏn p'ung), and
Songs from Everyday Life (Yiŏn), that developed from the seventeenth
century reveals the diversity of literature in classical Chinese.

Literature in classical Chinese is also significant because it contributed greatly to a widening of the scope of Korean literature and to the
creation of a romantic aesthetic and a rich world of contemplation.
Classical Chinese—the literature of the ruling class and the common
literary language—coexisted and was often in conflict with Korean
vernacular literature. At the same time, it functioned as a unifying
force for universalism, offsetting the localizing forces of literary indi-
vidualism and realism found in the oral tradition. Without the localizing influence of the oral tradition, the momentum for universalism in
the classical Chinese tradition would have most likely led to a total
dependence on the Chinese literary tradition, and to a shallow aristocratic literature. In the broad context of Korean literature, however,
literature in classical Chinese developed its own Korean literary individuality and, by adding diversity to the existing oral literary tradition,
expanded the range of possibilities in Korean literature.

Literature in hangŭl, which makes use of the Korean vernacular but
is written literature, developed in the space between oral literature and
literature in classical Chinese. The hyangga were vernacular lyric
poems that were written in the hyangch'al transcription system. Thus
hyangga originated from the oral literary tradition, and the ten-line
hyangga developed into lyrics that were sung to music. Hyangga declined in the early Koryŏ period, and little literature in vernacular
Korean developed until the invention of hangŭl in 1446 during the
reign of King Sejong. After the creation of hangŭl, Korean vernacular
literature was built on its use in national record keeping and translation
projects and in official literature. Hangŭl was first learned by male
members of the ruling class and then by their children. In general,
vernacular literature of this early period of the Chosŏn Dynasty developed first in poetry, which formed the basis for the later development
of narrative literature in hangŭl. Narrative poetry of the common peo-

ple appeared in the middle of the seventeenth century. Various phenomena of this period, such as the development of a market economy, the growth of commercial publishing, and the rise of the novel and yadam, "gossipy tales," were interrelated. As a result of these developments, vernacular literature in hangŭl proliferated and improved greatly in quality. Vernacular literature in particular underwent considerable changes in the direction of modern realism by taking advantage of the down-to-earth and practical currents of thought that arose as the social structure of the Chosŏn Dynasty began to weaken. Finally, after the turmoil of the late nineteenth and early twentieth centuries, literature in classical Chinese lost its base of support and oral literature also declined substantially. This left vernacular literature in a position of near total dominance in Korea.

In this process of development, Korean vernacular literature not only originated from oral literature and absorbed the legacy of literature in classical Chinese, it allowed for a diversity of channels of expression by people from the yangban to the peasants. Because of the diversity of classes involved in the creation, transmission, and enjoyment of literature, a wide range of experiences could be expressed in vernacular literature. The diversity and pluralism of vernacular literature overcame the limitations of the dualistic literary paradigm and the aristocratic system of the Koryŏ and Chosŏn dynasties and became the basis for a much more sympathetic national Korean literature.

Traditionally, literature dating from before the end of the nineteenth century—vernacular literature in hangŭl, oral literature, and literature in classical Chinese—has been classified as "traditional Korean literature," whereas vernacular literature that developed after that has been classified as "modern Korean literature." However, this classification is useful only for the convenience of scholars of Korean literature; it does not mean that there is a sharp division between these two made-up categories, or that they should be considered as separate entities. To understand Korean literature today, we need to overcome this distorted interpretation.

These issues will be dealt with in greater detail in "Traditional and Modern Literature," the first section of chapter 7.

3

Language, Style, and Meter

Literature is an art based on language. To gain a greater understanding of a national literature, as well as of individual works, it is therefore important to research linguistic aspects of literary language. Linguistic aspects of Korean literature have been largely ignored, however, particularly in the area of prose style. One of the main reasons for this is the lack of recognition in the academic community of the significance of the linguistic aspects of literature. In addition, there are fundamental difficulties inherent in the development of an effective methodology for researching literary style that combines methods of literary criticism and linguistics. In the 1960s research was largely based on a method that was centered on an analysis of the language and the internal structure of the work. This endeavor was generally successful, but it lost much of its impetus because research results were inaccessible to those who worked outside this relatively narrow field.

Research on stylistics has made little progress since that time. As the study of stylistics has progressed, researchers have advanced diffuse theories to explain the style of an individual writer or work, rather than developing a strong research focus. We need to move on from the unique style of the individual writer to consider groups. The style and language of one group in society exist within the style and language of a particular period, and these in turn relate to the historical and cultural context. Therefore, studies of linguistic developments, such as the creation of the third-person singular, *kŭ,* or of the use of the past tense in New Novels, or in the search for a unique literary style in every writer's work, should be conducted within their historical and cultural context.

There are many theoretical questions to consider, in light of previous research as well as in a more speculative way. Unlike the over-researched field of poetic meter, literary style will continue to attract new attention—despite the somewhat disappointing results of past research. If that research can contribute to future studies, it will not have been a waste of time and effort.

For the sake of clarity, "Korean literary style" in the following discussion will refer to prose literary style in works written in hangŭl or in earlier Chinese character-based phonetic transcription systems, such as hyangch'al.

1. The Korean Language and the History of Literary Style

History of Characteristics of the Korean Language

Most historical linguists have supported the theory that Korean is a member of the Altaic language family, but very little linguistic evidence of this exists, and many researchers remain skeptical about whether such evidence is obtainable. The language of ancient Korea has not been documented, but researchers have speculated that the languages of the emerging Korean states were closely related to those of parts of Manchuria. In the process of the conquest and absorption of various ethnic groups, these languages were reduced to the Koguryŏ language of the Puyŏ family and the Shilla, Paekche, and Karak languages of the Han family. The Karak language was later absorbed into the Shilla language. The Shilla and the Paekche languages were similar enough to be considered dialects of one larger language, whereas the Koguryŏ language was not closely related to the other two.

The Koguryŏ and Paekche kingdoms were defeated in 668 and 660, respectively, as the Shilla kingdom occupied parts of Koguryŏ territory and gained control over all the former Paekche territory; the development of a common ancient Korean language was thus enhanced by the Shilla language's absorption of the Paekche and Koguryŏ languages. This was one of the most important periods in the history of the Korean language. The Koguryŏ language most likely became the basis of the language of Palhae (A.D. 698–926), the Korean kingdom that extended over most of the northern two thirds of the former Koguryŏ territory. After the demise of Palhae, much of its former territory was taken over by the Koryŏ kingdom (918–1392), and the Palhae language was absorbed by the more powerful language of Koryŏ. The founding of the Koryŏ Dynasty in 936 greatly influenced the development of the Korean language and is one of the most significant events in its history. The ruling Koryŏ elite adopted many of the political and cultural practices of the Shilla elite.

Linguistically the Koryŏ language can be seen as a direct descendant of the Shilla language. The latter was based on the dialect spoken in Kyŏngju; the former on the dialect spoken in Kaesŏng. This meant that, for the first time, the new language was based on a central Korean dialect. With the founding of the Chosŏn Dynasty in 1392, the linguistic center of Korea moved to Seoul from Kaesŏng, but this fifty-kilometer move is not significant in the history of the Korean language. Modern Korean is the product of a thousand years of continuous change that began in the tenth century with the founding of the Koryŏ Dynasty, the capital of which, Kaesŏng, was located in the geographic center of the Korean Peninsula.

The changes in the Korean language and the characteristics of Korean literature are reflected directly and indirectly in the literary expressions and styles that have emerged since the tenth century. Unfortunately, little research has been conducted on this issue; investigation of the development of literary style from the Koryŏ period will help to fill the void.

One of the most important characteristics of Korean from a morphological point of view is that it is an agglutinative language. In agglutinative languages grammatical functions are indicated by combining the etymological root of a word with a suffix or a grammatical particle. The suffixes and particles are diverse and highly developed. Lexical choice and syntax are important in Korean, as they are in any language, but suffixes and particles carry the most weight in conveying meaning. Highly developed honorific expressions, which reflect a rigid social structure, and wide differences in regional dialects are all related to the use of suffixes and particles. The close relationship in Korean between meaning and the use of suffixes and particles is significant in the development of literary style in the language both of individuals and of various groups in society.

Syntactically, Korean is a subject-object-verb (SOV) language. The verb is placed behind the object or the complement that it governs, and modifying elements are placed in front of the word or structure that they modify. Regardless of how long and complicated, or how terse, a Korean sentence is, the main predicate appears after connecting words and modifying structures. Therefore the meaning of a sentence is not clear until the very end of the sentence. For example, it is difficult to determine the meaning of a sentence starting with *na nŭn tangshin ŭl kidari* ("I wait for you") if the final clause is omitted. The final clause could end in several ways, all of which change the meaning: *ryŏgo haetchiman, amuri saenggakhae poado* ("tried [to wait], but no matter how I look at it . . ."); *ki ttaemune onŭl ichŏrŏm* ("because [I wait] on a day like today"); or *chi anhsŭmnida* ("[I] do not [wait]"). Important linguistic functions such as negation, tense, and aspect are all expressed at the end of the predicate. Furthermore, the structure of the noun phrase, with its syntactically complex complement—in which the modifying phrase precedes the noun phrase—is such that the most important part comes at the end of the modifying phrase, again delaying the conveyance of meaning until the end of the phrase. Meaning is conveyed through the conversational setting and the structure of the sentence; these elements should be taken into consideration equally when analyzing meaning. Along with the various languages that have a similar grammatical structure to Korean, it is necessary to research literary style and sociolinguistics to understand the historical development and the way the above features are used by individuals and groups of people.

The language of ideas and the language of the common people tended to diverge. Philosophical, technical, and bureaucratic language included many lexical items based on Chinese characters, whereas the language of the common people was more heavily influenced by lexical items of Korean origin. This bifurcation is a result of the changing social and cultural conditions of the Koryŏ period.

The creation of this linguistic structure began as the Koguryŏ, Paekche, and Shilla kingdoms worked to establish centralized rule through the adoption of the Confucian civil service system, with its emphasis on knowledge of classical Chinese, and through the spread of Buddhism. Official histories and documents were written in classical Chinese; and Buddhist teaching on such issues as letting go of the self, the nature of man, and the principles of the universe were conducted in language that was heavily laden with classical Chinese vocabulary. Sharp class distinctions in the lexicon and in ways of expression did not, however, appear until the early Koryŏ period. Lexical items of Korean origin were overwhelmingly dominant during the Unified Shilla period (A.D. 668–935). The rich and expressive language of *Songs of the Ten Vows of Samantabhadra* (Pohyŏn shipchong wŏnwangsaeng ka) by the Buddhist monk Kyunyŏ (A.D. 923–973) and other surviving hyangga from this period use relatively few words of Chinese origin.

As it did in the overall structure of society, a two-tiered class system developed in the lexicon after the Koryŏ Dynasty established firm control over the country and existed until the end of the Chosŏn period in 1910. Elite groups in society wrote all official documents, historical records, scholarly writings, and literature in classical Chinese. As a result, lexical items that referred to social status and logical and abstract thought were based on Chinese characters, or at least derived from Chinese characters. Buddhist and Confucian texts, which played an important role in traditional religion and philosophy, contributed greatly to the spread of Chinese character-based lexical items. Lexical items of Korean origin, which are generally deeply expressive and highly descriptive, continued to proliferate and become more eloquent. The development of the expressive power of language and of the lexicon demonstrates progress in the language of the common people.

Literary Style in the First Half of the Chosŏn Period

After the development of hangŭl in 1446, Korean stylistics progressed gradually toward a more inclusive language, while at the same time maintaining the expressive power of the language of the common people that grew out of the specific linguistic and cultural circumstances. It is difficult to prove that the history of Korean stylistics began with the hyangch'al writing system in the Shilla period because the few surviving documents from that period are all poems. What follows is a summary of the history of prose literary stylistics after the development of hangŭl in 1446.

Literary stylistics of the fifteenth century were a product of government-sponsored translations of the Confucian classics, Buddhist sacred texts, and poetry in classical Chinese. These appeared in official collections such as *Songs of Flying Dragons* (Yongbi ŏch'ŏn ka), a heroic epic poem; *The Life of Buddha* (Sŏkpo sangjŏl), an epic biography; and *Songs of the Moon Reflecting a Thousand Rivers* (Wŏrin ch'ŏngang chi kok), an epic poem on the life of Buddha. All of these were completed in 1447. Translations of basic Confucian texts such as *Lesser Learning* (Sohak; Chinese: Xiaoxue), *Great Learning* (Taehak; Chinese: Daxue), *The Doctrine of the Mean* (Chungyong; Chinese: Zhongyong), *Mencius* (Maengja; Chinese: Mengzi), and *The Book of*

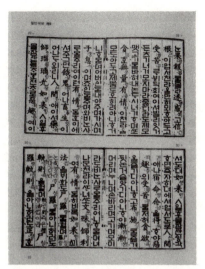

Page from *The Complete History of the Life of Buddha* (Wŏrin sŏkpo) illustrating early use of hangŭl with Chinese characters

Filial Piety (Hyo kyŏng; Chinese: Xiao jing) were very influential in the sixteenth century. The major Buddhist texts, such as *Śūraāmgàma-sūtra* (*Nŭng'ŏm kyŏng*), *Lotus Sutra* (Pŏphwa kyŏng; Sanskrit: Saddharma-pundarīka-sūtra), *Diamond Sutra* (Kŭmgang kyŏng; Sanskrit: Vajracchedikā-prajñāpāramitā-sūtra), and *Máhāvaipulya-pūrnabuddha-sūtra-prasannārtha-sūtra* (Wŏngak kyŏng) were translated at the Kangyŏng Togam, a royal center for the translation of Buddhist and Confucian texts that was established in 1457 and lasted until 1471. The *Annotated Poems of Du Fu* (Tushi ŏnhae), comprising all the poems of the Tang Chinese poet Du Fu (712–770), was published in 1481.

The history and style of these various forms—poetry and prose, original works and translation, religious texts and biographies—should be examined in greater detail for a complete understanding of Korean literature. There is little doubt that these works played a vital role in the development of Korean prose style because their subject matter and expressive power were models for writers to follow. Since style is dependent on the breadth and depth of language used before the development of written language, the types of writing mentioned above helped to expand the expressive range of the Korean language before the development of hangŭl. As language began to be written down, style became more specific, which helped to increase the expressive power of the language. Seen in this light, original works such as *Songs of Flying Dragons* and *Songs of the Moon Reflecting a Thousand Rivers*—which are characterized by a sense of balance typical of the terse style of the Korean language in the early Chosŏn period—are just as important as the translations of Confucian and Buddhist classics. Translation is not merely a mechanical process of changing text from one language into another. Rather, it is a creative process of conveying the experiences and system of logic of one language into another language. The first task of any fifteenth-century writer was to examine whether the experiences and system of logic expressed in classical Chinese could be conveyed in a detailed and stylistically appealing way in Korean. This endeavor was not only successful, as seen in the descriptive sentences produced in Korean, but also strengthened the Korean language by opening it up to positive influences from other languages.

Building on this early work, literary style entered new terrain with the emergence of the *naeganch'e* style ("internal [women's] style"), a more sophisticated style of writing in hangŭl that was rooted in everyday spoken language. The officially sponsored works mentioned above reflect the social position of the individual writer or group of writers, revealing the relatively stern writing style and outlook on life of official writers and compilers. The naeganch'e style developed in an entirely new direction. Relatively little research has been conducted on its development, but most scholars believe that it emerged in the late fifteenth and early sixteenth centuries.

Although hangŭl became known after *Correct Sounds to Instruct the People* (Hunmin chŏngŭm) appeared in 1446, male members of the aristocracy and officialdom continued to conduct their official and private business and literary activities in classical Chinese. The common people, on the other hand, due to their social and economic position, did not feel the need for literacy. Hangŭl was used by the middle or merchant class in business transactions, for record keeping, and for the education of their children, and by those in the royal palace who kept private diaries. Women were not expected to learn classical Chinese beyond the most basic level. With a few exceptions, the majority of women in the aristocratic and yangban classes used hangŭl for daily records of events and private correspondence with relatives. The 1475 book of classical Chinese moral lessons, *Naesun*, annotated by King Sŏngjong's mother, Queen Sohye, shows that aristocratic women used hangŭl mainly for annotating Confucian classics, which formed the core of every male child's education.

The term naeganch'e was created by contemporary scholars to describe this kind of writing in hangŭl. Women did not, however, use naeganch'e solely in their personal correspondence with relatives (in most family correspondence, men wrote on one side of the paper and women on the other). In addition, prose written in hangŭl by women— private records, diaries, travelogues, random notes, memoirs, and biographies—was in the naeganch'e style. Through the writings of literate aristocratic women in the male-dominated culture of the early Chosŏn period, the naeganch'e style enhanced the expressive power of hangŭl. Naeganch'e was also used by men and should be considered to be a purely Korean style that easily conveyed the ideas and feelings of everyday life, rather than one used only by women. A passage written in the naeganch'e style in 1596 by a yangban, An Minhak, on the death of his wife reveals the simplicity and honesty of this rich and clear language.

> I can't make clothes by myself but am trying to make cloth with a loom. I try my best every day but haven't managed to make much cloth. When you were alive, you wore a blouse with a tattered old skirt to save the good cloth for me. You must have been cold sitting on the unheated floor without warm clothes. I want you to know how sad I feel when I think of how much you suffered then. I refused many times when you asked me to sleep with you, but now I am alone in my sadness every night. I promise that I will revere you for the rest of my life. I will pray that your spirit, your soul, finds eternal peace.

Literary Style in the Last Half of the Chosŏn Period

The naeganch'e style of the sixteenth century came increasingly to express a diverse range of ideas and experiences, absorbing important elements from various other styles. Social and economic improvements among the common people, a greater interest in recording everyday life, and the spread of hangŭl were all part of the process of enrichment. Records of palace and aristocratic life such as *Diary from Sansŏng* (Sansŏng ilgi, 1639), *Diary from Hwasŏng* (Hwasŏng ilgi), *Diary of the Year Kyech'uk* (Kyech'uk ilgi, 1613), *Tale of Queen Inhyŏn* (Inhyŏn wanghu chŏn), and *Record from the Bottom of Sadness*

(Hanjung nok, composed 1795–1805); travelogues such as *Record of a Journey to Yanjing in the Year Muo* (Muo Yŏn haeng nok, 1798 ["Yanjing" refers to Beijing. —Trans.]), *Diary of Ŭiyudang* (Ŭiyudang ilgi, 1829), and *Diary of a Journey to Hamhŭng Province* (Chagyŏngji Hamhŭng ilgi, 1809); and prose works such as "Requiem for My Dead Needle" (Choch'im mun) and "A Debate Among a Woman's Seven Best Friends" (Kyujung ch'iru chaengnon ki) are all examples of prose writings of the last half of the Chosŏn period that reflect the influence of naeganch'e or a naeganch'e-like prose style. Although *yŏgŏch'e,* a literary style used in translations of classical Chinese texts, remained important after the fifteenth century, the influence of the naeganch'e style helped to make it smoother and more natural. An intensive examination of original materials is needed to show the underlying changes in these styles during the Chosŏn period.

Increased activity in the writing and selling of novels in the last half of the Chosŏn period played an important role in the spread of hangŭl and in the development of prose style literature in hangŭl. Traditional novels, the majority written in hangŭl, became more popular in the seventeenth century, which in turn stimulated commercial publishing and trading in books as commodities. There were two main types of trading in books: the wandering bookseller sold or exchanged books, mainly novels, along with other household goods, while the more specialized bookseller sold a wide variety of books from his printshop, usually located in a market town. Both types expanded the readership for novels, which created more demand for novels, and these developments contributed directly to the development of hangŭl stylistics. Furthermore, the publishing of popular novels (*panggakpon*) with interesting narratives and lifelike descriptions contributed to the expansion of literacy in hangŭl in the eighteenth century and afterward. (See chapter 6 for a detailed discussion of the rise of commercial publishing and the importance of popular novels.)

Naeganch'e was the basis of the literary style used in both traditional and commercially published novels in hangŭl. The literary style in these novels incorporated elements of translations of classical Chinese and of the spoken language of the common people. In times past, scholars argued that a large number of proverbs and idioms from classical Chinese was sufficient to prove that a novel was written in the translation, or yŏgŏch'e, style. There are very few instances in which the translation style dominates an entire novel written in hangŭl. Writers needed to attract the interest of the reader by writing in a colloquial style that took advantage of the natural expressions and ease of comprehension inherent in the language of the common people.

Based on the achievements of the naeganch'e style, works that partially absorbed yŏgŏch'e—such as heroic novels, fantasy novels, and "domestic" novels—generally appealed to readers in the upper classes of society. These novels made use of pedantic language and diverse expressions from classical Chinese in order to make the style of writing appear more sophisticated and to give the narrative a more serious tone. Novels that appealed to the common people had a larger readership and developed a literary style that was more closely rooted in their own colloquial language than was the naeganch'e style. In particular, novels that were based on p'ansori made use of a lively vernacular language that included the humor, both witty and vulgar, of the language of the common people. Since p'ansori narratives and novels depended on the use of a mixture of formal and colloquial language in differing situations, it is difficult to categorize this style.

Pulgyo kasa (Buddhist narrative poems), or the simple *ch'ŏnju kasa* (Catholic songs) and *tonghak kasa* (songs from the Tonghak rebellion in 1894)—which appeared for liturgical and religious purposes in the eighteenth century and the latter half of the nineteenth century, respectively—expanded the range of style in hangŭl literature to include a greater diversity of religious thought. The translation of the Bible and wider distribution of other sacred texts at the end of the nineteenth century played an important role in introducing hangŭl to ever greater numbers of people.

Literary Style since the Late Nineteenth Century

Literary style from the end of the nineteenth century to the 1910s developed from the spread of literacy and the refinements in writing that took place in the last half of the Chosŏn period. In the face of the internal collapse of the Chosŏn social order and the challenge posed by the forces of imperialism, classical Chinese lost its ideological legitimacy in the eyes of the common people. Thus, the literary style of this time not only built on existing literary styles, but also developed into a

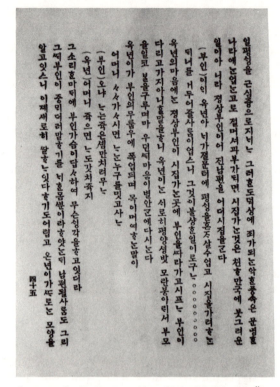

Page from early-twentieth-century New Novel (*shinsosŏl*)

language of persuasion and debate that included contemporary ideological and bureaucratic language and went beyond the confines of the
past by incorporating the language and experiences of the common
people in the written language to a degree previously unknown.

Literary style in this period can be divided into two broad types: the
mixed hangŭl and classical Chinese style as defined by Yu Kiljun, the
first Korean to study in Japan and the United States, in his *Things Seen
and Heard on a Journey to the West* (Sŏyu kyŏnmun) of 1895, and the
colloquial hangŭl style that appeared in *The Independent* (Tongnip
shinmun). Yun developed the mixed style, which was based mainly on
fifteenth- and sixteenth-century translations of classical Chinese texts,
for a highly literate readership that had basic knowledge of classical
Chinese. The following passage is taken from a scholarly journal similar to the *Korean Self-Strengthening Society Monthly* (Taehan cha-

ganghoe wŏlbo), the *Journal of the Northwest Association* (Sŏbuk hakhoebo), and the *T'aegŭk Journal* (T'aegŭk hakpo), which were published for enlightened scholars of classical Chinese who were familiar with Western ideas and who were in favor of opening Korea up to outside influences.

> Isn't it amazing how competition has developed among us human beings even though we have defeated all the other animals in the world? The world has become a smaller place, forcing people in all corners of the earth to complete with each other. This means that those peoples who are educated and powerful are superior to those who are uneducated and weak. The strong view the weak as barbarians and believe that they can do whatever they want, including committing mass murder, to the weak to bring them into subjugation. Thus the weak face the prospect of the gradual destruction of their culture and eventual extermination. The slaves taken from Africa and the North American Indians have suffered this fate. This is a tragedy, a terrible tragedy. The oppression of the weak by the strong is like the battle for supremacy on the earth between animals and human beings thousands of years ago. Competition between people is therefore natural, and the victory of the strong over the weak should also be accepted as natural.
>
> —from "Education Is Essential for Life"(Kyoyuk i
> pulhŭng imyŏn saengjon ŭl puldŭk), Pak Ŭnshik, 1906

Using the vernacular Korean style that developed from the naeganch'e style in the last half of the Chosŏn period, the scholars of this group were interested in reaching a broad readership and were not concerned about education or social class. The New Novel written in vernacular Korean incorporated many traditions that developed in hangŭl novels and collections of poetry and song in the latter half of the Chosŏn period. *The Independent*'s selection of this style for its debut in 1896 was an important event in the history of Korean literary style. The historical significance of *The Independent* and the ideology of its founders are not within the purview of this discussion; what is important is the desire to make use of hangŭl in a colloquial way to discuss the important social and ideological issues of the time, which reflected the steady growth in the use of hangŭl since its development in the fifteenth century.

The late nineteenth and early twentieth centuries saw a gradual decline in the use of the mixed style of classical Chinese and hangŭl and a shift toward a more colloquial language. This trend is clear if we compare articles and editorials in *Things Seen and Heard on a Journey to the West* with those in *The Korea Daily News* (Taehan maeil shinbo, 1904–1910), which was first published ten years later. It becomes even more apparent in the work of Shin Ch'aeho (1880–1936). The movement toward colloquial language gained impetus in the 1910s and by the end of this decade works written exclusively in hangŭl were considered the norm in Korean writing—except for special cases, such as the Declaration of Independence of 1919 (Kimi tongnip sŏnŏnsŏ), which precipitated the March 1 Movement and in which the mixed style was strictly maintained.

The critical role that Ch'oe Namsŏn and Yi Kwangsu played in creating a modern colloquial Korean language in this period of dramatic change should not be ignored simply because their importance has been emphasized repeatedly in past research. Through magazines such as *Youth* (Sonyŏn, 1908), *Red Chŏgori* (Pulgŭn chŏgori, 1912), *New Stars* (Saebyŏl, 1913), *Readings for Children* (*Aidŭl poi,* 1913), and *Bloom of Youth* (Ch'ŏngch'un, 1914), which appealed to relatively young readers, Ch'oe Namsŏn expanded the range of modern language, thus solidifying the adoption of a style that made almost exclusive use of colloquial Korean and hangŭl. Ch'oe championed the "movement for New Writing" in the magazine *New Stars,* to which he contributed a regular column entitled "Reading," which gave examples of "New Writing." Later he joined Yi Kwangsu in the New Writing Movement by writing a column in *Bloom of Youth* in which they stated their intention to write in a "purely literary style":

> All people need an education, but we [Koreans] need an education even more than others.
> The most important thing for us to do now is to get an education, and if we fail to do so, we will not be able to do anything else.
> Although we have made progress in education, we need to make greater efforts in the future. Although what we have learned may be useful, we need to learn from others because they have accomplished more than we have. If we do not do this voluntarily now, we will be forced to do so in the future.

It's time to wake up. Education is not something that we should leave to others; it is critical to our future, and we have to recognize this. Let's try our utmost to learn as much as we possibly can.

—from the preface of the inaugural issue of *Boom of Youth* (Ch'ŏngch'un), 1914

These two men built on many of the changes that had occurred in the latter half of the Chosŏn period and confronted the ever increasing demands for change in the early twentieth century; their accomplishment should be seen in this context, rather than as a sudden flowing of individual genius.

Literary style in the 1920s was also the beginning of what contemporary Koreans recognize as modern literary Korean. The influence of translations from classical Chinese faded, and the colloquial style that made almost exclusive use of hangŭl became the dominant style in literature as well as in journalism, nonfiction writing (although many newspapers and nonfiction works made limited use of Chinese characters), and almost all other forms of writing. This should be viewed as the culmination of developments throughout literary history rather than as a sudden break with the past. A social and cultural system that creates an environment of belief in which language can be an effective means of communication is necessary to the development of a style of writing capable of dealing with complex ideas and arguments in a modern society. Language and style are not simply the grammatical linking of vocabulary and meter but rather forms particular to a specific communicative situation. Korean literary style since the 1920s has confronted the issue of how to accurately and deeply express new experiences, ideas, and feelings so as to create a modern language that can be used by all members of society. The development of various writing styles—literary, scholarly, journalistic, and popular—that fit the needs of writers and express their individuality is built on a language that is open to all members of society.

2. Korean Poetic Meter

Introduction to Poetic Meter

Poetry makes much more use of the sound of language than prose does. Understanding rhythm is very important in understanding the poetic roots and traditions of an ethnolinguistic group. Since research on modern Korean poetry began in earnest, many scholars have been interested in rhythm in Korean poetry, particularly in the origin of meter, which is at the center of the structure of rhythm. Various theories have emerged to explain meter in Korean poetry: the syllabic theory, the dynamic theory, the tonal theory, the durational theory, and the segmental theory. Serious reservations have been raised about the first four theories, but the last, the segmental theory, has gained recognition and has become the basis of most research on Korean poetry since the 1970s. We shall first examine the limitations of the syllabic theory, which was the most influential of the theories, as well as being the oldest. Then, we shall examine poetic meter in Korean poetry from the standpoint of the segmental theory.

The idea of counting the number of syllables to explain the rhythm structure of Korean poetic meter was very influential after its emergence in the 1920s. Under close scrutiny, however, its limitations become clear. The problem of a set rhythm in *shijo* (short lyric poems), on which the syllabic theory was built, is a good example of these inherent limitations. According to syllabic theorists, the basic set-rhythm structure of shijo is as follows:

3	4	4 (3)	4
3	4	4 (3)	4
3	5	4	3

The problem with this theoretical set-rhythm structure is that very few shijo conform to it. Only about seven percent of extant shijo fit this pattern, and only about four to five percent of the *p'yŏng shijo* ("standard" shijo) do. The assertion of a "set" number of rhythms in the syllabic theory is not supported by the evidence from various genres of poetry, and we are left wondering whether there is any sort of meter in Korean poetry that is governed by a set number of syllables.

That a rigid breakdown of syllables fails to reflect and cannot account for the natural flow of poetic meter in Korean is made clear by the following well-known shijo:

1.

The sound of the rain on the rivers is funny somehow.
All the mountains are a mixture of red and green, and I'm smiling.
Let it be, and laugh to your heart's content; for the spring wind
   doesn't last long.

ch'ŏnggang e / pi tŭnnŭn sori / kŭi muoshi / uŭp kwandŭi
mansan / hongnok i / hwidŭrŭmyŏ / unnŭngoya
tuŏra / ch'unp'ung i myŏt nariri / u'ul ttaero / uŏra

—Prince Pongnim

2.

I was born just after the king I love was born.
We're bound to each other by a fate that even Heaven doesn't
   understand.
I'm one year younger than my beloved king.
Nothing compares to my feelings and love for the king.

i mom / samgishil che / nim ŭl choch'a / samgishini
hănsăuing / nokpun imyŏ / hanŭl morăl / il irŏnga
na hăna / chyŏmŏ itko / nim hăna / nal koeshini
i maŭm / i sarang / kyŏnjol tăi / noyŏ ŏpta

—preface to "Song to My Love" (Sa miin kok), Chŏng Chŏl

The first shijo was written by Prince Pongnim (who reigned as King
Hyojong from 1649 to 1659), and the second one is a section from
Chŏng Ch'ŏl's "Song to My Love" (Sa miin kok); Chŏng Ch'ŏl (1536–
1593) was one of the most prolific writers of shijo and *kasa* (poetic
song lyrics) in Korean history. In the first example, there are four
instances in which the number of syllables does not support the syllabic theory. In the second example, there are three examples that do
not fit the 3–4 or 4–4 syllabic pattern. Despite this fact, both of these
shijo sound natural and metrical to the native speaker of Korean. The
metric units indicated by the slash flow naturally because each element
is accepted as an equal unit in the overall structure of the shijo. The
3–5 and 2–4 syllable structure of "*ch'ŏnggang e / pi tŭnnŭn sori*" and
"*hăsăing / nokpun imyŏ*" are different according to the syllabic theory,
but a native speaker of Korean will recognize the metric structure
that makes these two shijo sound natural through harmony between
the smooth flow of the passage and the length of the individual

words. Theories that fail to take the native speaker's linguistic intuitions about poetic meter into account are ultimately useless. The merits of analyzing Korean poetic meter in terms of the segmental theory, which posits the regularity of sound as the basic element of poetic meter, are clear.

A Typology of Poetic Meter

In order to explain the segmental theory clearly, we need a survey of some of the major types of poetic meter from around the world:[*]

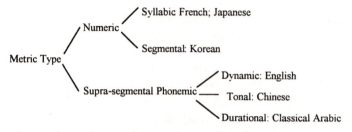

As the above chart shows, the typology of various languages, past and present, is divided into two main groups: numeric meter and suprasegmental phonemic meter. The numeric meter consists of the regular distribution of sounds without accent or stress, whereas the suprasegmental phonemic meter is dependent on the regular arrangement of fixed suprasegmental phonemes in a rhyming structure. Depending on how the rhythm alternates, this type of meter can be divided into the following three subcategories: dynamic meter, tonal meter, and durational meter.

The importance of rhythm is illustrated in the following example from English poetry:

> Shĕ wálks / ĭn beáu / tў, líke / thĕ níght
> Ŏf clóud / lĕss clímes / ănd stár / rў skíes;
>
> —Lord Byron, "She Walks in Beauty"

This poem is an example of iambic tetrameter—the most prevalent type of dynamic meter in English—which is composed of four feet.

---

[*]This organization of poetic meter was adapted from J. Lotz, "Metric Typology," in T.A. Sebeok, ed., *Style in Language* (Cambridge, MA: MIT Press, 1960). "Numeric meter" has been used in place of Lotz's "simple meter" and "suprasegmental phonemic meter" in place of his "complex meter." The subcategory "segmental meter" was added to account for Korean poetic meter.

For our discussion here, the diacritic mark ˘ in the above example refers to unaccented syllables and the accent ‾ to accented syllables, which follow each other to create the rhythm. This regularity of meter in English poetry is, in most cases, based on the idea of the foot, a unit of one or two unaccented syllables in combination with one accented syllable. The most important factor is the accented syllable on which the foot is dependent. Because of this, Jespersen and more generative phonologists have argued against the existence of the poetic foot in English. English poetic meter belongs fundamentally to the dynamic category because of its emphasis on the regular division between accented and unaccented syllables.

Chinese poetry, on the other hand, is built on the relationship of the four tones in Chinese—the even, the rising, the falling, and the "entering"—in a single line and in the overall composition of the poem: the *p'yŏng* (Chinese: ping) tone and the *chuk* (Chinese: ze) tone. The p'yŏng tone consists of only the even tone, whereas the chuk tone is made up of the remaining three tones. The following example is the first half of "Hoping for Spring" (Ch'unmang; Chinese: Chunwang) by Du Fu (712–770), a five-character-per-line regulated poem—known as the "modern style" in the Tang period (618–906)— In the following example, p'yŏng tones are indicated with an *X* and chuk tones with a *Y*:

Y Y X X Y   The nation is broken; only the mountains and rivers remain.
X X Y Y X   The city walls burst in spring with thick trees and grass.
Y X X Y Y   Struck with emotion, flows splash tears;
Y Y Y X X   Not wanting to leave, birds startle my heart.

Poetic meter in any given language is dependent at the most basic level on linguistic aspects of that language. Various efforts have been made to explain Korean poetic meter in terms of accented and unaccented syllables, high and low tones, or long and short syllables. This reflects a common view among researchers that Korean poetic meter is numeric meter. Unlike French or Japanese poetic meter, however, Korean poetic meter belongs to the subcategory of segmental meter. The *waka* in Japanese poetry is composed of 31 syllables arranged in a 5–7–5–7–7 syllabic distribution on five lines; the well-known haiku consists of 17 syllables in a 5–7–5 syllabic distribution on three lines. Any departure from the waka or haiku patterns destroys the integrity of the form.

Few forms of Korean poetry maintain a rigid number or order of syllables, as Japanese poetry does.

Segmental Meter in Korean Poetry

The Korean word *ŭmbo,* "segment," is also used to refer to "feet" in poetic meter found in the West. The word *segment,* however, will be used here to refer to Korean poetic meter. The idea of a beat composed of several sounds may be related to the word. This idea fits the metric structure of Korean poetry well. In the above example taken from Byron, the foot is composed of individual lexical items that do not reflect the grammatical structure of English. The border between one foot and another lies in the middle of the lexical elements. In Korean poetry, on the other hand, the boundary between one segment and the next clearly falls between syntactic divisions and metrically important syllables. Two more shijo, as well as the two that have already been presented, illustrate this point:

1.

Going home to my hut, I lie sleepless.
Staring out of my north window, I wait for dawn.
The nonchalant cuckoo makes my sad heart even sadder.
To get through the night, I look out anxiously at the fields in the
     distance.
Even the most entertaining farming songs sound dull to me now.
Knowing nothing of the real world, I sigh endlessly.

washil e / tŭrŏgandŭl / cham i wasŏ / nuŏshira //
pukch'ang ŭl / pigyŏ anja / săibăi rŭl / kidarini //
mujŏnghăn / taesŭng ŭn / i năi han ŭl / tounăda //
chongjo / ch'uch'ang hămyŏ / mŏn tŭlhŭl / paraboni //
chŭlgi năn / nongga to / hŭng ŏpsŏ / tŭllinăda //
sejŏng morăn / hansum ŭn / kŭch'iljul ŭl / morănăda //

—from "In Praise of Poverty" (Nuhang sa), Pak Illo

2.

The animals have lost their fields and their homes
Where should they go?

Carrying a bundle of forsythia,
I go over Arirang Hill.

Come, mother and father,
They say the land in Pukkando is good.

Keeping hold of my broken heart,
I go over Paektusan Hill.

pal ilk'o / chip irŭn / tongmudŭl a //
ŏdi ro / kayaman / choŭlga ponya //

koenari / putchim ŭl / chilmaŏ kigo //
arirang / kogae ro / nŏmŏ kanda //

abŏji / ŏmŏni / ŏsŏ oso //
pukkando / pŏlp'an i / chot'adŏra //

ssŭrarin / kasŭm ŭl / umk'yŏjwigo //
paektusan / kogae ro / nŏmŏ kanda //

—"New Arirang" (Shin arirang)

The average native speaker of Korean would most likely find the links in the chain of language, as represented by the single slash and the double slash, completely natural. Those sections that are divided by a single slash are segments. Each segment is composed of between two and five syllables, three- and four-syllable segments being most common. If we classify segments according to the number of syllables, then a segment of four syllables is average, a segment of three syllables or less is a short segment, and a segment of five or more syllables is a long segment. As the basic unit of poetic meter, the segment cannot grow or contract beyond the limits imposed by the number of sounds. There are no absolute rules in Korean poetry that govern the size or distribution of segments. In the first example in this section, the second, third, and fourth lines all begin with a segment of two syllables, but in terms of metric weight they are in balance with the three- and four-syllable segments in the shijo. Though the two-syllable segment and the four-syllable segment that follows it appear to be out of balance in this example, we cannot arbitrarily move the border over one syllable to achieve balance between these two segments because the dividing line between one metric unit and another in Korean poetry can only come at a syntactic, or at least a morphological, break in the flow of the sentence. This is clear in the second example in which all the divisions between segments correspond rigidly to syntactic breaks in each line.

The lack of metric equality in the segment in Korean poetry is preserved whether the last sound of each segment is lengthened or whether a slightly longer pause is placed between two segments. In the case of the long segment of five syllables, each syllable is shortened slightly to allow adequate time for a breath before the next segment begins. The line *ŏdi ro / kayaman / choŭlga ponya* (Where should they go?) from the second example above illustrates this clearly.

Major Forms of Meter in Korean Poetry

Korean poetry is typified by three main forms of meter: dimeter, a two-segment line; trimeter, a three-segment line; and tetrameter, a four-segment line. A line is generally composed of one of these.

Dimeter is used least, because the brevity of this form limits what can be expressed in one line. It is used mainly in songs with a rapid rhythm, such as work songs sung in the fields. The following is an example from Ch'ŏngdo County in North Kyŏngsang Province.

> *Ŭnghae ya,*
>   *ŭnghae ya.*
> Good work,
>   *ŭnghae ya.*
> This barley,
>   *ŭnghae ya.*
> We pound,
>   *ŭnghae ya.*
> The old people of the village,
>   *ŭnghae ya.*
> Let's care for them,
>   *ŭnghae ya.*
> Good work,
>   *ŭnghae ya.*
> Hooray!
>   *ŭnghae ya.*

> —"Song of Threshing Barley" (Pori t'ajak norae)

In the above example, breathing in dimeter becomes more rapid, which makes this more suitable for strong rhythms with a lot of repetition. If the element at the end of each line were weak, then the last element would flow into the next segment, changing the meter to tetrameter. Some scholars have argued on the basis of this that tetrameter is an extension of dimeter. Conversely, dimeter can be considered to be an abbreviated version of tetrameter.

Tetrameter is composed of four segments on one line, but the length of those segments is not equal. For the sake of simplicity, it was not noted in previous examples, but the line is typically divided in half by a pause, which is the second one that occurs in the line, and which is longer than the first or the third. The length of pauses in the following example is indicated by one to three slashes, with one slash indicating the briefest pause.

> Winter nights are so cold that snow flurries make their way inside.
> Summer days are long, and I wonder why it rains so much.
> When the flowers and the willows bloom in the spring, I'm busy in the fields.
> When the autumn moon shines in my room and the crickets chirp under the house,
> I take a deep breath and start to cry for no reason.
> It's hard to kill things that want to live.
> Trying to get over my troubled feelings, I drop back into helplessness.

> *kyŏul pam / ch'ago ch'an che // chach'oenun / sŏtkŏ ch'igo ///*
> *yŏrŭm nal / kilgo kil che // kujŭn pi nŭn / mŭsŭ ilgo ///*
> *samch'un hwayu / hoshichŏl e // kyŏngmul i / shirŭm ŏpta ///*
> *kaŭl tal / pang e tŭlgo // shilsol i / sang e ul che ///*
> *kin hansum / chinŭn nunmul // sokchŏl ŏpshi / hemman mant'a ///*
> *amado / mojin moksum // chukkido / ŏryŏulsa ///*
> *torohyŏ / p'ulch'yŏ heni // irihaya / ŏihari ///*

> —"Song of Resentment" (Kyuwŏn ka), attributed to Muok

Because of the sense of balance in tetrameter, it is a safe form that is suitable for evocative recitation. Most kasa were written in tetrameter because the narration could be developed fully without the limitations imposed by most poetic forms. Tetrameter was used extensively in shijo and in many *minyo* (folk songs); it was also the basic form in the *shibi kasa* [long kasa known as "the twelve kasa."—Trans.] and short p'ansori songs.

Trimeter is used less than tetrameter, but more than dimeter. Excluding the modern period that began in the late nineteenth century—when trimeter gained rapidly in popularity—this form was used mainly in lyric folk songs, which required strong melodies. This is because trimeter is characterized by an unequal relationship among the three segments on a line: the third segment receives more emphasis than the first and second. Furthermore, the pause after the second segment is generally, though not always, greater than the pause after the first segment. Given these facts, trimeter is structurally closer to tetrameter, as seen in the following example.

> What happened to the good land in front of the house?
> Weren't the gourds growing well?
>
> The field has been torn up for a road.
> The house has been torn down for a railroad.
>
> Those who talk a little end up in court.
> Those who work a little end up in a mine.
>
> *munjŏn ŭi / okt'o nŭn // ŏtchi toego / ø*
> *tchokpak ŭi / shinsega // wenmaringa / ø*
>
> *pat ŭn / hŏllyŏsŏ // shinjangno toego / ø*
> *chip ŭn / hŏllyŏsŏ // chŏnggŏjang toene / ø*
>
> *malkkaena / hanŭn nom // chaep'anso kago / ø*
> *ilkkaena / hanŭn nom // kongdongsan kanda / ø*

> —"Arirang" (Arirang)

The mark ø in the above example represents a pause for breath at the end of each line. Trimeter has two emotionally moving pauses at the end of each line that are longer than the pauses in tetrameter. This is why trimeter is more prevalent in melodic lyric folk songs and why modern poets such as Kim Sowŏl and Kim Yŏngnang made extensive use of this form. Metaphorically speaking, tetrameter is a steady walk, whereas trimeter is a dance that stirs emotion with strong movements and abrupt pauses.

The seven-segment heptameter and the five-segment pentameter in Korean poetry belong to the same category as the trimeter. The *ch'angga* (long songs) of the late nineteenth and early twentieth centuries used heptameter and pentameter extensively. It was previously believed that ch'angga were Western-style songs that came to Korea from Japan, because heptameter and pentameter with each syllable as one segment are the most common forms of meter in Japanese poetry. This argument, however, is not supported by close scrutiny of Korean poetic meter. In contrast to Japanese poetic meter, in which the number of syllables (feet) in each line was rigidly fixed, to 5–7–5 in haiku, for example, or to 5–7–5–7–7 in waka, heptameter and pentameter in Korean poetry are built around the traditional trimeter in combinations of either three, four, and five syllables, or four, three, and five syllables. Many folk songs are also composed in trimeter that fits the above pattern. Conditions at the end of the nineteenth century no doubt contributed to the spread of the ch'angga form. It is impossible, however, to change suddenly from a meter with deep linguistic and poetic roots in one culture to a foreign meter. The 7–5 and its related forms, the 8–5 form and the 6–5 form, are variations of the basic trimeter.

The Issue of Poetic Meter Before the Fourteenth Century

The large amount of original material dating from the Chosŏn period has allowed researchers to define the basic forms of Korean poetic meter, but many questions remain regarding poetic meter from before that time. This applies particularly to works that predate the Koryŏ period. Two competing theories have been put forth to describe the poetic meter of ancient poetry—Koguryŏ songs (*Koguryŏ kayo*), Paekche songs (*Paekche kayo*), and hyangga—all of which were written before the development of hangŭl. The first suggests that tetrameter was the most prevalent form, and the second that trimeter was the most common.

Given that doubts remain about whether there is enough evidence even to describe accurately poetic meter in hyangga, any attempt to come to an understanding of poetic meter of the pre-Koryŏ period requires careful consideration. A tonal system clearly existed in fifteenth-century Korean, but evidence shows that the system started to break down in the sixteenth century. Scholars researching poetry of the pre-Chosŏn period must consider whether tonal meter existed in Korean poetry before the fifteenth century.

Scholars are in broad agreement that the Koryŏ period was dominated by trimeter. This is evident from collections of Koryŏ kayo such as *Canon of Music* (Akhak kwebŏm, 1493), a *Collection of Courtly Songs* (Akchang kasa, mid-sixteenth century), and *Musical Scores for*

Title page from *Musical Scores for Songs and Poems* (Shiyong hyangakpo)

Songs and Poems (Shiyong hyangakpo, ca. 1504). Tetrameter began to appear in "Spring Overflows the Pavilion" (Manjŏnch'un pyŏlsa), the last section of the *kyŏnggich'ega* (kyŏnggi-style songs and poems), supporting the hypothesis that this form appeared toward the end of the Koryŏ period. There are very few extant Koryŏ kayo, and all of these works are parts of collections of court music, which is a cause for doubt about how widespread tetrameter was at the time. The dominance of trimeter in the above three collections of court music is in keeping with the use of this form in melodically developed genres of poetry such as lyric folk songs. If tetrameter first appeared at the end of the Koryŏ period, this raises the question of whether trimeter was the dominant poetic form in the early Koryŏ period and before. Further research is needed in this area, but given later developments in Korean poetic meter, it seems that dimeter, trimeter, and tetrameter all existed in the Koryŏ period as well.

Traditional Poetic Meter and Modern Poetry

Modern free-verse poetry first appeared in Korea in 1915 and developed a unique rhythm and a new way of expression that represented a clear break with traditional meter and form. Contrary to popular assumption, however, modern Korean poetry has deep roots in traditional poetry. The organization of sounds that were chosen to reflect the depth of poetic expression reached a high level of development, based on the selective re-creation and adaptation of previous forms of poetry. This is evident in the work of various poets, particularly Kim Sowŏl, Kim Yŏngnang, Cho Chihun, Pak Mogwŏl, Pak Tujin, and Sŏ Chŏngju. After the release of Shin Kyŏngnim's collection *Farmers' Dances* (Nongmu), contemporary poets have also showed a greater interest in using traditional poetic meter. Some examples of the use of trimeter by modern poets are given below. The lines and pauses are organized to enhance the meaning and allow for an appropriate breath in the flow of the poem.

1.

In the mountains, flowers bloom,
oh, how they bloom.
Fall, spring, and summer through,
oh, how they bloom.
In the mountains,
in the mountains,
the flowers
bloom so well left alone.

san enŭn / kkot p'ine /
kkot i p'ine //
kal pom // yŏrŭm ŏpshi /
kkot i p'ine //

san e /
san e /
p'inŭn kkot ŭn //
chŏmanch'i / honjasŏ / p'iŏ inne //

—from "Mountain Flowers" (Sanyuhwa), Kim Sowŏl

2.

> In my heart somewhere,
> A river flows endlessly.
> The morning sun rising up,
> I frolic in the clear silver waves.
>
> *nae maŭm ŭi / ŏdindŭt / hanp'yŏn e // kkŭt ŏmnŭn /*
> *kangmul i / hŭrŭne //*
> *totch'yŏ orŭnŭn / ach'im / nalbit i // ppanjilhan /*
> *ŭngyŏl ŭl / todone //*

—from "The Endless River" (Kkŭt ŏmnun
kangmul i hŭrŭne), Kim Yŏngnang

3.

> The sweet eyebrows of my deepest love,
> I wiped them clean in the dreams of a thousand nights,
> and shipped them off to heaven.
>
> *nae maŭm sok / uri nim ŭi / koun nunssŏp ŭl //*
> *chŭmun pam ŭi / kkum ŭro / malkke ssisŏsŏ //*
> *hanŭl eda / omgiŏ / shimŏ noattŏni //*

—from "Winter Heaven" (Tongch'ŏn), Sŏ Chŏngju

The expressive trimeter is the most common form in modern and contemporary poetry, but tetrameter is also often used.

1.

> Blossoms fall,
> the wind isn't to blame.
>
> Sparse stars behind the beaded curtain
> fade away one by one.
>
> As the cuckoo cries,
> the distant mountains draw near.
>
> *Kkot i / chigirosoni /*
> *param ŭl / t'atharya //*
>
> *churyŏm pakke / sŏnggin pyŏl i /*
> *hana tul / sŭrŏjigo //*

kwich'okto / urŭm twi e /
mŏŏn san i / tagasŏda //

—from "Falling Blossoms" (Nakhwa), Cho Chihun

2.

Hey, sun, rise up, rise up. Rise up, gentle sun, with your fresh clean
  face.
Eat your way through the darkness as you rise over the mountains.
  Eat your way
through the darkness trying to stay the night as you rise over the
  mountains.
Rise up, gentle sun, with your love-burnt face.

hae ya / sosara. / hae ya / sosara. // malgak'e / ssisŭn ŏlgul / koun
  hae ya / sosara. // san nŏmŏ / san nŏmŏsŏ / ŏdum ŭl / salla
  mŏkko, // san nŏmŏsŏ /
pam saedorok / ŏdum ŭl / salla mŏkko, // igŭl igŭl / aettin ŏlgul /
  koun hae ya / sosara. //

—"Sun" (Hae), Pak Tujin

Some modern and contemporary poets have avoided using any one
particular meter in favor of various forms that fit natural pauses in the
flow of the poem, thus blurring the distinction between free verse and
traditional meter.

Can I not go home,
though I fought hard?
The red blood on the walls, the ancient cries
frighten me, frighten me, though I fought hard.
After I wake, it's all over.
Oh, you rough road,
I wander you yet again.

mot toragari /
irŏsŏttado //
pyŏk wi ŭi / pulgŭn p'i // yet pimyŏngdŭl ch'ŏrŏm //
sosŭrach'yŏ / sosŭrach'yŏ / irŏsŏttado // han pŏn /
cham tŭlgo namyŏ/ kkŭt kkŭnnae //
a a / kŏch'in kil /
nagŭne ro / tu pŏn tashi nŭn //

—from "No Return" (Pulgwi), Kim Chiha

As illustrated in the above examples, traditional poetic meter did not disappear but continued to influence modern and contemporary poetry in various ways. The influence of traditional poetic meter in these poems is not always easy to see on a first read; it is revealed on a closer study of the underlying rhythm. Many modern and contemporary poets aim to create a unique rhythm in each work that goes beyond the more rigid traditional forms. Forms of meter that have evolved over a long history do not suppress creativity but serve as models of the rhythmic possibilities in Korean poetry. Future poets will no doubt take Korean poetry in new directions while continuing to draw on poetic resources from the past for guidance and inspiration.

—————— **4** ——————

Genres of Korean Literature

Literature and Genre

In attempting to gain a complete understanding of a specific genre of Korean literature, many scholars outline the unique characteristics of various literary genres. Although this traditional method of literary analysis may seem out of date, it is still widely used by scholars because it is a convenient way of introducing various types of literature. In this chapter, I will discuss how various types of Korean literature fit into five broad literary genres.

Adherence to a traditional literary analysis does not necessarily mean the logical fallacies in this type of analysis must be ignored. We need to question analyses that force all types of literature into simple categories that can be arranged neatly like bottles of chemicals in a laboratory, or that stick to a rigid, textbook-like classification to such a degree that a clear understanding of each genre gets lost between the cracks. To avoid this, we need to investigate the concept of genre before we begin to discuss the various genres of Korean literature in detail.

Some scholars argue that literature is the composite of many individual works, but a closer investigation reveals that this is not necessarily so. A work of literature is not something that is suspended in midair by itself. It is rather a system of meaning that comes from the complex relationship between past and present works, and writers and readers who are bound together by various literary traditions and conventions, which are an integral part of a language and its literature. "Understanding literature" is not simply understanding the text itself but includes an understanding of the human experience, through reference to the literary traditions and conventions that surround a particular work. When we deal for the first time with a work with an interesting opening line, we are reminded, either consciously or unconsciously, of other works that have a similar structure, grammar, and form. We can also gain an understanding of the work by imagining what will happen as the story unfolds. If we did not have these reference points, our understanding of the work would be slow and vague.

This is also true in the creation of a work of literature. Writers follow the methods and traditions of the world that surrounds them, and they also put this world of experience and thought into their work. The resulting works then become part of the existing body of literary conventions and, in turn, influence subsequent works.

The term *genre* refers to various levels of literary convention that describe the human experience aesthetically and that are common to many different works. Genre is a system of literary description that helps put works into several clearly organized categories, but it is open enough so that each work of literature can be discussed on its own merits. All works of literature are unique in their own right, but they are inevitably related in some way to the conventions and styles practiced in a specific area of literary creation. Even experimental art that rejects the limitations of convention needs "negative" conventions to exist. When the expression and development of experimental art is accepted as something meaningful, it becomes a new convention that defines it as experimental artistic activity. In this sense, all works of art and literature are products of an individual's unique life experiences and emotional needs.

Though genres are useful in understanding literature, they should not be isolated from each other by rigid boundaries. Some works of literature do not fit conveniently into any of the major genres, and some works overlap several genres, making them difficult to classify. Historical genres such as shijo, p'ansori, dream records (*mongyurok*), sonnets, and Greek tragedy existed before they came to be recognized as such. A genre comes into existence at a certain point in time or is the result of a sudden change in a dominant form of literature that had existed for a long or short time.

Genre is more than an organized system of principles and unique characteristics that are a convenient means of unifying works of literature under one particular name; rather, it consists of the broad features that are extracted from various works that have a certain affinity with each other. This varies according to the time period and the culture, but individual works, while corresponding to the defining characteristics of the genre, often have features that defy the standard definition of it. In the latter case, we need to understand how genres overlap and evolve. In addition, some genres are flexible enough to include a variety of works, not just those that conform to a particular set of conventions. If there was a time when genres were believed to comprise basic, unchangeable rules, then there was also a time when creative individuality and diverse points of view were welcomed. When we look at the literary history of many nations we find that in certain eras, attempts were made to maintain a stable system of genres, whereas in others old and new genres competed with each other. In discussing literary genres, we need to maintain a degree of flexibility that allows us to include the diverse historical evolution of a particular genre.

Broad Genres and Narrow Genres

Because historical and modern genres are so numerous, Asian and Western scholars have tried to define several broad genres that accurately include all types of literary convention. The contents of these genres are diverse, and are usually divided into a system of two, three, four, five, or seven categories. Opinions vary greatly, however, on how broad genres should be defined. We are interested in defining the contours of Korean literature rather than discussing theoretical issues relating to literary genre. Most scholars of Korean literature have followed a system of four comparatively broad literary genres; I will discuss this system as it applies to Korean literature in this chapter.

This system of classification divides literary works into four categories based on certain general characteristics and attempts to explain the relationship among the narrow historical genres that make up each of the four. Literary scholars differ on how they define these four basic genres, but I will adopt the system developed by Professor Cho Dong-il [Cho Tongil] of Seoul National University, which is based on the addition of the "didactic genre" to the three traditional genres: the lyric, the narrative, and the dramatic. This method of classification is particularly important in developing a theory of genre adequate to cope with the diverse history of East Asian literature. The three-genre method of classification commonly applied to modern Western literature, which emphasizes imagination, is ill-suited to the study of Korean literature because Korean, Chinese, Japanese, Vietnamese and Ryūkyū Island literature—literature of the Chinese character cultural zone (hanja munhwakwŏn)—has traditionally placed greater emphasis on honest expression of the author's feelings than on creative imagination. Records written in literary style before the nineteenth century that include fiction and poems are examples of this mixture of genres in one particular work. No one has found a definitive term for this genre, which includes personal accounts, written records, and documents promoting a certain religion or ideology, but Cho Dong-il's use of the term *didactic* is suitable to describe it.

This method of analysis does not solve all of the problems of applying a theory of genre to Korean literature; on the contrary, it causes more problems than it solves, as is evident from the following two questions: (1) Are the four broad genres—the lyric, the narrative, the dramatic, and the didactic—based on clear divisions that divide them from one another according to certain conditions, or are they based on a continuum that allows for intermediate genres at various points along that continuum? (2) Do the broad genres exist regardless of cultural and temporal differences, or are they a tool that can be used to explain how the various narrow genres relate to each other?

I will attempt to answer the above questions by arguing that the latter view of each is correct; that is, that as a system of broad genres is a concept developed to explain various historical genres, we can combine these narrow genres into one unified genre. However, historical genres still overlap, allowing us to place literary works that have characteristics belonging to several of the broad genres on a continuum.

This approach has several benefits with regard to Korean literature. First, it is impossible for the broad genres to be subsumed in a complete or universal system that fits any literature in any era, contrary to what those who believe in cultural universality argue. An understanding of the system of broad genres as the theoretical model of a cultural phenomenon reflects a particular worldview and attitude toward literature at a basic level; at a more superficial level, it stimulates research and debate among literary scholars about the theory of genre. Thus, this approach is more beneficial because it raises the interest of researchers in finding culture-specific definitions of genre and helps them to develop more effective explanations of how genres function in various cultures. Of course, not all theories about how to establish and classify various genres are equally beneficial, but many well-developed theories of genre have emerged over thousands of years of literary discussion. These genres are thus rooted in the historical evolution of the broad genres.

Those scholars who argue for universal genres often force various literary styles and genres into one broad category to fit their universalistic arguments. Such logic affirms a static structure and traps scholars into forcing various historical genres into one of the broad genres: all lyrics into the lyric genre, all narratives into the narrative genre. It is all too easy to simplify the evolution and change of historical genres for the sake of explanation. This view of genre fails to provide an adequate explanation of the frequent changes in how genres relate to each other as reflections of the dynamics of literary creation. For example, if we took a restrictive view of the distinction between the narrative and didactic genres, we would have difficulty in explaining how facts became fables and how fables evolved into legends and novels. In addition, works such as Korean narrative songs and English ballads contain a great deal of narration. In many cases, narrative is used to resolve a conflict within the structure of a lyric work rather than simply for the sake of interest. Thus, we need to deal with the issue of whether to define a mixed genre that adheres to features of several broad genres. Broad genres cannot escape this fundamental problem.

To illustrate the above points clearly, I have devised the following graph, which describes how the broad genres relate to each other. Instead of adopting terminology based on clearly defined nouns, such as lyrics, narrative, drama, exposition, I have decided to use adjectives— lyric, narrative, dramatic, didactic—to identify each respective genre. This gives each genre more flexibility and allows it to include a wider range of works. Various historical genres are located at intermediate points along the horizontal and vertical axes. Certain genres on the graph may be very close to one of the broad genres, whereas others may be more distant. Such a graph is an oversimplification, but it is useful as a visual aid.

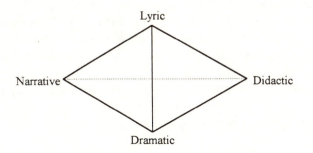

Various historical genres lie inside the diamond that is formed by the broad genres. These historical genres grow, evolve, and fade away with the flow of time. Historical genres are not simply points but extended spaces that occupy part of the interior of the diamond. Parts of any given historical genre may be closer to or relatively further from one of the broad genres. Genres can be found at various intermediate points in the above graph because they combine features of several genres. Literary historians have debated how to handle historical genres such as kasa, *kajŏn* (fictitious biographies), and classical Chinese narrative, but a satisfactory answer has yet to emerge because these historical genres have characteristics in common with one or more of the broad genres.

Thus, locating the historical genres inside the diamond is not as easy as it seems if we adopt an open approach to defining the broad genres. However, we need to have a rough outline of how the historical genres relate to the four broad genres, and in the case of those that do not fit any one of the four, we need a fifth broad genre, which I call the "intermediate and mixed genre." We also need to be aware that certain works and features of some historical genres that are close to one of the broad genres may overlap with one or more of the other broad genres.

In view of the above discussion, the various historical genres in Korean literature can be placed in one of the five broad genres in the following way:

1. Lyric genres: ancient songs (*kodae kayo*), hyangga, Koryŏ folk songs (*Koryŏ sogyo*), shijo, narrative shijo (*sasŏl shijo*), *chapka* (light songs), lyric folk songs (*sŏjŏng minyo*), most poetry in classical Chinese, new poetry (*shinch'eshi*) of the nineteenth century, most modern poems (*hyŏndaeshi*)
2. Narrative genres: myths (*shinhwa*), narrative poems (*sŏsashi*), legends (*chŏnsŏl*), folk tales, narrative folk songs (*sŏsa minyo*), narrative shaman chants (*sŏsa muga*), p'ansori, the classic novel (*kojŏn sosŏl*), the new novel (*shinsosŏl*), the modern novel (*hyŏndae sosŏl*)
3. Dramatic genres: mask dance (*t'alch'um*), puppet theater (*kkoktukkakshi norŭm*), new theater (*ch'anggŭk*), *shinp'agŭk*, modern drama (*hyŏndaegŭk*).

4. Didactic genres: *akchang* (court music), *ch'angga*, essays (*sup'il*), diaries (*ilgi*), travelogues (*kihaeng*), various types of literature in classical Chinese (*hanmunhak*).
5. Intermediate and mixed genres: *kyŏnggich'ega,* kasa, kajŏn, dream records (*mongyurok*), yadam

The rest of this chapter is devoted to a detailed discussion of each of the historical genres of Korean literature.

1. Lyric Genres

Ancient Songs (Kodae Kayo)

It is difficult to know whether Korean literature originated in lyric or narrative poetry, but the peoples of northeast Asia and the Korean Peninsula who were the ancestors of the Korean people probably had a wide variety of songs. Most of these songs had a religious function or were sung as prayers during hunting or farmwork. Many probably dealt with everyday hopes and aspirations in addition to being ceremonial songs sung in thanks for the blessings of nature or to invoke a supernatural power through praise, eulogy, and confession. Their ceremonial function in ancient Korean society is apparent in the following examples taken from [a Chinese source] the "History of Wei" section of *The History of the Three Kingdoms* (Samguk chi; Chinese: Sanguo zhi) by Chen Shou (233–297).

> On New Year's Day, according to the Yin version of the lunar calendar, the people in the kingdom of Puyŏ hold a festival in honor of the heavens. At this festival, which is called "The Festival of Welcoming Drums" [*Yŏngo*], they drink, dance, and sing endlessly. People of all ages fill the streets of the village day and night, singing and making merry for days on end.
>
> In the kingdom of Mahan, the people hold a festival in honor of the gods after finishing the spring planting in May. They drink and sing for days on end at this festival. They dance in large groups, moving back and forth and repeatedly bending their bodies toward the ground and rising up again. They move their hands and feet to the rhythm of their bodies.
>
> The people of Koguryŏ like to sing and dance. Men and women in villages throughout the country gather every night to sing and dance.
>
> In Chinhan, people like to dance and sing while drinking and playing the zither [*kŏmungo*].

Transmitted in classical Chinese, the "Song of the Turtle" (Kuji ka, A.D. 42), one of the few songs surviving today, is clearly an incantation, but we can interpret the "Song of the Konghu Zither" (Konghuin, 108 B.C.) as a lyric poem because it contains a great deal of lyric grief. The "Song of Nightingales" (Hwangjo ka, 17 B.C.), which was sung by King Yuri, the second king of the Koguryŏ kingdom, is a terse and honest lyric poem:

> Nightingales flutter above,
> Man and woman, nestling together.
> Deep in loneliness, I wonder,
> Who will come home with me?

The organization of this poem is very simple, but this is a complete and balanced poem. The nightingales next to the lonely man are an important symbol in this poem: the lightness of flying, the heaviness of the man's lonely heart, and the melancholy hymn at the end all contrast with each other. These contrasting elements emphasize the longing and loneliness in the song simply and directly.

The "History of Koguryŏ" (Koguryŏ pongi) section of *The History of the Three Kingdoms* (Samguk sagi, 1145) describes the origin of this song as follows: A nightingale sang it to King Yuri when he was resting underneath a tree on his way home after losing a princess whom he loved. Although this song refers to the king, it was probably sung among the common people of the time.

Both of these ancient songs have come down to us in classical Chinese in four lines of four characters each. This unified form not only reflects the influence of the translators of the poems, who modeled their translations on *The Book of Songs* (Shi kyŏng; Chinese: Shi jing), the earliest collection of Chinese classic poems, but also the traditional structure of ancient songs, in which one line or one verse of a song was made of four syllables. The appearance of the four-line form in hyangga that have features in common with folk songs also lends support to the argument that this form was characteristic of ancient Korean songs.

Hyangga

The term *hyangga,* which was used to define a genre of Shilla Dynasty poetry, comes from a combination of terms that refer to Chinese poetry

Hyangga, "Requiem for My Sister" (Che mangmae ka)

and Sanskrit poetry. It refers to poems that used the hyangch'al system of Chinese characters to represent Korean pronunciation faithfully. Although the use of the hyangch'al system is considered a necessary condition for a poem to be classified as a hyangga, most hyangga, as evident in *Memorabilia of the Three Kingdoms* (Samguk yusa, ca. 1285) do not meet this requirement because they were written down long after they were composed as oral poems.

Not only do hyangga include works with oral origins as well as poems composed in writing, they also are extremely diverse in form and content, a fact which makes it difficult to view hyangga as a unified genre based on a clearly defined set of characteristics. Although some researchers place all works written in hyangch'al in the hyangga genre, the term *hyangga* refers to a genre of poetry in Korean that corresponds closely to Tang Chinese poetry and Sanskrit poetry.

The people of Shilla used many other terms in addition to the more general *hyangga*. This matter is difficult to clarify because so few original sources remain, but, as a genre, *hyangga* is a general term that refers to a diverse collection of individual works.

The diversity of hyangga shows that it is not a genre unified by a dominant poetic form but a collection of individual works in a variety of poetic forms. Of the twenty-five extant hyangga, fourteen are found in *Memorabilia of the Three Kingdoms* and eleven are found in the "Songs of the Ten Vows of Samantabhadra" (Pohyŏn shipchong wŏnwangsaeng ka, 973) section of *The Life of the Great Monk Kyunyŏ* (Kyunyŏ chŏn, 1075). "Song of Sŏdong" (Sŏdong yo, ca. 599), "Ballad" (P'ungyo, ca. 632–647), "Song of Offering Flowers" (Hŏnhwa ka, ca. 702–731), and "Song of Offering Flowers Before Buddha" (Sanhwa Kongdŏk ka, ca. 760) are composed of four lines; "Ode to the Hwarang Chukchi" (Mo Chukchi rang ka, ca. 692–702 ["hwarang" refers to mounted warriors of the Shilla Dynasty. —Trans.]) and "Song of Ch'ŏyong" (Ch'ŏyong ka, 879) of eight; the "Song of the Comet" (Hyesŏng ka, ca. 579–631) and "Ode to the Hwarang Kip'a" (Ch'an Kip'a rang ka, ca. 742–765), "Requiem for My Sister" (Che mangmae ka, ca. 742–765), and the eleven poems in "Songs of the Ten Vows of Samantabhadra" are in the ten-line form. This diversity of form is not limited to the number of lines but extends to the overall structure of the poem. In particular, ten-line hyangga are divided into three sections, two of four lines and one of two lines, and the expression of emotion is concentrated at the beginning of the two-line section; expressively, therefore, it differs entirely from the four- and the eight-line forms.

Most literary historians have interpreted this variation of form as a reflection of the development from the four-line form with its roots in simple folk songs to the eight-line form, and finally to the highest form of hyangga, the ten-line form. Natural as this evolution may seem, it does not fit the history of hyangga; in fact, the four- and eight-line forms continued to exist alongside each other. Of the existing four-line hyangga, "Song of Tuṣita Heaven" (Tosol ka) was composed as late as 760, and the eight-line form continued well into the Koryŏ period, as evident in the "Chant for Two Great Generals" (To ijang ka, 1120). Thus, although the three forms of hyangga may have developed one from another, they also existed alongside each other as independent forms.

The contents of hyangga are also diverse. All of the ten-line hyanggas were composed by individuals, but the four-line hyangga "Ballad" is clearly a folk song, and the eight-line "Song of Ch'ŏyong" is a shaman chant, while "Song of Offering Flowers" is generally considered to be something between a folk song and a shaman chant.

Hyangga are diverse in content because the genre not only evolved from the four-line form with its origins in folk songs to the ten-line form with its emphasis on the writer's emotion, it also maintained the four-, eight-, and ten-line forms in the process of evolution. Thus the history of the development of the hyangga is one of important literary change from oral forms of literature such as folk songs and shaman chants to poems composed in written language by individuals.

Because hyangga are so diverse, it is difficult to classify them according to the social origins of their authors. If we classified the existing hyangga by social class, we would force differing works into the same category, thus ignoring conflicting arguments about the effects of social class on the development of the hyangga. Thus, the only conclusion that we can draw about the hyangga from the existing evidence is that the four-line hyangga originated in folk songs, whereas the ten-line hyangga originated in the writer's emotion; we can only speculate about the influence of social class. One theory holds that the four-line hyangga was composed by all classes of society, whereas another theory holds that the ten-line hyangga was composed by the upper class, such as mounted *hwarang* warriors and Buddhist monks. The hyangga were not unique to the upper classes, but the ten-line hyangga reflect the interests and sensibilities of the upper classes more than do the four-line hyangga.

All of the ten-line hyangga are divided into three sections: the first section, of four lines, introduces the subject of the poem; the second section, also of four lines, intensifies or alters the emotion of the subject; and the third section, of two lines, starts with an exclamation and ends with a strong conclusion. To illustrate this point I will use an example from "Requiem for My Sister" by Wŏlmyŏng, a famous Shilla Buddhist monk:

> The road to life and death
> Stands fearfully before us.
> Without saying good-bye,
> Have you left me?
> The early morning wind in autumn
> Scatters leaves here and there.

> Though from the same branch,
> They know not where they've gone.
>
> Oh, my dear sister, to see you again in
>   Amitābha's Paradise,
> I shall wait, perfecting Buddha's way.

The above hyangga deals with the basic issue of death. The writer is paying tribute to his younger sister, who died young. The agony that the writer feels at his sister's death appears in the first four lines of the poem. This is revealed in the melancholy question "Without saying good-bye, have you left me?" about the suffering of death that the writer feels in a world in which life and death exist alongside each other. The writer broadens the agony that he feels into anguish at the transience of existence. By drawing a contrast between the wind, which symbolizes the power that rules over all finite forms of life, and the leaves, which symbolize the worthlessness of the individual, and by voicing his thoughts in the form of a question, the writer reveals a deep sense of powerlessness. The exclamation at the beginning of the last two lines is not only an expression of extreme emotional suffering but also an appeal for divine intervention. The poem ends by embracing the Buddhist vision of going beyond the transience of worldly existence to achieve enlightenment.

This emotional effusion and structure of resolution are appropriate for subjects such as the sincere expression of prayer or the sublime admiration of existence, which are found in many famous works; for example, "Ode to the Hwarang Kip'a," "Prayer to Amitābha" (Wŏnwang saeng ka, ca. 661–680) and the poems in "Songs of the Ten Vows of Samantabhadra," which are full of clear, profound emotion and prayer. This reflects the influence of the traditional Buddhist worldview. Terms such as "extremely lofty meaning" or "pure words and beautiful phrases" are applied to the ten-line hyangga because hyangga in this form contain highly developed rhythm and lyric elegance.

Koryŏ Folk Songs

After the founding of the Koryŏ Dynasty in 918 A.D., literature in classical Chinese developed as hyangga declined, causing poetry in Korean to return to the medium of oral literature. Thus, no lyric genres other than poetry in classical Chinese remain from this period. Al-

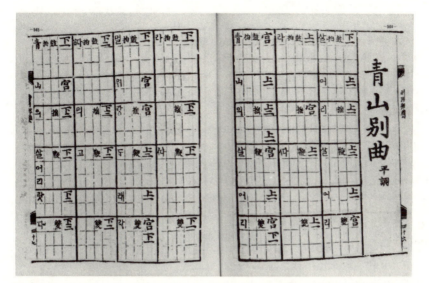

Score for the koryŏ sogyo, "Song of the Green Mountains" (Ch'ŏngsan pyŏlgok)

though very few primary sources exist, we are able to make a few educated guesses about how native Korean literature evolved at this time. Except for the *kyŏnggich'ega,* native Korean lyrics from the period are generally called *Koryŏ sogyo* or Koryŏ folk songs, although some scholars refer to them as *kosokka, changga,* or *pyŏlgok.*

Though *Koryŏ sogyo* is a convenient term for all native Korean lyrics other than the kyŏnggich'ega, this is by no means a genre unified by a set of common characteristics. A closer look at the works in question reveals that not all of them are folk songs, a fact which calls into question the appropriateness of the word *sogyo.* The problem with changing the terminology in our discussion here is that *Koryŏ sogyo* (Koryŏ folk songs) is the most commonly used term in the literature, and many of the songs in this category refer to the everyday life and aspiration of the common people.

All of the Koryŏ sogyo, except for those that are translated as *akpu* in other books, appear in three books: *Canon of Music* (Akhak kwebŏm, 1493), *Musical Scores for Songs and Poems* (Shiyong hyangakpo, ca. 1504), and *Collection of Courtly Songs* (Akchang kasa, mid-sixteenth century). These books comprise musical scores for court music from the early Chosŏn period together with a few sections containing Koryŏ sogyo. The Koryŏ sogyo that have come down to us are not representative of the lyrics of the Koryŏ period but are selected works of Koryŏ court lyrics that persisted into the early Chosŏn period and were recorded in written form in the above books and then published in the early Chosŏn period. We must therefore be careful not to make generalizations about Koryŏ period lyrics from an analysis of the extant Koryŏ sogyo.

In terms of form, the Koryŏ sogyo are divided into two major types: independent line verse and linked verse. "Song of Chŏngŭp" (Chongŭp sa) and "Song of Chŏng Kwajŏng" (Chŏng Kwajŏng kok, ca. 1160) are similar in form to the ten-line hyangga, which can be viewed as the last stage of the hyangga or as the first stage in the evolution from hyangga to Koryŏ sogyo. The linked-verse form in which most of the well-known Koryŏ sogyo, such as "Song of the Green Mountains" (Ch'ŏngsan pyŏlgok), "Tongdong," "Song of Sŏgyŏng" (Sŏgyŏng pyŏlgok ["Sŏgyŏng" refers to present-day P'yŏngyang. —Trans.]), "A Mandu Shop" (Ssanghwajŏm; "mandu" refers to Korean dumplings that are steamed, fried, or used in soup. Trans.), and "Spring Overflows the Pavilion " (Manjŏnch'un pyŏlsa), all from the early to mid-fourteenth century, are interesting because a refrain or a short utterance is inserted in the middle of the song. In terms of poetic meter, the trimeter is dominant, but some works are written in other meters. The following is an example of a trimeter song in linked-verse from "Song of Sŏgyŏng":

> Sŏgyŏng, *ajŭlga.*
> Sŏgyŏng is the capital but,
> > *Oh, tuŏryŏngsyŏng, tuŏryŏngsyŏng, taringdiri.*
>
> We made it, *ajŭlga.*
> We love our beautiful small capital
> > *Oh, tuŏryŏngsyŏng, tuŏryŏngsyŏng, taringdiri.*
>
> Rather than lose you, *ajŭlga.*
> Rather than lose you, I'll stop making cloth
> > *Oh, tuŏryŏngsyŏng, tuŏryŏngsyŏng, taringdiri.*
>
> If you love me, *ajŭlga.*
> If you love me, I chase after you with tears in my eyes
> > *Oh, tuŏryŏngsyŏng, tuŏryŏngsyŏng, taringdiri.*

—anonymous

The extant Koryŏ sogyo can be divided into the following five groups: folk songs, court dancing music adapted from folk songs, Buddhist songs such as "Muae" and "Song in Praise of Guanyin" (Kwanŭm ch'an), shaman chants such as the Song of Ch'ŏyong" and "The Great King Kunma" (Kunma taewang) and songs composed by individuals. The reasons for placing Buddhist songs and shaman chants in special categories are self-evident, but the three remaining categories are more difficult to classify.

Although songs such as "Song of Threshing Rice" (Sangjŏ ka), "Song of Maternal Love" (Sa mo kok), and "Are You Leaving Now?" (Kasiri) have come down to us as court music, they retain many features of folk songs, which justifies the use of the term "sogyo" to refer to them. Folk songs such as "Chesŏnggang," "Kŏsabyŏn," "Wŏljŏnghwa," and "Tamna yo" appear in classical Chinese translations in such works as The History of Koryŏ (Koryŏ sa, 1451) The Collected Works of Ikchae (Ikchae chip, 1363), An Augmented Survey of the Geography of Korea (Tongguk yŏji sŭngnam, 1481), and The New Reference Compilation of Documents on Korea (Chŭngbo munhŏn pigo, 1908). Many of these works include such themes as love between couples or between parents and children, sarcastic criticism of social conditions, and descriptions of the everyday life of farmers. Some of these folk songs were brought to the royal palace by singers and royal maids and were either adapted to court music or sung in their original form. Thus, most Koryŏ sogyo have more affinity with folk songs than with the court music of the time. The following example, Sangjŏ ka, with its light tone and simple, clear language, was sung by workers as they threshed rice:

> Tŏlk'ŏdŏng, I'm milling away, hiae.
> Though the rice isn't very good, hiae,
> I'll give some to my parents first, hiyahae,
> And eat the rest myself, hiyahae.

Most lyrics that derived from folk songs were revised in the process of being included in collections of court music scores and thus lost much of their original, folk characteristics. Most of these revisions took place in the latter half of the Koryŏ period, a period dominated by the pleasure-seeking lifestyle of the royal palace. Works such as "Secret Lives at Court" (Hujŏn chinjak), "A Mandu Shop," and "Spring

Overflows the Pavilion" belong to this category. In the process of revision, some lines and words were condensed and omitted so that the lyrics of the song would be acceptable for use in the royal palace. Thus songs of this type are no longer considered folk songs, despite their folk origin.

Lyrics composed by individual writers have also survived. "Chant for Two Great Generals" comes from the period when hyangga were in decline, and "Song of Chŏng Kwajŏng" is a vestige of the hyangga form. Most works of this type are listed in the "Akchi" and "Yŏljŏn" sections of *The History of Koryŏ* by the title, author, and motive for composition. Scholars disagree on whether "Song of the Green Mountains" originated as a folk song or whether it was composed by a person who was a scholar or aristocrat. When written for music, lyrics composed by individual writers are divided into two major categories: lyrics in praise of the king, and lyrics about the elegant life of the aristocracy.

To summarize, the term *Koryŏ sogyo* is a convenient label for various lyrics that differ in form, origin, and purpose, but it does not represent a genre based on a set of well-defined characteristics. Excluding works that developed from shaman chants, such as "Song of Ch'ŏyong," "Song of Offering Rice at the Village Alter" (Sŏnghwangban), and "Song of the Great King Samsŏng" (Samsŏng taewang), which have a dramatic element, most of the Koryŏ sogyo are lyric poems, but the way of expression and the origin and character of these lyrics differs so much that it is difficult to classify these works into clearly defined groups. In addition, the existing Koryŏ sogyo do not represent the entire history of native Korean poetry of the Koryŏ period because most of these works were adapted and changed to fit the interests of the court and the aristocracy and the musical conventions of court music, a fact which accounts for the great many Koryŏ sogyo that deal with themes such as love and merrymaking.

Shijo

Of all genres of traditional Korean literature, *shijo* comprises the largest number of extant works and has had the widest appeal over a long period of time. Shijo gained its strength as a poetic form from precise and controlled language, graceful and clear poetic aesthetics, a concise three-line, twelve-segment form, and a lyric structure that allows individual variation while restricting the range of thought. As defined by a unified poetic structure, shijo is the genre with the clearest set of defining characteristics and the broadest appeal among those engaged in literary activity since the ten-line form of hyangga.

In its basic form, the shijo is composed of four segments (*ŭmbo*) repeated three times in one poem (the tetrameter/three-line structure). The word *ŭmbo* refers to rhythmical segments in a line of verse, but differs from the English concept of metric feet because Korean rhythmical segments do not distinguish between stressed an unstressed syllables with the segment. Of the segments—the basic unit of poetic meter in shijo—the four-segment form is the average length in frequency of use; segments that are shorter than that are called "short segments," and those that are longer are called "long segments." The general structure of shijo is summarized in the following chart (the numbers in parenthesis refer to the most common alternatives to this structure:

3	4	4 (3)	4
3	4	4 (3)	4
3	5	4	3

The first songwriters were no doubt full of worry.
Did their worries find a better voice in song than in words?
If song cast their worries aside, then I too shall sing!

norae / samgin sarăm / shirŭm to / hado halshya //
nillŏ / ta mot nillŏ / pullŏna / p'udot tănga //
chinshil ro / pŭllil kŏshimyŏnŭn / na to pullŏ / porira //

—Shin Hŭm

The structure of the first two lines creates a relatively regular flow that indicates that the poem will continue and is thus an open form of poetic meter. The combination of short and long segments at the beginning of the last line stops the flow of the previous two lines to create a sense of tension; the end of the line brings the poem to a close with a sudden relaxation of this built-up tension. The last line always begins with an exclamatory phrase and ends in a phrase that reveals the author's attitude toward the subject in the form of a command or another exclamation. The shijo is structurally stable because of the simplicity of the three-line form; as a result of this formulaic principle, shijo has helped raise poetic expression to a high level.

Literary scholars do not agree on when the forms of shijo became fixed. One theory holds that shijo evolved from the three sections of the ten-line hyangga; another holds that the origin of shijo lies in the three-line, tetrameter type of *Koryŏ sogyo*, such as "Spring Overflows the Pavilion" (Manjŏnch'un pyŏlsa); and yet another theory holds that shijo evolved from folk songs in the late Koryŏ period.

Although the origin of shijo might be in the latter part of the Koryŏ period, it did not flourish as a genre until the Chosŏn period. The tightly controlled language and form of the shijo fit the aesthetic sensibilities of the yangban class in the Chosŏn period because it allowed the yangban to express their innermost feelings elegantly. As Yi Hwang noted in his "Postscript to the Twelve Songs of Tosan" (Tosan shibi kokpal, 1565) poems in classical Chinese could be recited but not sung, indicating that, despite a strong preference for classical Chinese, some yangban viewed native Korean genres positively.

Many exceptional shijo poets emerged in the first half of the Chosŏn period: Yi Hyŏn (1467–1555), Yi Hwang (1501–1570), Kwŏn Hyomun (1532–1587), Chŏng Ch'ŏl (1536–1593), and Shin Hŭm (1566–1628). The dominant theme among these poets was Confucian ethics and life lived in harmony with nature to escape the stresses and conflicts of society. Together, Yun Sŏndo's (1587–1671) "The Fisherman's Calendar" (Ŏbu sashi sa, 1651) and "New Songs from the Mountains" (Sanjung shingok, ca. 1642–1645) not only give us the most detailed portrayal of an idealized life in harmony with nature, but also represent one of the linguistic and aesthetic peaks of the shijo genre. The following shijo are examples of an ideal life in harmony with nature:

1.
> When night falls on an autumn river, it turns cold.
> I cast my line into the cold, but nothing bites.
> Loading the lonely moonlight into my boat, I go home
> empty-handed.
>
> —Prince Wŏnsan

2.

> A lonely pine stands by the river's edge. Why does it look so brave?
> Tie up your boat, tie up your boat.
> Don't loathe the clouds; they only hide this dirty world.
> *Chigukch'ong chigukch'ong ŏsawa*
> Don't loathe the noise of the waves; they only block the noise of the
>   real world.
>
> Oh, the sun is setting, and it's time to go home to rest.
> Bring your boat to dock, bring your boat to dock.
> I walk slowly down the sunset-tainted road covered deep in snow.
> *Chigukch'ong chigukch'ong ŏsawa*
> Until the cold moon sets over the hills in the west, I shall sit by my
>   window
> Looking out at the lonely pine.
>
> —"Winter" (Tong); "The Fisherman's Calendar"
> (Ŏbu sashi sa), Yun Sŏndo

The fisherman in the above poems is not a person who makes a living by fishing; rather, he symbolizes a reclusive yangban who attempts to get close to nature so as to transcend mundane concerns. The "lonely pine" and the moonlight shining on the empty boat express the desire for a life free of worry. Images of clouds, waves, snow, moonlight, and solitary thought are used to create a lonely atmosphere.

In the second half of the seventeenth century, shijo, which had been exclusively the province of the yangban class, began to be composed by a variety of people who were not yangban. In this period, shijo, which had been sung according to a clearly defined technique, became simpler and less technically demanding to sing and so appealed to a wider audience. Collections of shijo, such as *Songs from Green Hill* (Ch'ŏnggu yŏngŏn, 1728) by Kim Ch'ŏnt'aek (n.d.) and *Songs from the East* (Haedong kayo, 1755 ["East" refers to Korea. —Trans.]) by Kim Sujang (b. 1690) were published, further popularizing shijo. Common people who liked shijo adopted the form as a way to express themselves clearly, not as a form of high poetry. The commoners were also attracted to shijo because it allowed them to express their feelings and experiences freely in Korean, rather than in classical Chinese, which many commoners did not know. Along with this trend, the subject matter of shijo became more diverse. And as yangban domination of shijo waned, the influx of new writers, including anonymous ones, enriched the genre with a new set of feelings and experiences. This change is clear in the following examples:

1.

> Putting away my long sword, I sit down to think.
> All that I believed in turned into a dream one afternoon .
> Forget it! Words cannot change my fate.

> —Kim Ch'ŏnt'aek

2.

> Hey, you, you cranes bobbing up and down as you forage among
>   the red weeds on a sandy beach.
> How can you bob up and down on an empty stomach?
> Hunger is my shame, so I too must bob my head up and down.

> —*Song of the Peaceful Scent from the South*
> (Namhun t'aep'yŏng ka), anonymous

The first example shows the conflict over status that Kim Ch'ŏnt'aek, who was born into a family of minor local officials, must have felt. The poem invokes the Chinese four-character proverb *handan chibo* ("treading water") to express Kim Ch'ŏnt'aek's depression and agony over being mistreated in a society in which one's fate was determined by birth. In the second example, we see active conflicts in society; this differs greatly from early shijo imbued with yangban sensibilities about harmony with nature and Confucian values. Symbols from nature, such as white beaches, red weeds, and swans, that appeared in shijo of the early Chosŏn period gave way to more realistic symbols in the latter part of the period, reflecting an interest in focusing on real-life problems instead of on the contemplation of beauty. Themes and ways of expression from the early Chosŏn period survived into the later Chosŏn period, but the changes discussed above represent important developments that deserve further study.

Narrative Shijo

The term *narrative shijo* (*sasŏl shijo*) originated as a description of a subcategory of shijo composed in a looser, more narrative form rather than in the well-defined standard form. Narrative shijo are now classified as a separate genre; in terms of form, the last line is similar to that of standard shijo, but the first and second lines become longer, a dramatic departure from the common four-segment (tetrameter) structure. Some scholars attempt to divide narrative shijo into categories such as "mid-length shijo" and "long shijo." Although narrative shijo can be so categorized, the difference in form and content between standard shijo and narrative shijo is more important than the modest difference between mid-length and long examples of the latter; this clear difference justifies the use of these two genres of shijo.

A few scholars take the view that narrative shijo came from folk songs that existed alongside standard shijo in the early and middle Chosŏn period, which contradicts the broadly accepted theory that narrative shijo are a deviant form of standard shijo. These scholars use the term *manhwangch'ŏng* instead of "narrative shijo" to define this genre. Unlike standard shijo, works in this category came from folk songs of the common people and thus refer to the experiences of the common people. These songs probably emerged well before the beginning of the eighteenth century. Scholars who support this theory base their definition of narrative shijo on the musical features of the genre, the melody and rhythm.

Narrative shijo extended the range of poetry of the late Chosŏn period by bringing in the wit, sarcasm, and earthy language of the common people. Unlike the standard shijo of the yangban class, with their refined form and contemplative beauty, the narrative shijo are full of the energy of everyday life expressed in a rough yet vibrant language. The governing principle behind the narrative shijo is the aesthetic of laughter, which is felt in the sharp irony with which everyday life is described, the bitter sarcasm directed against the rigid ideology of the Chosŏn period, and in witticisms about the drudgery of life in the country. Love and sex are also common themes and are at times portrayed strongly and explicitly. The first of the following two examples shows one woman's view of men; the second example is a cry of resentment against the king by a soldier injured in battle. The feelings of the common people and the subtleties of honest expression in these works are what make narrative shijo a unique genre of Korean literature.

1.

Look at the handsome man in the white clothes over there.
I run over the little stone bridge and then over the big stone bridge.

Oh, how I wish he could be my husband!
If he cannot be mine, I hope that one of my friends gets him.

—anonymous

2.

I strap a bow, a club, and knives to my waist. Oh, how I hate the old
   Chinese Emperor Xuan Yuanshi for inventing war.
Before we learned to fight, we lived in peace and harmony for
   eighteen thousand years.
Just look at how we have learned to make weapons and kill each
   other since!

—anonymous

We should be careful not to simplify the discussion of the contents and form of narrative shijo such as the examples above from a contemporary point of view. Although the sexual explicitness and the sarcastic sense of humor in most narrative shijo can be interpreted as a reaction against the prudery of the Chosŏn period, these tendencies do not represent the rise of an alternative system of values in that period. In coming to terms with the transience of life, composers of narrative shijo often reinterpreted the meaning of life pessimistically, seeing self-absorption in the pleasures of the flesh as the only way of escape. In interpreting narrative shijo in this way, we need to be aware of new issues arising from the rough and often crude contents of these works, which emerged from the social climate of conflict, desire, and sensibility of the last half of the Chosŏn period, and which diverged from the original style and form of shijo in the first half of that era.

Lyric Folk Songs

Folk songs (*sŏjŏng minyo*) is a general term used for the genre of oral poetry that is rooted in the everyday life of the common people. Unlike p'ansori, shaman's chants (*muga*), and chapka, which require special training, folk songs are easy to sing. Because folk songs have their roots in the diverse experience of the common people, the contents, forms, and functions of folk songs are extremely diverse. Folk songs have existed from the beginning of Korean literature until today and have adapted successfully to the changes in Korean literature over thousands of years. Some types of folk songs have evolved into written songs or poems composed according to specific sets of rules. The problem of how to define this genre conclusively remains. Like written poetry, folk songs as a genre contain features of lyric and narrative genres, depending on the character and function of the song. Other folk songs include elements of the didactic genre.

Despite this diversity, however, folk songs clearly show features typical of a distinct genre in form and content. These works are also known as "lyric folk songs," but the term *folk song* will be used in the following discussion.

Folk songs can be divided into two types: functional folk songs and nonfunctional folk songs. Functional folk songs are those sung as an accompaniment to work and religious ceremonies and by those looking after children. Most lyric folk songs, however, belong to the class of nonfunctional folk songs. Because nonfunctional folk songs can be sung for entertainment by anyone at any time, there are few restrictions on content and form. Overall, nonfunctional folk songs are more elaborate musically and in terms of literary content. The subjects of these songs usually relate to the hope of overcoming various problems in life and to emotions such as worry, sadness, and happiness. These works have a relative clarity of form and theme because they came out of a desire to express emotion in lyric song. Songs such as "Arirang" and "Toraji," which have come down to us in various regional forms, are examples of nonfunctional lyric folk songs.

> *Arirang arariyo*
> Please help me over Arirang Hill.
> I don't know if it's spring or fall.
> The sun behind the mountains and the stars show me the way.
> Hey, boatman, help me get to the other side.
> The weeds and the thistles are in full bloom.
>
> —"Chŏnsŏn Arirang" from Myŏngju County
> in Kangwŏn Province

Among the functional folk songs, most lyric songs are work songs, but some are ceremonial songs. The most common type of lyric ceremonial songs are those related to death, which are sung in a sad tone and to a slow beat. In the case of functional folk songs, each type of song is not divided along strict lines between lyric and narrative songs but according to the purpose and character of the song. Thus songs that are sung during rice planting in the spring follow a tetrameter, two-line form, and the contents of these songs are based on a series of lyrics about farm life that are linked together in a chain. Songs sung by children at play generally follow a regular pattern, and few of these songs can be considered lyric folk songs.

Folk songs are divided into three categories according to the way they are sung: alternating verse, rounds, and one-person improvisations. Songs that are short and sung by one person generally belong to the lyric category. Songs in alternating verse and rounds vary in content and form, but regardless of whether a song is lyric or narrative, alternating verse allows for a great deal of improvisation and individual creativity. In rounds, the meaningful verses are sung alternatively by a group, but in alternating verse, one person sings a meaningful verse while the group sings a refrain that is repeated throughout the song. This refrain makes these songs more open to improvisation than are rounds. In terms of lyricism, this means that alternating verse is more flexible and allows greater individual variation in expression. The well-known folk songs "Kanggang suwŏllae" and "K'waejina ch'ingch'ing nane" are examples of this type of song.

Below are two examples of the alternating verse form and of a round. The first example is from a song that accompanies rice planting. One verse is in two lines with the first line sung by one group and a second group responding with the second line. This song can also be sung by one group.

1.

> *Ŏŏru sangsadiya*
> The little purple flowers in my garden,
> *Ŏŏru sangsadiya*
> The old and the young, they're all bent over.
> *Ŏŏru sangsadiya*
> The old trees in my garden,
> *Ŏŏru sangsadiya*
> Like my true heart, they're all depressed.

> —"Rice-planting song" from Kŏch'ang County
> in South Kyŏngsan Province

2.

> I count the years since I have seen the smiling face of my love.
> Don't worry, don't feel bad; you can see him another time.
>
> Of all the fish in the sea, carp is my favorite.
> Of all the fruit on trees, pears are my favorite.
>
> Oh, towel, oh towel, towel of loyalty that my love made for me,
> If I lose you, I lose my love.
>
> I can't sleep. Oh, how I lie awake. It's beginning to drive me crazy.
> Tuck me in, tuck me in, tuck me in with cool ramie cloth from
>   Hansan Village.
>
> —"Rice-planting song" from Yŏngyang County
>   in North Kyŏngsan Province

The contents and language of lyric folk songs derive from the blunt language of the common people. Songs that deal directly with the lives of the common people in witty and lively as well as sad and bitter language are found in many cultures, but the distinction between happiness and sadness is particularly profound in Korean folk songs because the common people in Korea suffered extreme hardship under a system of land ownership that favored the aristocracy of the Koryŏ period and the yangban of the Chosŏn period.

Poetry in Classical Chinese

Like lyric folk songs, "poetry in classical Chinese" is a general term, rather than one designating a literary genre that is defined by a set of specific characteristics. Poetry in classical Chinese is very diverse: some poems describe historical events through the use of narrative and, at times, nonpoetic ways of presentation. Putting aside the issue of such poetic genres as poetic composition (sa; Chinese: ci), rhyming prose poetry (bu; Chinese: fu), and lyric poetry (sa; Chinese: ci) for the moment, the forms of poetry in classical Chinese are also diverse: old-style poetry of five or seven syllables (koshi; Chinese: gushi), broken-off lines (chŏlshi; Chinese: juegou), regulated verse (yulshi; Chinese: lushi), regulated couplets (paeyul; Chinese: pailu), and songs (akpu; Chinese: lefu). Forms such as regulated couplets and songs, which are comparatively long forms, also include works that do not fit the characteristics of a lyric genre. Most works in classical Chinese, however, represent the lyric expression of the literate classes of society. Only lyric poems in classical Chinese will be discussed in this section.

Poetry written in classical Chinese goes back to an era when ancient folk songs were transcribed into classical Chinese, but it was not until aristocrats such as the *yuktup'um* scholars emerged in the Unified Shilla period that writing poetry in classical Chinese became widespread among the literate classes of society. Later, writing poetry in classical Chinese not only became an integral part of education among the aristocracy and yangban from the Koryŏ period to the end of the Chosŏn period, but also their main method of lyric expression. For yangban literati, writing poetry in classical Chinese was an essential tool of instruction and a way of gaining prestige. Classical Chinese literature used terse language to refer to the cosmos, nature, and human life. Mastering classical Chinese, with its complex rhyming system and erudite historical metaphors, took a long time and required not only a great deal of self-control and discipline, but also a gift for poetry. The following poem by Im Che (1567–1608) is an example of the five-characters-to-a-line form:

> I wake up at dawn and light the incense.
> Sitting down to read, I open *The Doctrine of the Mean*.
> As I read the wisdom of *The Doctrine of the Mean,*
> For the first time, I come to know the essence of human nature.
> The moonlight shines gently on the lotus pond.
> Though the snow covers the fresh plum blossoms, I know spring is
>   here.
> As I read, *The Doctrine of the Mean* moves me ever more.
> My heart shapes everything in the world.
>
> —Im Che

Shinch'eshi (Tang-period "modern-style" poetry) forms such as regulated verse (*yulshi;* Chinese: *lushi*) and broken-off lines (*chŏlshi;* Chinese: *juegou*) were more common than old-style poems of five or seven syllables (*koshi;* Chinese: *gushi*), but the proportion of poetry written in the old style was greater in Korea than in China, despite the limitations imposed by the brevity of this form. Modern-style poetry, which was not popular in China itself, was even less so in Korea.

Poetry in classical Chinese was read according to the Korean pronunciation of each Chinese character, a practice which contributed to the development of an indigenous way of recitation that differed from the tone-based Chinese method.

The subjects and poetics of Korean classical Chinese poetry corresponded closely to those of Chinese poetry, the work of To Yŏnmyŏng (Chinese: Tao Yuanming), Yi Paek (Chinese: Li Bai), Tu Po (Chinese: Du Fu), Paek Nakchŏn (Chinese: Bai Letian), So Tongp'a (Chinese: Su Dongpo), Hwang Chŏnggyŏn (Chinese: Huang Tingjian), and Mae Yoshin (Chinese: Mei Yaochen) serving as models of "good" poetry in classical Chinese. However, response to and interest in Chinese poetry took Korean poetry in classical Chinese in new directions at certain points in the history this genre. As a result, the works of a given poet were interpreted differently at different times. The biggest task in researching poetry in classical Chinese is to define how individual poets were affected in various periods not only by the reception of Chinese forms, but also by the integration of these forms into existing Korean poetry in classical Chinese. In addition, we need to be aware that poets writing in classical Chinese were influenced both consciously and unconsciously by the prevailing cultural attitudes of a particular period of Korean history. Greater cultural independence from Chinese forms of composition in the last half of the Chosŏn period contributed to the development of a form of expression that was more deeply rooted in Korean culture and history. This trend reached its peak in works of poetry by shilhak scholars, such as Chŏng Yagyong's (1762–1836) *Korean Poems* (Chosŏn shi), Pak Chiwŏn's (1737–1805) *Korean-style Poems* (Chosŏn p'ung), and Yi Ok's (n.d.) *Songs from Everyday Life* (Yiŏn). In the middle of the seventeenth century, nonaristocrats began composing poetry in classical Chinese as literary activity grew among the growing class of merchants and traders known as the *chungin*.

Though limited, the following two works help illustrate the diversification of poetry in classical Chinese in the last half of the Chosŏn period. Written while he was in internal exile in 1809, the poem by Chŏng Yagyong is a section of his long poem, *The State of the Fields* (Chŏngan kisa, 1809), in which he described the suffering of local farmers under conditions of famine and brutal political oppression. Written in the clear language of the ancient style of *The Book of Songs* (four characters on a line) the poem sharply criticizes the social injustice that peasants suffered in the late Chosŏn period. The poem by Yi Ok deviates from established poetic forms in a different way; these poems offer us a new look at the poetic inspiration of their authors.

1.

> I am gathering greens, gathering greens.
> They're not lush, but meager.
> All the good herbs and greens have withered away.
> The sprouts and shoots have all dried up.
> The grass and trees have been scorched by the sun.
> The wells have dried up.
> The water bugs have disappeared from the rice paddies.
> Even the clams have vanished from the sea.
> Those in power know nothing of this.
> "Famine," that's all they can say.
> We may have to live this way until autumn.
> They say they can't help us until next spring.
> My husband scours the land like a beggar to put food on the table.
> If he died, who would ensure that he gets a proper funeral?
> Oh, oh, dear heaven,
> How can you be so cruel?
>
> —from "Gathering Greens" (Ch'aeho); *The State of the Fields* (Chŏngan kisa, 1809), Chŏng Yagyong

2.

> My husband should have finished his duty by now.
> He usually comes back when the moon sets.
> If I go to bed first, I know he'll be angry.
> But if I wait up, he'll wonder what's wrong.
> When I was young, I wanted to have a son.
> Now, I think I'd be better off without him,
> because he turned out to be just like his father.
> The rest of my life will be filled with tears.
>
> —from "Songs from Everyday Life" (Yiŏn in), Yi Ok

Scholars have yet to develop a theory that explains the historical development of Korean poetry in classical Chinese in relation to the lives of the authors of these poems. In investigating these issues, we find that poetry in classical Chinese is not simply poetry written in a foreign language, but rather an important genre of Korean poetry that helped to push it into new areas of expression in the face of considerable stylistic and formulaic limitations.

Hŏduga

Before they begin the first lines of a p'ansori work such as *Song of Ch'unhyang* (Ch'unhyang ka) or *Song of Shim Ch'ŏng* (Shim Ch'ŏng ka), p'ansori singers sing what are known as *hŏduga* to loosen their vocal chords and to attract the attention of the audience. Hŏduga are also called *tanga,* but to distinguish them from *shijo tanga,* the common technical term for hŏduga is *p'ansori tanga.* Because p'ansori permitted many changes in rhythm and vocalization over a wide and diverse range of sound, singing to the written score literally would not only have been too demanding for the singer, but would have made it difficult for the p'ansori singer to reach out to the audience naturally. From a literary point of view, hŏduga communicate a feeling of loneliness, and from a musical point of view, they have smooth moderately paced melodies (*p'yŏngikcho*).

Literary scholars estimate that from forty to fifty hŏduga were commonly performed, but only twenty of these have survived. These works are purely lyric, and most contain a series of Chinese proverbs about various ethical dilemmas. Hŏduga depicted everyday life in a formal and stylized language, which makes it difficult to identify a clear set of characteristics that define this genre. Most hŏduga, however, expressed sadness about the meaninglessness of life or described the joys of communing with nature. The lyricism of hŏduga contrasted nicely with p'ansori, which originated as narrative, because the former raised the level of excitement before the latter was performed.

As the use of Chinese proverbs shows, almost all hŏduga were imitations of ancient literary styles, and this meant that singers had to express their feelings in a relatively rigid language. This leaves few works of high literary value; the hŏduga gained their literary strength from the passion of p'ansori singers. The following example is from *Old Rivers and Mountains* (Mango kangsan), a relatively short hŏduga that contains fewer Chinese proverbs than usual:

> I've traveled all over Korea, but where is the mountain called Mount Samshin? It goes by one of the following three names: Mount Pongnae, Mount Pangjang, and Mount Hoyŏn. I walked through Mount Pongnae, carrying a bamboo walking stick and enjoying the refreshing wind. I saw the bright moon rise over the hill on the east side of Kyŏngp'odae Beach. I visited Ch'ŏnggan Pavilion and Naksan Temple on my way. I

climbed to the top of Mount Pongnae and looked down at the scenery below. I saw many peaks and valleys open to the sky. The water bubbling over the waterfalls looked as if it were flowing from the Milky Way. This wasn't a place fit for ordinary people but for Daoist immortals. I was there at the beginning of spring. Red flowers, green leaves, dancing butterflies, and singing birds were all enjoying the spring together. I hadn't seen the beauty of Mount Pongnae for myself for a long time. After all my travels, I finally got here. Mount Pongnae was more beautiful than I remember it. Listen, everybody! Don't laugh at the changes in the world! How can you stop the leaves from turning and the flowers from dying? I know how. I'll tie up the sun in the west with a willow thread and hang the moon in the east from a cinnamon tree. That way we can enjoy ourselves forever!

—from the *Old Rivers and Mountains*
(Mango kangsan), anonymous

Chapka

Chapka is a genre of entertaining songs that were performed by professional and semiprofessional singers in street markets in the last half of the Chosŏn period. From a musical point of view, chapka were much more popular with the common people than the *shibi kasa.* At the same time, they were musically and compositionally more elegant and entertaining than folk songs. Although there are some shijo and folk songs that are similar to chapka in terms of composition, these works will be excluded from the literary genre of chapka because they conform more closely to the defining characteristics of those genres.

Because chapka emerged from various songs, meter and overall organization are very loose, making it difficult to describe the structure of a typical chapka. The tetrameter, which is the most common meter in shijo, appears randomly in chapka. *Kasa,* for example, follow a continuous flow of verse, whereas chapka are also unique in that verses are independent of each other; some works have a refrain between verses. Chapka borrow phrases from well-known shijo and poems in classical Chinese, as well as from folk songs, shibi kasa, and p'ansori, but these can appear at any point in the song. Chapka are diverse in form and extremely flexible in their ability to absorb parts of other genres. This diversity and flexibility is clear in works such as "Song of Plum Blossoms" (Maehwa sa) and "Song of the Gull" (Paekku sa), in which the link between various phrases is not clear, and in works in which the musical refrain occurs where it does for no particular reason.

One of the major reasons that chapka were so diverse and open to influences from other literary genres is that singers from the lower classes of rural society sang them in the marketplaces for the common people, to make money. In attempting to entertain these people, the singers needed to use various musical and literary devices to attract the interest of the busy audience in the market place.

Chapka did not exist as an independent form of folk song, but developed from the beginning of the eighteenth century as a mixed form of song for the common people. Although the origin of songs for commercial entertainment based on adaptations of folk songs may go back as far as the Koryŏ period or earlier, it was not until the last half of the Chosŏn period that the expanding market economy created active local markets where chapka singers could reach audiences that were willing to pay for entertainment.

The subjects of chapka are diverse, but these works tend to deal with everyday issues such as love, boredom, drinking, misfortune, humor, and nature. Most chapka—"Song of Melancholy" (Sushim ka), "Song of the Yellow Rooster" (Hwanggye sa), "Yukchabaegi," and "Ballad of Wings" (Nalgae t'aryŏng), for example—depict joy and sadness, or describe life's hopes and failures. At a deeper level, chapka affirm an optimistic view of life by showing that joy can overcome the feeling of meaninglessness in everyday existence. Water, mountains, trees, flowers, and birds appear in chapka as subjects related to enjoying life in the present rather than as metaphysical subjects related to the order of the universe. Originating as songs sung to entertain people in the marketplace, chapka differed from the restrained poetry that appealed to the yangban class and from the earthy folk songs, which were closely connected with farm life.

The following section from "Song of Making Merry" (Panyu ka) is an example of the diverse form and subject of the chapka:

> You there, come on, come on, let's go play.
> Let's go play on a boat. *Chidudŏnggiyŏra tunggedungdŏngjiro,* let's
>   go play.
> The woman here, the woman there, all the women of the village cast
>   a spell on men.
> Come back Miss Kye, the great *kisaeng,* come back to Hŭiyangdo.

Enamna e ilsonni ton patso.
My old lover has forgotten all about me; I'm no longer in his
    dreams.
I haven't forgotten you; don't you remember me?

You there, come on, come on, let's go play.
Let's go play on a boat. *Chidudŏnggiyŏra tunggedungdŏngjiro,* let's
    go play.
Oh, the pain of breaking up; oh, the pain. My old lover is an enemy
    for life.
Come back, Miss Kye, the great *kisaeng,* come back to Hŭiyangdo.
Enamna e ilsonni ton patso.
Breaking up is like setting fire to the grass and trees.
Who can put out that fire?

You there, come on, come on, let's go play.
Let's go play on a boat. *Chidudŏnggiyŏra tunggedungdŏngjiro,* let's
    go play.
I'm dying, I'm dying. I'm dying because of you.
After I die, I'll search for you far and wide.
Come back, Miss Kye, the great *kisaeng**, come back to Hŭiyangdo.
Enamna e ilsonni ton patso.
They killed the great Chinese general Hangu with an old iron
    hammer.
Wake up, wake up. Wake up to the meaning of the phrase "break
    up."
You there, come on, come on, let's go play.
Let's go play on a boat. *Chidudŏnggiyŏra tunggedungdŏngjiro,* let's
    go play.

—"Song of Making Merry" (Panyu ka)
[*Kisaeng were female entertainers in traditional Korea. —Trans.]

New Poetry and Modern Poetry

In the midst of the turbulent changes of the late nineteenth and early
twentieth centuries, "New Poetry" (shinch'eshi) such as Ch'oe
Namsŏn's "From the Sea to Boys" (Hae egesŏ sonyŏn ege, 1908) and
"On Flowers" (Kkot tugo) emerged as an experimental form that made
a clear break with all previous styles of poetry. As indicated by the
name, New Poetry broke with the previous poetic forms in an attempt
to create a freer style of poetry along the lines of Western poetry of the

time. A form that attempted to create a sense of unity by ending each line of a stanza with the same syllable, New Poetry was not free verse because it followed a set rhyming scheme just as previous forms of poetry had. Nevertheless, New Poetry played an important role as a transitional genre between traditional forms and modern Korean poetry as we know it. In embracing the spirit of enlightenment, New Poetry dealt with hopes for the new era and projected an optimistic view of life. The following example, Ch'oe Namsŏn's "On Flowers" is divided into two stanzas, and the repetition of sounds from the first stanza in the second gives an interesting structural unity to the poem.

> I welcome flowers with joy,
> but I do not want them carried away,
> because their beautiful movements capture my eyes,
> and their sweet fragrance bathes my nose.
> I welcome them with joy
> because they bring the spring breeze
> that replaces the cutting north with warm breath,
> and that replaces bitter hate with deep love,
> to save the millions of people who are
> trapped under bone-chilling ice and buried in
> blood-freezing snow pits.
>
> I look at flowers with joy,
> but I do not look at them with giddy joy,
> enchanted by their smiling faces drenched in peace,
> possessive of the wealth of their lush shapes.
> I look at them with joy because
> —though outside beauty covers inner poverty
> and quick flashes usually fizzle out—
> flowers, and only flowers,
> neither seek ephemeral glory,
> nor give in to what stands in their way.
> Instead they hold the seeds of the lives of millions.

After the transitional period that resulted in New Poetry, modern poetry, which first appeared in magazines such as the *Light of Scholarship* (Hak chi kwang,1914) and the *T'aesŏ Literature and Art* (T'aesŏ munye shinbo, 1918–1919) in the years 1915 to 1920, became part of the Movement for a New Literature that emerged immediately after the March 1 Movement (*Samil undong*) in 1919. From this formative period to the present day, modern poetry has included not only lyric poems but also many narrative poems, and a smaller number of dramatic poems. The narrative and dramatic poems, however, were written for special purposes; the lyric poem is the most common form in modern poetry.

Although most modern poems are lyric, the genre of modern poetry is extremely diverse in form and style. Because modern poets attempt to give their poems a unique style in the tradition of free verse, modern poetry lacks any sort of standard rhythm. As poetry embraces a wider range of experience and ideas regarding which subjects, values, and type of language are felt to be "poetic," it is natural for a wider range of works to contain a lyric quality of some sort. Modern literary criticism, which puts great emphasis on individual creativity rather than attempting to place a particular work in a particular literary genre, has also contributed to the diversification of modern poetry. Criticism focusing on the theory of genre has given way to criticism of poetic movements and styles and of individual poets.

Thus it is almost impossible to summarize all of the relevant characteristics of modern Korean poetry, but a summary of the history of modern poetry before the liberation from Japanese colonial rule on August 15, 1945, is useful in understanding the development of modern poetry.

After a period of transition in the decade 1910 to 1920, modern poetry fluorished in the 1920s in various literary magazines and journals such as *Creation* (Ch'angjo, 1919), *Ruins* (P'yehŏ, 1920), *Rose Village* (Changmich'on, 1921), *White Tide* (Paekcho, 1922), *Genesis* (Kaebyŏk, 1920), and the *Chosŏn Literary World* (Chosŏn mundan, 1924). The common theme of poets such as Kim Ŏk, Hwang Sŏgu, Hong Sayong, Yi Sanghwa, Pak Yonghŭi, and Pak Chonghwa was the agony of the lonely individual in a morally corrupt world. The reality that appears in their poems is one of evil and darkness; only escape into the worlds of death or imagination makes a meaningful life possible. This dark romanticism is a result of the sudden destruction of traditional society and culture and the experience of colonial oppression. In this sense, the agony of intellectuals who were powerless to effect change became the typical poetic emotion of this era. One of the outstanding works of this period is "To My Bedroom" (Na ŭi chimshil ro, 1923), in which the poet, Yi Sanghwa (1901–1943), uses "bedroom" as a metaphor for the world of death.

After 1924, modern literature diverged into two main groups, the "new wave" group and the KAPF, a group of proletarian writers. New wave writers emphasized aesthetics and the inner experiences of the individual, whereas KAPF writers emphasized an activist social conscience, with which they confronted the social contradictions of the times. This division was not simply between right and left on the political spectrum. Some poets who were associated with the romantic poetry of the early 1920s, such as Pak Yonghŭi (b. 1901), became doctrinaire leftists, whereas Yi Sanghwa refused to participate in any sort of ideological organization in poems such as "To My Bedroom" and "My Stolen Field" (Ppaeatkin tŭl edo pom ŭn onŭnga, 1926). Kim Ŏk turned to the language of folk songs to create a unique style of poetry.

Kim Sowŏl (1902–1934) and Han Yongun (1879–1944) were two major poets of the mid-1920s who did not participate in any movement or follow trends. The work of these two poets shows how self-identity of the 1920s had become divorced from real human values. These themes were especially poignant amid the darkness of Japanese colonial rule. The poetry of Kim Sowŏl deals subtly with losing one's love ("*nim*") and with fleeting feelings of sadness that come from a tragic view of the world that divides the self from real human values. Han Yongun, on the other hand, based his poetry on an optimistic view of life and a Buddhist view of the world in an attempt to achieve a poetic consciousness that could overcome the existing divisions in the world. The following example is from a poem that Han Yongun dedicated to the Indian poet Tagore. It clearly shows how Han used prose-style rhythm to give his poetry great depth.

> My friend, my dear friend, smiling at your new-found love,
> tears will not make the fallen blossoms go back to their branches.
> Please do not shed tears on the fallen blossoms, but on the dust
>   below the tree.
>
> My friend, my dear friend,
> No matter how much you like the scent of death, you cannot bring
>   your lips to a skull.
> Please do not cast a net over their grave with golden melodies, but
>   place a flagpole smeared in blood above their grave.
> But, after listening to your song, the dead earth moves again with
>   the spring wind.

Modern Korean poetry became even more diverse in the 1930s. Much of this diversity was an expansion of the developments of the 1920s. Increased Japanese political oppression in the 1930s caused all ideological movements to go underground, which meant that poetry that criticized existing social conditions declined or was forced to use indirect methods of criticism. Themes such as self-examination of the inner world of thought, descriptions of urban life, and interest in the world of nature appeared in the poetry of this time. Thus, the poetry of the 1930s took poetic expression and sensibilities to new levels of accomplishment rather than taking on new and difficult subject matter.

The first major poetic movement to emerge in the 1930s was the "pure-poetry movement," which centered on poets such as Pak Yongch'ŏl, Kim Yŏngnang, and Shin Sŏkchŏng, who were involved in the publication of the poetry journal *Poetic Literature* (Shimunhak), founded in 1931. These poets defined "pure poetry" as poetry that has hidden lyricism and detailed language and feelings unrelated to any social or ideological cause. Kim Yŏngnang (1903–1950) was one of the key figures of the pure-poetry movement.

From the middle of the 1930s, however, experimental trends that fell into the general category of modernism appeared. These various "isms," such as imagism, surrealism, Dadaism, and intellectualism, closely mirrored trends in Western poetry. The imagism in the work of Kim Kwanggyun and the surrealism and Dadaism in Yi Sang are good examples of the modernist poetry of this era. But cultural trends and forms of poetry are not simply surface problems, they are reflections of the times in which they were written. It is unclear whether the work of the modernists followed international trends in poetry from the beginning or not. Perhaps the most valuable contribution of the modernist poets was the synthesis of their own strong emotions and what they considered "modern," and their vivid descriptions of the dark side of urban life under Japanese colonial rule.

As the modernists were reaching the peak of their success in the last half of the 1930s, another group of poets with decidedly different attitudes emerged. This group rejected the urbanism and the dry intellectualism of the modernists in favor of humanistic themes that dealt with everyday life and the relationship between man and nature. Poets such as Sŏ Chŏngju, Ham Hyŏngsu, and Yun Ch'igyŏng, who portrayed the former, are classified as members of the "life school," and poets such as Pak Mogwŏl, Pak Tujin, and Cho Chihun, who dealt with man and nature, are classified as members of the "nature school" or "ch'ŏngnyo school." The nature school poets went beyond reality and built an imaginary environment of harmony that offered the hope of inner salvation. In comparison, the life school poets examined the urge to live and the fear of death in strong language. The following poem by Sŏ Chŏngju (b. 1915), "Self-Portrait" (Chawasang), is an example of this school:

> My father was a slave who never came home.
> My old white-haired grandmother and a
> Korean date blossom were all that was around.
> My mother said that she wanted to eat an apricot dried by the
>   moon, but . . . to catch the wind, her son was lying on the
>   dirt below a lamp with dirty fingernails.
> They say my thick hair and big eyes look like my grandfather's,
>   who, they say, did not return after going out to sea in the year
>   of the Kabo Reforms.
>
> The wind raised about eighty percent of me during my
>   twenty-three years.
> As time moves on, I'm more embarrassed than ever.
> Some people see a criminal in my eyes,
> some people see a fool in my mouth, but
> I don't have any regrets.
>
> On a bright sunny morning,
> the poetic dew on my brow
> is always mixed with drops of blood.
> Sun or shade, I stick out my tongue,
> panting like a sick dog, and here I am.

Yi Yuksa and Yun Tongju explored the desire to create an independent identity with which to confront the growing oppression of the late Japanese colonial period.

2. Narrative Genres

Myths

Myths are stories that are handed down from previous generations and are intended to reinforce beliefs in members of a certain group. Myths go beyond daily experience, and because they offer an explanation of how a past or present deity or other supernatural power rules over human society and nature, they are related to a past or present ethnic group. Myths are supernatural in their attempt to go beyond daily experience, universal in their attempt to communicate a lasting moral message, and communal in their attempt to express the collective experience and idealism of a particular ethnic group. Ethnic groups with differing origins and ways of life have different myths. The rise and fall of various myths coincided with the emergence of early ethnic groups and states, rather than as a result of exchange and conquest among various ethnic groups.

The formative period of Korean myth coincided with the formation of the three kingdoms of Koguryŏ, Paekche, and Shilla, from the second century B.C. to the first century A.D. Myths continued to undergo changes as they were transmitted from generation to generation, changes that were based on the myths that had already emerged during the three kingdoms. Myths surviving from this time include myths about the origin of the Korean people such as those of Tangun (founder of Old Chosŏn, the first Korean kingdom), Chumong (the founder of Koguryŏ, who reigned as King Tongmyŏng, 37–19 B.C.), Pak Hyŏkkŏse (the founder of Shilla, 57 B.C.–A.D. 4), T'alhae (king of Shilla, 57–80), Alji (leader of a Kim clan in Shilla), and Suro (king of Kaya, A.D. 42–199). These myths that developed in the Koryŏ period explain the origin of the kings of the Koryŏ Dynasty to give their rule greater historical legitimacy. In addition to myths relating to the origin of the Korean people and kingship, myths such as the three-family myth in Cheju Province discuss the origin of a particular clan. Other types of myths include those that discuss the origin of local village deities and shamanistic myths that explain the origin and power of various shamanistic beliefs. Curiously, myths related to the origin of the universe have not survived, except for those few that have become folk legends. One possible explanation is that these myths had previously existed but disappeared as the ethnic groups that later became the Korean people moved from central to northeast Asia and then into the Korean Peninsula.

One of the most prominent motifs in Korean myths, as evident in the foundation myth, shijo, is that the king descended from the sky and then moved from the west to east and from north to south. In the Tangun and Chumong myths, the son of the king of heaven came from the sky and impregnated a bear, who gave birth to Tangun, the founder of the Korean people. Chumong, the son of heaven, moved south to escape the internal strife of Puyŏ and founded the new kingdom of Koguryŏ. Pak Hyŏkkŏse and Suro were born from the power of heaven and rose to be rulers of their respective kingdoms. A good example of this type of myth is "The Lay of King Tongmyŏng" (Tongmyŏng wang p'yŏn, recorded by Yi Kyubo in 1241) from the *Memorabilia of the Three Kingdoms* (Samguk yusa, ca. 1285), in which Chumong comes to the fore by performing great deeds.

> The founder of the kingdom of Koguryŏ was King Tongmŏng, whose surname was Ko and whose given name was Chumong. The birth of Ko Chumong and the founding of the Koguryŏ kingdom occurred in this way.
>
> In a dream, the gods ordered King Puru of the kingdom of North Puyŏ to move his kingdom to East Puyŏ. King Puru died and Crown Prince Kŭmwa ascended the throne.
>
> One day King Kŭmwa was passing Ubalsu on the southern slope of Mount T'aebaek when he met a beautiful young woman. He gazed at her and asked her who she was. She responded, "I am the daughter of Habaek, the god of water. My name is Yuhwa. One day, as I was enjoying the fine weather with my younger sisters, I met an imposing man. He said that he was Haemosu, the son of the gods. He took me to a house by the Amnok River near Mount Kkoeŏungshin. He made love to me, and then took himself off, never to return. My parents scolded me furiously, saying that they wouldn't bother to find me a good husband and would banish me from the house. They banished me to this place as punishment."
>
> King Kŭmwa was troubled after hearing the woman's confession. He led Yuhwa to a dark room. Strangely, a light shone into the room, illuminating Yuhwa's body. Yuhwa tried to avoid the light, but it followed her about the room. Yuhwa conceived and ultimately laid an egg the size of a chicken's egg.
>
> Shocked that a woman could lay an egg, Kŭmwa threw it to a dog and a pig, but they refused to eat it. He then threw it onto a path used by horses and oxen, but they refused to tread on it. Next he threw it into a field, but the wild animals and the birds sheltered the egg with their bodies and their wings.
>
> King Kŭmwa tried again and again to destroy the egg, but could not, and he finally returned the egg to Yuhwa, in frustration, who gently placed it in a warm and safe place.
>
> Breaking through the shell, a baby boy was hatched. The baby

looked strong and destined for fame. At the age of seven, the boy far surpassed other boys in strength and courage. He made a bow and arrows all by himself, and when he shot it for the first time, he hit a bull's-eye. He became known throughout East Puyŏ for his skill and was given the name Chumong, or "Great Archer."

King Kŭmwa sired seven princes, and they customarily practiced archery and went riding and hunting with Chumong. But none of these seven princes could approach Chumong's skill. Taeso, one of the princes, was envious of Chumong, and he complained to King Kŭmwa, "Chumong was not born of a human mother. If we fail to banish him now, we will live to regret it." King Kŭmwa did not agree with Prince Taeso and made Chumong his chief hunter.

On hearing a prophetic warning not to let Chumong ride, the King forced him to work in the stables. Chumong was entrusted with the task of choosing the best horses from the herd for the king, so Chumong was left with all the bad horses. Prince Taeso conspired with the other princes and the king's ministers to destroy Chumong. Chumong's mother Yuhwa got wind of this plot and secretly informed Chumong.

"People in the palace are plotting against you," warned Yuhwa. "With your power, you'll win favor wherever you go. Get away from here while you can."

Chumong had three loyal friends that he could rely on. He left East Puyŏ with them, riding a noble horse that he had nursed back to health.

Taeso, the other princes, and the king's ministers learned of Chumong's escape and pursued him, shooting in vain at his steed.

Chumong and his friends reached Ŏmsu, where they were halted by a deep blue river. There was no way to cross it, and Taeso and his supporters were getting closer and closer. In desperation, Chumong faced the river, crying, "I am the son of the gods, and the grandson of Habaek, the god of water. Today, I am fleeing for my life, and my enemies are right behind me. What should I do?"

As soon as Chumong had spoken, thousands of fish and clams rose up in huge waves. They joined together to form a bridge across the river. Chumong and his friends quickly crossed the bridge of fish and clams. As soon as Chumong and his friends were safe on the other side of the river, the fish and clams destroyed the bridge by sinking back into the river. Taeso and his supporters reached the river but found no way to cross it.

Chumong and his friends arrived in Solbonju and founded a village there. Lacking the materials to build a palace, they pitched a tent safely upstream and named their new kingdom Koguryŏ. Chumong decided that everyone should take the surname Ko. Chumong was twelve years old at the time [the original text gives his age as twenty-two]. He was crowned the first king of Koguryŏ in the twelfth year [37 B.C.] of the reign of Emperor Xiao Yuan of Han China.

Foundation myths, in addition to being shaman myths transmitted through shaman songs such as those of Chumong and T'alhae, have come down to us in the form of narratives of "the life of a hero." According to Professors Cho Dong-il and Kim Yŏlgyu, characters in foundation myths have the following general characteristics: (1) noble birth, (2) unnatural birth, (3) supernatural power, (4) a period of emotional and physical suffering, (5) meeting with a savior, (6) overcoming all difficulties, (7) achieving victory in battle, and (8) becoming devine heroes. The potential to overcome difficulties is more important than the difficulties themselves; this shows that these myths are related to an optimistic view of life that emphasizes accomplishment in the present rather than the hope of reward in the afterlife. This type of narrative structure had a strong influence on the "heroic novels" that emerged in the last half of the Chosŏn period.

Legends

One major difference between legends and myths is that legends are more believable because the hero is an average person who does not possess special powers or an aristocratic background. Legends are presented as true stories and often include references to existing rocks, lotus ponds, and old trees and to the actual house sites of houses. These references differ according to region. In order to establish a sense of reality, legends are set in a particular time and place and do not depend on a sudden event or miracle to resolve the conflict in the story. This gives legends the somewhat dark and tragic atmosphere for which they are known.

More original sources of legends than of any other genre of Korean narrative literature currently exist, and many of these sources have been gathered in recent years. These sources are limited, however, because they lack the orality of the original legends. The legends found in *The History of the Three Kingdoms* (Samguk sagi, 1145), *Memorabilia of the Three Kingdoms* (Samguk yusa, ca. 1285), *An Augmented Survey of the Geography of Korea* (Tongguk yoji sŭngnam, 1481), *Veritable Records of King Sejong* (Sejong shillok chiri chi, 1454) and various local histories (*ŭpchi*) are useful in understanding history as well as the development of narrative literature.

Legends can be classified according to theme, motif, regional origin, and social origin. We will look at the social origin of legends in terms of etiological explanations of natural phenomena, historical legends, and religious legends.

Legends that seek to explain natural phenomena originated in the attempts of common people to explain various natural and social phenomena. These legends generally deal with the origin and character of things such as topographic features, forces of nature, historical customs, and animals and plants. Some of these stories are very similar to the folk tales (*mindam*) discussed in the next section, but because they are closely related to the natural characteristics of a particular region, they are generally classified as legends. Legends that deal with place names and local topography continue to live on in the farming and fishing villages of Korea.

Most of the existing legends are historical legends. Because the original events and figures have been modified in the process of oral transmission, these legends inevitably distort historical reality to varying degrees, but they also reflect the values and imagination of the common people as portrayed by characters and events in the narrative. In this sense, historical legends emerged from the consciousness of the common people and are a form of orally transmitted history. More historical legends emerged after periods of national or regional crisis. Many of these legends included heroes who really lived and common people who were noble in their humble lives. Classic novels such as *Record of the Imjin Wars With Japan* (Imjin nok, ca. 1600), written after the Japanese invasions of 1592 and 1598, fall into this category. We still find many legends relating to historical events such as these two Japanese invasions and the Tonghak Rebellion of 1896. In legends that relate to deep social division, such as were caused by these events, protagonists remained silent observers.

Religious legends deal with the folk beliefs of the common people. These legends range from those that deal with purely religious matters to those that introduce figures such as the *mirok* (Sanskrit: Maitreya) future Buddha, who promises to create a new world on earth by overthrowing the established order of the times. Legends that promise salvation emerged at the end of the Shilla, Koryŏ, and Chosŏn periods, times of increased national insecurity; many of these legends were based on religion or on uprisings by the common people during these periods of change and insecurity.

The regional diversity of legends has been mentioned above, but some legends transcend a particular region and are found in similar form throughout the country. An example of this phenomenon is "Legend of the Boy General" (Agi changsa chŏnsŏl) in which a boy general of humble origin dies tragically despite his intelligence and strength. Although the contents of this story vary from region to region, the overall flow of the narrative is the same throughout the country. This story reflects the severity of the latent conflict between the common people and the aristocracy in Korean society in the Chosŏn period. The following version of "Legend of the Boy General" comes from the village of Tŏkpatche in Ch'unsŏng County in Kangwŏn Province:

> A woman gave birth to a girl after only a one-day pregnancy. Unfortunately, the girl's parents died while she was still a young girl. She couldn't find a suitable place for their graves, so she buried them in an ordinary plot of land. One day a passing monk asked to spend the night in the house. The minute the girl agreed, the monk realized that she was an orphan.
>
> "You, the mistress of the house, are an orphan, aren't you?" asked the monk.
>
> "Yes, I'm an orphan."
>
> "How did you find a plot for your parents' grave so quickly?"
>
> "I couldn't find a good plot because I'm poor, so the best I could do was to bury them in an ordinary plot of land."
>
> "Did you, now? Well, I know of a good place, so let's go look at it tomorrow."
>
> The next morning they packed a lunch early and went to look at the grave site, which was located in the village of Pŏngaet'ŏ in Tongmyŏn. This village is also known as Tŏkpatche. Now it goes by the name of Hongchŏn County.
>
> "This is good place for your parents' grave," said the monk when they arrived in Tŏkpatche. He looked around and found three large stone figures of a soldier.
>
> "I understand," said the orphan.
>
> After the monk had left, the girl returned to her home village, dug up her parents' bodies, and moved them to the new grave plot. She became pregnant right after that and gave birth to a baby boy. One night, she noticed that the baby was sweating very much. She thought that strange. The boy continued to sweat for four days while his mother watched

over him. What was making him sweat so much? Suddenly, the boy got up, opened the door, and walked out of the house. Once outside, he seized a plow, and began to push it back and forth for exercise. After playing with the plow for a long time, he went back into the house and ran into his mother's arms. When she hugged him, she realized that he was covered with sweat. She turned to the boy's father.

"It's incredible," said the woman.

"What's the matter?" asked the man.

"How can a two-month-old baby run out of the house and play with a plow and exercise all night? What should I do with him?"

"Kill him," replied the man. "He could be a loyal child or he could turn on you. In any case, you can't just let him be." So, they put the baby into a bag, and after wiggling around for a few minutes, he died. Four days after they killed the baby, a monk came to the house.

"I heard that a baby was born in this house, and I'd like you to give him to me," the monk said.

"There's no baby here," replied the woman.

"Stop lying and give him to me at once. I'll take him away. Just bring him to me," the monk demanded.

The woman denied having given birth to the baby, and the monk continued to ask for him. Finally, she confessed the truth.

"I was worried that the baby might turn on us, the whole Pak family, so I killed him. I know that you're going to be angry with me," said the woman.

"I was meant to have fostered that baby. Do you know what is going to happen now? You're going to have two more babies, and you are to hand them over to me," said the monk, who then went on his way.

Two days later, the woman heard noises in the courtyard. She went there and found a dragon on its knees causing a commotion. Suddenly it jumped up and fell over dead in the courtyard. A pear tree sprang up on that spot. If you go to the village of Kumŏng today, you will find "the dragon's pear tree" in the exact place where the dragon died. It is said that Mistress Pak tried to have two more babies, but couldn't, which meant that she couldn't get married. She dug up her parents' grave but ended up being smothered by the weight of their dead bodies.

Legends have existed throughout Korean history, but a large number of new legends emerged in the late Chosŏn period as the market economy developed. Many of these legends were recorded in writing as *yadam* or incorporated into novels, thus contributing greatly to the development of narrative literature at this time.

Folk Tales

Mindam are folk tales that, to capture the interest of the speaker and the listener, begin with an intriguing statement such as "In a time and place far away, when tigers smoked pipes. . . ." The main characters in these folk tales are commoners who endure a period of hardship but who overcome these difficulties through good fortune and end up living a happy life. Everything is possible in folk tales, a fact that reflects the optimistic imagination of the common people, who needed to believe that all difficulties could be overcome.

Unlike legends, folk tales are not based on historical facts, actual or assumed, and do not vary greatly from one region to another. In some folk tales the main character goes beyond traditional ethnic and cultural borders and ends up traveling around the world. Although it is doubtful whether similar folk tales emerged from a common root, desires and interests common to all people appear most clearly in folk tales. Most folk tales follow a mechanical structure in depicting the conflict between events and the main character. This structure is closely related to the strong appeal of folk tales among the common people. The simplicity and clarity of the organization of folk tales not only helped them spread, but allowed them to deal with the diversity of human experience in an honest way.

Folk tales can be classified in various ways, depending on the basis of classification. I will classify folk tales into three broad classes: animal, basic, and humorous.

In animal folk tales, the protagonist may be an animal. This category can be further divided into basic stories about animals, animal ghost stories, and humorous stories about animals. Some of the former, which use animal characters to express the conflicts of human society in animal form, were incorporated into novels in the late Chosŏn period. *Tale of the Tortoise and the Hare* (T'okki chŏn), *Tale of Sŏ Taeju, the Rat* (Sŏ Taeju chŏn), and *Tale of a Male Pheasant* (Changgi chŏn) originated from folk tales.

Basic folk tales can be divided into real-life folk tales and fantasy folk tales, depending on the role of the main characters in the plot. The first are faithful to reality to a certain degree, whereas fantasy folk tales describe supernatural characters and events. The following example is from a folk tale that has striking similarities to stories from other parts of the world. This story is a prophecy folk tale, which is one type of fantasy folk tale. The beauty of the story is found in the simple lessons that it teaches.

A long time ago, there lived a husband and wife. While the wife wove, the husband went to market to buy rice. When he saw a skilled fortuneteller entertaining a crowd of onlookers, he too wanted to have his fortune told. He knew that it would cost more than he could afford and that he wouldn't be able to return home and face his wife, but he had his fortune told anyway.

Said the fortuneteller, "Do not keep going on ahead if you are fearful. Dance when you're afraid. Step discreetly when you're happy."

Instead of going home, the man ran away. He came to a big river and boarded a boat to get to the other side. The boat was crowded, and it was a windy day. The wind was so strong that it almost capsized the boat. Remembering the fortuneteller's words, the man cried out, "I'm scared; take me back!"

"Are you sure?" asked the master of the boat.

"Yes," said the man.

The boat returned the man to shore and set off again across the river. A strong gust of wind then blew up, capsizing the boat in the middle of the river. The man believed the fortuneteller's words more than ever. Taking a pathway leading from the river, the man soon came to a mountainous area with no houses but strewn with human skeletons. As he walked, he saw yet more skeletons. Suddenly he sensed something staring at him. Turning around, he saw a tall figure with bright eyes dancing. Remembering the fortuneteller's advice to "dance when you're afraid," he began to dance. The tall figure gradually shrank back to the size of a normal person.

"My hopes have been fulfilled,"said the figure, "thanks to you. I'm the spirit Mach'o, and I was evil in heaven. The spirits told me that if someone danced in front of me, all my evil deeds would be forgiven. For a long time, nobody danced before me, but now you have set me free. I will do anything for you."

"I want to be rich," said the man.

"Very well, I'll give you a secret ginseng field," the spirit said. "Cross two hills and you will find the field when you come to an area of small rocks open to the sun."

The man followed the spirit's instructions and found the field. When he pulled up what looked like radishes, he found an endless supply of ginseng. He was so pleased that he pulled up as much ginseng as he could carry and took it home. His wife was very pleased. He remembered the fortuneteller's advice to "step discreetly when you're happy." Then he noticed a suspicious character with a sharp knife laying in wait under the veranda.

"Ah, so you want to kill me," the man said. "I'll give you this house, my wife, my children; just put your weapon down now."

The man gave everything away. Then he sold all of his ginseng, which brought him enough money to move to Seoul and live a life of luxury.

—adapted by Cho Hŭiung

Humorous tales, which are more numerous and diverse in Korean literature than in many other literatures, can be divided into the following subcategories: tales of braggadocio, tales of foolish behavior, tales of deception, tales of mockery, and tales of competition. The first three are useful in gaining an understanding of Korean humorous folk tales. Folk tales that show human weakness—the flatulent daughter-in-law, the stingy father, the foolish son-in-law, blundering relatives—are most common in this category. Rather than poking fun at people through cold sarcasm, however, these folk tales create an atmosphere of humorous forgiveness. From this we can get a sense of aspect of the traditional Korean outlook on life.

Narrative Shaman Chants

Some scholars have argued that narrative poetry existed in ancient Korean literature, though no original sources are extant. Myths about the founders of dynasties, such as Tangun and Chumong, have come down to us in prose translations in classical Chinese, a fact which indicates that these foundation myths were originally in narrative rather than lyric form. "The Lay of King Tongmyŏng," in which Chumong overcomes all difficulties to found the Koguryŏ kingdom, is a good example of a foundation myth in a narrative poetic form. The people of Koguryŏ held regular ceremonies to worship Chumong and his mother Yuhwa. This story was probably transmitted orally in ceremonies that created group solidarity by reaffirming the divine origin of the group.

Narrative shaman chants (*sŏsa muga*) are shamanistic myths in the form of narrative poems that were transmitted by shamans in ceremonies that evolved from the official ceremonies held during the period of the three kingdoms. Those that have been passed down have changed significantly over time, but we do not know to what degree. Foundation myths, such as those about Tangun, Chumong, and Pak Hyŏkkŏse, incorporated various elements from shaman chants of the more powerful ethnic groups that formed each of the three kingdoms. Narrative shaman chants about the origin of various gods have probably come down to us through *kut*—shamanistic ceremonies—that express polytheistic beliefs. In this sense, narrative shaman chants are important not only as reflections of ancient Korean views on human beings and the cosmos, but also as valuable sources of information about the historical development of Korean narrative literature.

In addition to narrative shaman chants, there are also sermon-style shaman chants, which express religious ideas and a shamanistic view of the world without following a set plot or making use of a protagonist. Lyric shaman chants express basic emotions such as hopes and lamentation and serve as prayers. Together, these three types of shaman chants alternate in the structure of a *kut,* a Korean shaman ceremony. From a literary point of view, however, narrative shaman chants are considered much more important.

Narrative shaman chants are narrative poems in that they relate the life of the protagonist in song and speech, but they are shamanistic myths in that they discuss the origin of a particular god or spirit. In performing a kut, the shaman (*mudang*) invokes one or more spirits. This type of chant is called an invocational shaman chant because the shaman tries to show her divinity by calling up a particular god or spirit. [Most shamans in Korea were women. —Trans.] Thus this type of chant displays the spiritual powers that only the shaman possesses and that enhance her aura of spirituality. Later, however, this type of chant became popular with the common people as a form of entertainment. The invocational shaman chant also involved audience participation as reflected in chants for a bountiful harvest inland and chants for a bountiful catch on the coast.

In a kut, the shaman sings and recites the narrative chant accompanied by various Korean musical instruments, such as the *changgo,* the *kkweanggari,* the *ching,* and the *nallari.* The atmosphere of these songs is not entirely stern and serious, but depends on the purpose of the kut and the characteristics of the spirit that is being called up. In the shamanistic view of the world, Daoist and Buddhist supernatural worlds and the afterlife exist on the same level as the real world, and spirits, ghosts, and demons have the same feelings and desires as human beings do. Protagonists overcome their difficulties in very realistic ways, even though the narrative includes elements that often go beyond reality. At certain points, the shaman creates a comic atmosphere by adding wit and humor that reflect everyday life.

The following is an example of the Princess Pari form of narrative shaman chant. The most important goddess, Princess Pari, has the power to open a road between this life and the afterlife to guide them safely to the next life. The following section describes how Princess Pari became the most important goddess:

    1. A king in a certain kingdom (names vary according to version) sired seven princesses in a row.

    2. Angry at not being able to have a son, the king sent away his seven daughters.

    3. Every time he sent away a princess, the animals and the birds looked after her, taking her far away before finally parting with her.

    4. The cast-off princesses, known as Pari Kongju, were saved and raised by Buddha or a supernatural force.

    5. The king and queen fell mortally ill as punishment for having banished their daughters.

    6. The soothsayer told the king that the only way to cure the disease was to obtain medicine from the world of the dead.

    7. Six of the princesses refused to go to the world of the dead to find the medicine to cure the king and queen.

    8. The seventh princess, Princess Pari, agrees to find the medicine.

    9. Princess Pari sets off on a mission to the world of the dead to find medicine for the king who had banished her.

    10. After overcoming many difficulties, she arrives in the world of the dead and goes to great trouble to find the medicine. According to a version of the story transmitted in the Seoul area, Princess Pari meets a general, marries him, and gives birth to seven children.

    11. Princess Pari finally obtains the medicine that the king needs and returns to the world of the living.

    12. She returns only to find that the king has already died and is being borne in a funeral procession.

    13. Princess Pari uses the medicine and other rare materials to save the queen.

    14. In the end, Princess Pari turns into the goddess of the road between the worlds of the living and the dead.

Through various types of kut, narrative shaman chants not only met the religious needs of the common people but also exerted considerable influence on the development of p'ansori and classic novels, while being themselves influenced by folk songs. The hero-based structure of narrative shaman chants that began in ancient myths probably contributed to the development of heroic novels. The close relationship between narrative shaman chants and p'ansori music and performance is a topic of continuing interest to literary critics and historians.

P'ansori

In contrast to narrative shaman chants, which are fundamentally spiritual, p'ansori is oral narrative poetry that deals with real life. P'ansori is based on a high level of musical expression mixed with a fair amount of humor. In addition to the literary qualities of narrative and humor, p'ansori relies on various musical and performance devices. Because of the importance of performance in p'ansori, some scholars consider it a dramatic genre. On a deeper level, however, p'ansori are narrative; the dramatic elements accompany the narrator. Certain features of p'ansori, such as the gestures of the singer, the stage and set, and the singer's occasional dance, are all dramatic expressions. The active performance of p'ansori under the sponsorship of Wŏngaksa, the national theater company from 1908 to 1909, was possible because of the dramatic elements inherent in p'ansori. In the case of the one-singer p'ansori, however, the overall flow of the story follows a narrative structure, thus making it difficult to argue that the dramatic elements are more important than narrative ones.

Scholars have proposed various theories to explain the origin of p'ansori, but the most probable theory is that p'ansori emerged from narrative shaman chants and kut in Chŏlla Province in southwestern Korea. The narrative shaman chants of the Chŏlla region resemble p'ansori in the long story lines, the mixture of song and speech, and the musical structure and way of singing. In addition, most of the famous p'ansori singers have come from this part of Korea.

P'ansori probably began to develop as an independent art form in the late seventeenth and early eighteenth centuries. Early p'ansori seem to have been simple in form and content, but in time p'ansori singers had to develop a rich musical and performance repertory to attract the interest of a paying audience. By the mid-eighteenth century, p'ansori had developed into a high form of musical narrative poetry.

P'ansori singers open their performance by singing a well-known folk tale in an interesting way, rather than by making up a new story. Thus, existing p'ansori works evolve musically over time as they are transmitted from one generation to another and are influenced by other types of music. This evolution has given us the twelve p'ansori works that are collected in the early-nineteenth-century *Kwanyujae,* compiled by Song Mansŏ.

Of these twelve works, five—*Song of Ch'unhyang* (Ch'unhyang ka), *Song of Hŭngbu* (Hŭngbu ka), *Song of Shim Ch'ŏng* (Shim Ch'ŏng ka), *Song of the Water Palace* (Sugung ka; also known as T'okki chŏn [Tale of the Tortoise and the Hare]), and *Song of the Red Cliff* (Chŏkpyŏk ka)—have come down to us with scores. Of the other seven works, *The Ballad of General Pae* (Pae pijang t'aryŏng), *Tale of a Male Pheasant* (Changkki chŏn), *Tale of Stubborn Mr. Ong* (Ong Kojip chŏn), and *Ballad of a Ghost's Revenge* (Karujigi t'aryŏng) survive as prose stories, whereas only a general outline, found in various records, remains for *Tale of Maehwa of Kangnŭng* (Kangnŭng Maehwa chŏn), *The Ballad of Musuk* (Musuk i t'aryŏng), and *Tale of a Fake Daoist Immortal* (Katcha shinsŏn chŏn). In *The History of Korean Musical Composition* (Chosŏn ch'anggŭk sa), Chŏng Kapshik includes *Tale of the Maiden Sugyŏng* (Sugyŏng nangja chŏn) as one of the twelve works, omitting *Tale of a Fake Daoist Immortal,* but we have no evidence of the existence of *Tale of the Maiden Sugyŏng*.

These twelve works have come down to us in this haphazard way because p'ansori, which emerged from the common people, started to reflect the prevailing taste of the yangban as was adapted by that class toward the end of the eighteenth century. Popular wit and sarcasm is a key element of the seven works without scores; the five works with scores mingle that wit and sarcasm with an overlay of the yangban sensibility.

P'ansori emphasized interest and emotional feeling at particular points in the performance rather than in the entire structure of the performance. This was because singers expanded and elaborated on narrative and musical sections in the performance that were of particular interest to them. This created gaps and contradictions in the flow of the narrative in p'ansori and in novels based on p'ansori. Despite these problems, a unique narrative structure that matched the needs of the genre developed. The overall structure of p'ansori helped liberate the audience from everyday reality by mingling song with speech, humor with sadness. The idea that p'ansori is said to make the audience laugh and cry simultaneously comes from the effect of this repetitive pattern of emotional tension and release.

Because it was designed to appeal to a wide audience, p'ansori narrative not only mingles prose and poetry but also includes diverse types and levels of language. Thus, literary phrases in classical Chinese contrast with earthy colloquialism and proverbs, and classical Chinese phrases mingle with phrases from the shamans' kut. In addition, many elements from folk songs and other sung genres of literature appear at various points in p'ansori.

One of the most interesting features of the p'ansori literary form is the use of various speech levels. Speech levels indicate how speakers adjust their language according to their relationship with the addressee and the context of the conversation. In p'ansori music, overall harmony is composed of long and short notes; a similar pattern is followed in the style of p'ansori writing. Furthermore, in parts of the narrative concerning upper-class characters, not only is the rhythm refined and graceful but the narrative is presented in a serious and solemn tone. On the other hand, when reference is made to characters of low social status, or when a character is ridiculed, the rhythm and narration reflect the simple, lively language of the common people.

The first example below is from the scene in *Song of Shim Ch'ŏng* in which Shim Ch'ŏng, the main character leaves her house. The second example is the scene in *Song of Hŭngbu* in which Nolbu beats Hŭngbu after he returns from buying rice.

1.

> *Aniri* (spoken narration):
> All of the villagers came out and held Blindman Shim's hands. Blindman Shim could not move, as his daughter Shim Ch'ŏng was leaving him.
>
> *Chungmori* (slow sung narration):
> "Don't go, don't go. You can't just leave me like this. Oh, look at me. I lost my wife and now my daughter," said Blindman Shim as he fell to the ground.
> The villagers held on to Blindman Shim while Shim Ch'ŏng followed a boatman. Shim Ch'ŏng held on to her skirt so that it wouldn't drag and let her hair down over her ears. Flowing like rain, her tears soaked the collar of her blouse. She floundered from side to side several times as she tried to keep up with the boatman. Looking at the village on the other side of the river, she shouted, "Hey, girl from the Chin family, don't you

remember the fun we had on Tano Day last May? Take good care of your parents. I just ran away from my dying father today."

All of the villagers burst into tears. The heavens also knew what had happened. How could the sky have become full of dark clouds so quickly? The green mountains frowned, the sound of the rivers turned to a cry of sadness, the beautiful flowers withered and lost their color, and even the green willows wept.

With all the spring birds crying, Shim Ch'ŏng asked one of them, "Nightingale, whom have you parted from? Why do you cry as if you were vomiting up blood? Your cries are like those of a homeless cuckoo crying its heart out in the mountains at midnight. Do you think that a girl like me who sells herself for a living will be able to return to her home?"

A flower carried by the wind brushed against Shim Ch'ŏng's cheek. She took it in her hand, asking, "The spring wind is impartial; is that why it blows a flower my way? Emperor Wu's Princess Shouyang in Han China had a crown of flowers, but how does a woman on her way to death crown herself?"

Crying at one step, pausing for breath at the next, she finally reached the edge of the river.

—adapted by Han Aesun

2.

Chajinmori (fast sung narration):

Look at how Nolbu behaved. He lifted the wooden stick that he cut on Mount Chiri above my head, and said:

"Listen, Hŭngbu! You want some of my stored rice, but do you really think I'm going to dig into that big rice box in the southern veranda and give some to you? You want some harvested rice, but do you really think I'm going to share all those bundles of rice in the paddies with you? You want to borrow some money, but do you think I'm going to risk any of the jade in my strongbox on you? You want some chicken feed, but how do you think I can feed hundreds of chickens if I give some to you? You want some pig slop, but I've got pigs waiting to be fed; you want some cooked rice, but I've got hungry dogs and puppies to feed. Getting rich is my good fortune, and living in poverty is your fate. I couldn't care less whether you have clothes to wear or food to eat!"

Like lightening on a summer day, Nolbu beat Hŭngbu as if Hŭngbu were a jealous little girl or naughty boy climbing over the garden wall.

"Ah, Nolbu, I understand, I understand," said Hŭngbu as Nolbu hit him once more.

"Ah, ah, you're going to break my legs, Nolbu. I'll never visit you again. I'll never ask for anything. Please, please stop!" cried Hŭngbu. He jumped up and ran into the garden but found the main gate locked. There was no escape.

Aniri (spoken narration):

Hŭngbu tried to escape by going into the house. Nolbu's wife was making dinner quietly in the kitchen but heard the sound of someone dying in the garden and came out of the kitchen to see what was going on. She looked around and saw Nolbu beating his younger brother Hŭngbu and realized that Hŭngbu was trying to come into the house to escape. She waited at the front door, rice flail in hand, like a hunter waiting for elk in the forest, as Hŭngbu approached.

"Oh, sister-in-law, dear sister-in-law, save me, please save me," pleaded Hŭngbu.

—adapted by Pak Pongsul

The social point of view presented in p'ansori changed as the genre developed. The singers, however, came from the lowest class of Chosŏn society, and until the end of the eighteenth century, so did most p'ansori audiences. Thus, in its formative stages p'ansori reflected the outlook and sensibility of the common people. This influence declined slightly at the beginning of the nineteenth century when p'ansori became popular with the yangban class, and from this point on, the form developed the commoner–yangban duality that makes it unique in the history of Korean literature. In looking at the overall worldview and aesthetic sensibility of p'ansori, we find an attempt to escape from the rigidity of the Confucian-dominated society of the Chosŏn period.

As p'ansori were disseminated in book form, p'ansori novels emerged as an important genre of the classic novel; such novels played an important role in stimulating the development of "common-people-based" realism toward the end of the Chosŏn period.

Narrative Folk Songs

Narrative folk songs center on a particular character or event. Unlike the lyric folk songs, which are brief, narrative folk songs are lengthy and express an attempt to resolve a conflict.

Narrative folk songs have not been studied in detail, but according to *Research on Narrative Folk Songs* (Sŏsa minyo yŏngu, 1979) by Cho Dong-il [Cho Tongil], most narrative folk songs were sung by women as an accompaniment to weaving. Because weaving takes a long time and follows a regular rhythm, verses were long and comparatively simple. The lyrics of these songs also fit the genre. In addition, there were dramatic narrative folk songs that were sung mainly by men in p'ansori.

Weaving was done exclusively by women in traditional Korea, and narrative folk songs dealt with the everyday concerns of home life, as well as with problems in romantic relationships between men and women.

Narrative folk songs were sung by common people and were therefore relatively simple in terms of content and expression compared with the professional narrative in p'ansori, with narrative shaman chants, and with the prose narrative in the classic novel. They are more vivid, however, because they come out of the experience of real life. In particular, narrative folk songs that were sung to accompany weaving are interesting as works that show the inner concerns and hardships of women in the restrictive family system of the Chosŏn period. The following is taken from "Song of a Newlywed" (Shijip sari norae).

On the fourth day of marriage, I went into the fields, hoe in hand.
"Field hand, field hand, let's go to till the fields."
The fields are hard as a courtyard, rough, and wide as Mount Nam. I tilled, one, two, three, four rows, and then it was time for lunch.
"Field hand, field hand, let's go back and have lunch."
Hardly am I back at the house when my father-in-law said, "You come back here like lightning with hardly any work done, and you expect to have lunch?"
My little mother-in-law rose and thrust her face into mine. "You think you've worked hard enough to eat lunch. Ha!"
As I shake, the oldest of the village children slowly comes over. "You think you've worked hard enough to eat lunch. Ha!"
I was starving and thought that they were crazy. . . .
I plopped some cold rice, which looked as if it had been cooked three years ago, into his rice bowl. He asked for some soybean paste, so I plopped some on a small dish. I added a worn-out spoon that I found on top of the clothes box.
I opened the clothes box and found the skirt that my father had made and the white skirt that my mother had made. Taking them out, I tore off one piece and made it into a monk's cowl; I tore off a second piece

and made it into trousers; I tore off a third piece and made it into a knapsack. I put a net bag over my shoulders and said,

"Mother-in-law, I'm leaving. I can't stand married life."

"I'm leaving, I'm leaving, and nobody's going to stop me."

I ran to my husband's room. "Husband, dear husband, I can't stand married life, so I'm leaving. I'm leaving," I said.

He said, "Don't go, don't go. Listen to what I have to say. Whatever you do, don't leave me. My parents won't live forever. That boy won't live forever. Listen to me. Don't leave me."

His fingernails and toenails were clean because all he did was study. I had dirty fingernails and my feet were in the fields all day. I couldn't hold back my tears any longer.

"I'm getting out of here."

So I ran away to Tonghae Temple, and they let me in. An old monk, a young monk, and a child monk were sitting inside. I asked the senior monk to hear my case and to cut off my hair, but he replied, "Do you think I can admit someone who's just run away from her family?"

"Don't worry, just cut off my hair. Senior monk, junior monk, cut off my hair, and after that, let's go beg for alms in my home village. Please, cut off my hair. We have no time to waste."

The senior monk cut off one tiny lock of hair. I began to cry. He cut off another lock and I sobbed like a squashed watermelon in mid-August. I set down my net bag and said, "Junior monk, my friend, let's go to my home village and beg for alms. Let's go."

We arrived at the village. "Hello, we've come to ask for alms. Alms, please. Will anyone give alms in this house?"

When my mother opened the front gate and saw me, she said, "That monk looks like my daughter."

I said, "Excuse me, but don't say that. Many people look alike in this world."

My father opened his door and said, "That monk looks like our daughter."

I said, "Excuse me, but don't say that. Many people look alike in this world."

My elder brother's wife said, "That monk looks like my sister-in-law."

I said, "Excuse me, but don't say that. Many people look alike in this world."

A dog jumped into the house through an open window. Wagging his tail, he pulled on the end of my skirt as he ran in. Seeing the happy dog, I picked him up and began to cry.

As I cried louder, everybody realized who I was, and my mother came forward. She tore off my monk's cowl, trousers, and knapsack. She said, "My child, my child, what's the matter? What happened to you? Let's go into the living room. What happened? What in the world did they do to you?"

—from Yŏngchŏn County in North Kyŏngsang Province

Another important issue here is that although such folk songs are classified as narrative because they revolve around a main event or character, they sometimes go beyond the traditional bounds of narration. This phenomenon, which is also found in certain types of Western literature, such as the ballad, serves to give the work a particular emotional tone, rather than focusing on the narrative expressions used to describe the main event. Because weaving songs have lengthy plots, they are classified as a narrative genre, but shorter songs, such as those about marriage, use narrative to help women overcome difficulties of everyday life.

The Classic Novel

"Classic novels" are those that were written up until the end of the nineteenth century. Here, the word *classic* does not denote "books that have timeless, universal value" but rather works that appeared before a particular time in history. The classic novel has also been called "the old novel" and "the ancient novel." Some scholars use the term "novel of the strange" to refer to the entire range of classic novels. However, this term is not suitable because not all classic novels are stories about strange events. The Korean word for novel, *sosŏl,* denotes all forms of story-based fiction regardless of length. In the following three sections, the word "novel" thus refers to short stories, novellas, and novels. The titles of those works that would be classified as short stories in English are placed in quotation marks, whereas the titles of those that would be classified as novellas and novels are italicized.

A theory that explains the origin of the classic novel satisfactorily has yet to emerge, but clearly *Tales of Kŭmo* (Kŭmo shinhwa, ca. 1445–1468) by Kim Shisŭp (1435–1493) marks the beginning of the emergence of the classic novel. The culture and social structure of the Chosŏn period were still intact in the late fifteenth century when this work was written, but by dealing biographically with the worries and

Page from metal-printed classic novel

conflicts created by worldly desire under the weight of Confucian
ideology, worries and conflicts felt by Kim Shisŭp himself, *Tales of
Kŭmo* presented social conflicts that could rightfully be included in
novels at the time. By the end of the sixteenth century, the novel, under
the influence of Hŏ Kyun (1569–1618), author of *Tale of Hong
Kildong* (Hong Kildong chŏn), had begun to deal directly with contradictions in society rather than by means of biographical methods.*
From the seventeenth century onward, the novel flourished, and it
appealed to and reached an ever growing audience; the eighteenth and
nineteenth centuries were the era of the novel. Not only were a large

---

*Some scholars doubt whether Hŏ Kyun first wrote *Hong Kildong chŏn* in
hangŭl, but it is impossible to know for sure because none of the existing versions
of the novel were written by Hŏ Kyun himself; all are products of extensive
revisions during the process of printing over many centuries.

number of novels of good quality published, but these centuries also witnessed the rise of commercial publishing and the book trade.

Because a great many novels have been lost, it is difficult to determine the true number of classic novels, but about six hundred classic novels have been verified, and no doubt more will be discovered in the future. Many novels exist in several versions, and some of these versions are so different that it is more accurate to regard them as separate but related works. By looking at the relationship among plot, character, theme, and style, we can separate classical novels into the following categories: heroic novels, fantasy dream novels, historical war novels, p'ansori novels, family novels, and novels in classical Chinese.

Early heroic novels took their form from *Tale of Hong Kildong* and developed from that point on. This form became one of the most popular in the eighteenth and nineteenth centuries. Heroic novels are defined by several major characteristics: (1) the protagonist is of humble origin and becomes an aristocrat; (2) the protagonist falls on unexpected hard times; (3) the protagonist finds a savior and overcomes his predicament; (4) after developing his strength and wisdom, the protagonist reenters society; (5) the protagonist defeats evil forces and becomes a hero. In this structure, the protagonist is usually a handsome genius, and the overall tone of the work is serious and solemn.

Because the protagonist of most of these novels is a soldier, this type of novel is also called the "war novel." The term is not appropriate, however, because not all heroic novels have military protagonists. In addition, most heroic novels establish a duality that includes the supernatural world and the real world, and because the protagonist is brought down from the supernatural world to the real world by his own failures, heroic novels are also called "human incarnation novels." This term, however, is not appropriate because the heroes are not always incarnations of a supernatural being. Nevertheless, works that deal with the tragic fall and dramatic rise of the protagonist and that are elaborate tales of war and the duality of the world clearly comprise the majority of heroic novels. *Tale of Yu Ch'ungnyŏl* (Yu Ch'ungnyŏl chŏn) fits this pattern, and despite individual differences, well-known works such as *Tale of Cho Ung* (Cho Ung chŏn), *Tale of Kim Pangul* (Kim Pangul chŏn), *Tale of So Taesŏng* (So Taesŏng chŏn), *Tale of Chang P'ung* (Chang P'ung chŏn), *Tale of Hyŏn Sumun* (Hyŏn Sumun chŏn), and *Tale of Sukhyang* (Sukhyang chŏn) are all heroic novels. The following scene from *Tale of Yu Ch'ungnyŏl,* is from the part in which Yu Ch'ungnyŏl and his mother barely escape death at the hands of Chong Handam. This section exemplifies the characteristically serious and grim tone of descriptions of the danger in which protagonists find themselves.

> Ch'ungnyŏl's mother clutched his hand as they hid behind the wall. The bright light lit up a huge stack of white dishes. When the light faded away, the house became quiet. One night, all the people were gone from the house, though two soldiers were guarding the main gate. They couldn't escape through the main gate, so they waited quietly behind the wall. The moon rose and lit the garden. They noticed that the wall was too high to climb, and that their only way of escape was though the opening that carried water into the house. Holding on to Ch'ungnyŏl's clothes, his mother followed him through the hole. After reaching the other side, Ch'ungnyŏl noticed that his mother's fair skin had been cut by sharp stones and her white face was smeared with mud. He was overcome by shock and sadness and began to cry. Ch'ungnyŏl picked up his mother and followed a narrow pathway. Looking at the southern sky, he ran with all his might until he came to the foot of a huge mountain. The mountain was so high that its summit was obscured by dark clouds. He then realized that this mountain was the site of the altar to the Heavens. His mother was pleased at the sight of the mountain, but as the altar came into view, she burst into tears and held on to Ch'ungnyŏl.

> "Do you know what this mountain is?" she said. "I gave birth to you here when I came here to pay our respects to our ancestors. Don't you know where your father is? When I look at this mountain, I want to see him. Tears are not enough to express my sorrow."

> On hearing her words, Ch'ungnyŏl held her hand and wept. "Could it be that I was born here during a ceremony for my ancestors? Tell me, god of the mountain, if this is true. Why don't you answer me?" Ch'ungnyŏl demanded as he cried.

> When his mother heard this, she fell silent. After Ch'ungnyŏl comforted her, she regained her strength and took the lead. The two crossed Lake Pŏnyang and approached the village of Hoesu, where the sun was shining over the mountains to the west. They could tell it was suppertime because smoke was rising from the houses in the village. The river birds had flown into the willow trees for the night and a crow was cawing mournfully as it flew in the clear sky. Looking out to sea, they could see the mast of a fishing boat shrouded in the evening fog. The smoke from the village was scattered in all directions by the last rays of the sun. This scene soothed his mother, and she held Ch'ungnyŏl's hand

as they walked by the bank of the river, looking for a boat, but none appeared. As they looked up at the sky, they felt a deepening sense of helplessness.

—from a Chŏnju woodblock-print

Heroic novels, which are built on the fall and rise of an aristocratic hero of humble origin, developed from the union of two different literary outlooks: the real-life outlook, an investigation of personal desire and the confusion of the Confucian system of values in the Chosŏn period; and the nostalgic outlook, a search for heroes, an attempt to create a feeling of stability by returning to the same system of Confucian values. The degree of conflict between these two outlooks obviously varies from work to work, but on the whole, heroic novels contain more nostalgia for the Confucian system of values that served as the ruling ideology of the Chosŏn Dynasty than do p'ansori novels or family novels. Though the protagonist in heroic novels upholds the Confucian ethics of filial piety and loyalty, underlying themes such as ambition, fame, and love clearly reflect the dreams and experiences of people as the system of Confucian values weakened in the last half of the Chosŏn period.

Fantasy dream novels and war novels are subcategories that are closely related to heroic novels. Most of the few remaining dream novels were written from the end of the seventeenth century—the time in which *A Dream of Nine Clouds* (Kuun mong, ca. 1689) by Kim Manjung (1637–1692) appeared—to the end of the nineteenth century. Most dream novels have the following plot: (1) The protagonist lives in a supernatural world but is stuck in a worldly existence; (2) in a dream, the protagonist is reborn as a hero; (3) the protagonist awakes from the dream and dies slowly in three stages. This plot closely resembles ancient Korean and Chinese myths and dream stories such as "Dream of Choshin" (Choshin mong) in *Memorabilia of the Three Kingdoms* (Samguk yusa, ca. 1285) and the Tang period *Account of the Southern Branch* (Namga ki; Chinese: Nanke ji).

Dream novels vary considerably. Unlike the unification of the transcendental Buddhist values with the worldly Confucian values in the plot of a work such as *A Dream of Nine Clouds,* the nineteenth-century work *Dream of the Jade Pavilion* (Ungnu mong) deals with basic human desires and thus moves toward realism. The real-life story that takes place in the dream section of these works has much in common with the plot of heroic novels, but because the dream section plays an important role in the overall plot, the dream novel is considered a separate genre.

In focusing on the hero's superhuman military accomplishments, historical war novels, such as *Tale of Im Kyŏngŏp* (Im Kyŏngŏp chŏn), *Tale of Lady Pak* (Pak ssi chŏn), and *Record of the Imjin Wars with Japan* (Imjin nok, ca. 1600), are similar to war novels, and works in each category show the influence of the other in plot and literary style. The historical war novel differs from the war novel because the former portrays actual events and people, such as the Imjin Wars of 1592 and 1598. Although such works are based on actual historical events and people, they are mostly fictitious accounts of events the memory of which was passed down orally among the common people from one generation to the next. Unlike the protagonists of heroic novels, who achieve greatness and add to the prestige of their families, protagonists in historical war novels are usually heroes from the common people who fight dramatically against the cunning and ruthless ruling class.

Because p'ansori were transmitted in writing, the p'ansori novel did not develop a plot structure of its own, but adopted the narrative style, characterization, and worldview of p'ansori itself. Works such as *Tale of Ch'unhyang, Tale of Shim Ch'ŏng, Tale of Hŭngbu, Tale of the Water Palace* (also known as T'okki chŏn [*Tale of the Tortoise and the Hare*]), *Tale of a Male Pheasant,* and *Tale of Stubborn Mr. Ong* all deal with the problems of average people, and these works are characterized by a unified worldview that places emphasis on the here and now.* None of the protagonists in p'ansori novels have superhuman abilities, and these novels emphasize how the characters deal with the events of the story as they unfold. In terms of literary style, p'ansori novels not only mingle prose and poetry but also combine a great deal of wit, sarcasm, and slang with elegant and refined language. In addition, while taking the spicy sarcasm and rich humor that reflect the concerns of everyday life from p'ansori, these novels incorporated a broader worldview into the literature of the late Chosŏn period.

With respect to plot, in the following example from *Tale of Ch'unhyang,* in which Kunno's soldiers try to capture the beautiful

---

*'P'ansori works that end in *ka* (song) were orally transmitted through singing, whereas those works that were novelized end in *chŏn* (tale). Works that end in *ka* are translated as *Song of;* those that end in *chŏn* are translated as *Tale of*—Trans.

Ch'unhyang, we see how Ch'unhyang charmed the soldier into complacency so that she could make her escape.

> Ch'unhyang ran over happily, smiling and clapping her hands. "Look at that customer. What a pleasant surprise; I'm so happy to see him." . . . Ch'unhyang took Yi P'aedo's hand and brought him inside, saying, "Come in. Let's drink and have fun. What brought you here? Did you come to see me out of boredom? Did the wind carry you here?" She was so happy that she thought she must be dreaming. She had longed to see him, but now he was here. She was overjoyed. When you miss someone so much, it's easy to be swayed by their sweet talk. Look at these two people!
>
> Ch'unhyang doesn't usually act this way, but today's events were a very big surprise. She usually acts like a fairy in a palace, but now we know who she really is. Oh, he held her hand in his gentle white hand. When she touched the back of his neck, his rough neck bones melted like ice on a river.
>
> —from *Old Song of Namwŏn* (Namwŏn kosa)

There are many different versions of the three most popular p'ansori novels, *Tale of Shim Ch'ŏng,* the *Tale of Ch'unghyang,* and *Tale of Hŭngbu.* In addition to changes that took place in the process of reprinting these novels for the commercial market, which grew considerably in the eighteenth and nineteenth centuries, the novels were transmitted orally in various versions over the years. P'ansori novels grew in popularity from the eighteenth century on, particularly among the common people. As p'ansori novels grew in popularity, novels based on drama and written in a style that appealed to the common people developed a growing readership. *Tale of Yi Ch'unp'ung* (Yi ch'unp'ung chŏn), *Diary of Three Daoist Immortals* (Samsŏn ki), and *Tale of O Yuran* (O Yuran chŏn) are examples of this type of novel. Novels that portrayed human society sarcastically through the use of animals, such as *Tale of Sŏ Tongji, the Rat* (Sŏ Tongji chŏn) and *Record of a Rat's Trial* (Sŏok ki), also appeared at this time. All of these novels belong to the category of "commoner novels" because of their popularity with the common people.

Certain works by Pak Chiwŏn (1737–1805) and Yi Ok (n.d.) that have the characteristics of novels are classified as "novels written in classical Chinese," and those of Yi Ok are called "short stories in classical Chinese." This type of work appealed to those groups in society that were proficient in classical Chinese but in terms of contents it departed sharply from traditional yangban literature. Everyday life and social problems of the time were depicted clearly through the lives of a variety of people—merchants, peasants, wealthy landowners, thieves, *kisaeng* (female entertainers in traditional Korea), and shamans.

Most of the novels discussed above had one character, or one important character. This meant that there was very little character development beyond the protagonist. In most of the novels that were discovered in the Naksŏnje, the private quarters of the royal family, the plot was built around the lives of many members of an extended family through several generations; this type of novel is called the "family novel" or "epic novel." Except for works such as *Ch'ŏngsusŏk, Falling Spring and Rising Clouds* (Naksŏn tŭngun), *Record of Repaying Gratitude* (Poun kiurok), and *History of the Two Branches of the Hyŏn Family* (Hyŏn-ssi yangung ssangnim ki), which have been studied extensively, most of the remaining works have yet to be studied in detail. Family novels emerged toward the end of the eighteenth century and became popular with women in the royal palace through the activities of increasingly active book sellers in Seoul. The works were extremely long, most of them thirty or forty volumes. *Treasure of Bright Pearls in the Moonlight* (Myŏngju powŏlbing), a novel based on three generations of family life, is in 235 volumes. The characters in these novels are average members of the yangban class searching for power, wealth, and love in the real world. This differed sharply from other genres of the classic novel, whose heroes either had supernatural powers or accomplished miraculous deeds.

Except for a small number, classic novels were written by anonymous authors. This reflects the fact that not only was there little regard for novel writing at the time, there was also a lack of respect for individual creativity. In reviewing the historical evidence, we find that yangban and literate commoners first wrote novels as a means of self-expression, but then began to write them to appeal to a growing market. Many novels underwent considerable revision during the process of printing and reprinting, giving rise to a large number of different versions of the same work. Classic novels were popular with yangban children and children of the middle-class, which comprised merchants and artisans, and with commoner men. How classic novels were distributed to their readers is a topic of particular interest, to be discussed in further detail in chapter 6.

The New Novel

From the end of the nineteenth century to the early twentieth century, classic novels were published as "six-*chŏn* novels" using metal typesetting methods imported from the West. [A *chŏn* is a hundredth of a *won*, the Korean unit of currency. —Trans.] By this time, however, they had lost their dominant position in the history of Korean literature, as new novels that reflected the concerns of writers in this era began to appear from the middle of the 1900s. The term "new novel" originated in advertisements of that time that attracted the reader's interest by making a distinction between staid "old novels"—classic novels—and exciting "new novels." Although writers attempted to create an entirely new literary tradition in the new novel, they could not break away completely from the traditions set by the classic novel. Thus, the new novel represents the transition from the classic novel to the modern novel of today.

The New Novel emerged after Korea was opened to the outside world in the late nineteenth century and traditional values were challenged by a previously unknown way of life. The readership for fiction, which had been growing since the late Chosŏn period, began to grow at a much more rapid pace. The development of commercial publishing companies resulted in increased production of books, lowering their price and contributing to their distribution in society. The vernacular newspapers that began printing in the 1900s ran a serialized novel to attract readers. Some authors of these serialized novels were steeped in the tradition of classic novels, whereas others were new to writing and had chosen it as a career. From a literary historical point of view, the development of the new novel was influenced by Japanese novels, which had been influenced by Western literary trends since the Meiji Restoration in 1868. Some critics also claim that the new novel was influenced by Chinese novels of the time. However, the new novel not only derived from these two outside influences, but also absorbed literary features from classic novels; structurally, it bore a resemblance to the heroic genre of the latter.

Because many early new novels began as newspaper serials, they dealt with topics that were of interest at the time, such as modernization, national strength, educational reform, and changes in social customs. *Tears of Blood* (Hyŏl ŭi nu) by Yi Injik (1862–1919), which was serialized in *The Independence News* (Mansebo) in 1906, was the first new novel, although sarcastic short stories written in the same form

Cover of the New Novel *Tears of Blood* (Hyŏl ŭi nu)

had appeared slightly earlier. "A Driver's Misunderstanding" (Chabu ohae, 1905) and "A Conversation with Sogyŏng" (Sogyŏng kwa anjun pang i mundap, 1905), which appeared in *The Korea Daily News* (Taehan maeil shinbo), and "An Embarrassing Thought" (Illyŏmhong, 1906) and "The Dragon and the King" (Yongham wang, 1906), which appeared in *The Korea Daily* (Taehan ilbo), are good examples of early short stories in this period of rapid social and cultural change.

Because the earliest works dealt with everyday life, they attracted the interest of a wide readership, stimulating more authors to write in the new style. Yi Injik's *Voice of the Devil* (Kwi ŭi sŏng, 1908), *Mount Ch'iak* (Ch'iaksan, 1908), and *Silver World* (Ŭnsegye, 1908); Yi Haejo's *Snow-Covered Temples* (Pingsangsŏl, 1908), the *Magic Sword* (Kumagŏm, 1907), and *Liberty Bell* (Chayujong, 1910); Ch'oe Ch'anshik's *Color of an Autumn Moon* (Ch'uwŏlsaek, 1912); and An Kuksŏn's *Cry of a Wild Goose* (An ŭi sŏng, 1912), and

Minutes from a Meeting of Animals (Kŭmsu hoeŭi rok, 1907), are examples of popular new novels. *Silver World* was based on a drama, *The Ballad of Ch'oe Pyŏngdo* (Ch'oe Pyŏngdo t'aryŏng, 1908), and depicted an actual event in society at the time. The author added an additional section at the end to conclude the story. By incorporating a late-Chosŏn-period animal story in the plot, the author of *Minutes from a Meeting of Animals* treated social problems of the time sarcastically. As the popularity of the new novel spread, writing as a profession gained greater respect in society, encouraging authors to develop their own unique writing styles. Both of these developments stand in sharp contrast to the social attitudes toward writing during the Chosŏn period.

Unlike the classic novel, which was built around the life of one main character, the new novel was centered on the development and resolution of a particular problem. Most of the problems in the new novel were closely related to social and political problems of the time. The flow of time in the classic novel was strictly chronological, whereas in the new novel, time was given a more open interpretation. Retrospection was used to transport readers into the past. The new novel also used vernacular speech and portrayed events more realistically, changes that allowed the form to better reflect the real-life experience of contemporary readers.

Despite these innovations, however, the new novel was deeply rooted in the traditions of the classic novel. The traditional dichotomy between good and bad is clearly apparent in the stance of the new novel: modern equals good; traditional equals bad. The new novel also relied on coincidence to move the plot along, and the crisis–salvation–victory plot of the heroic genre of classic novel was incorporated into many new novels. In response to the pressures of a new era, the new novel drew on outside literary traditions to create a new form of literature while preserving many of the traditions of the classic novel.

Except for a few notable cases, most new novels extolled the modernization of Korea through the importation of Western culture and technology, things that promised a better future and were viewed with sympathy and envy. Protagonists in the new novel turned to Japanese or Western people for help in overcoming crises, which often they were able to resolve only by going overseas to study. Despite this boundless optimism for the Western way of life, many new novels ended up as shallow propaganda for modernization. The works of well-known authors, such as Yi Injik, projected Japan as a model for Korea to follow—ironically, just as Japan was about to subject Korea to harsh colonial rule (1910–45). This interpretation of Korea's destiny contrasts sharply with the struggle against Japanese imperialism that was being waged at the time.

The Modern Novel

The new novel, written mainly for escapist entertainment, lost its literary value after the Japanese takeover of Korea in 1910 and the modern novel emerged. The modern novel combined a more realistic description of contemporary life with influences from Japanese and Western literature that had been incorporated into Korean literature through the new novel. Works by Hyŏn Sangyun and Yi Kwangsu, which first appeared in *The Light of Scholarship* (Hak chi kwang), a literary magazine published by the Korean Students Association in Tokyo, are typical examples of early modern novels. Although these works are highly subjective and are not well organized in terms of plot and style, they managed to overcome the blind admiration for Westernization and the simplistic plots of the new novel to dig deeper into the problems of Korean society under colonial rule.

Heartlessness (Mujŏng, 1917), a well-known novella by Yi Kwangsu, is considered by most critics to be the first modern novel in Korea. Although some critics argue that *Heartlessness* is written in language similar to that of the classic novel and the new novels and that the plot is based on coincidence, it remains a landmark in the history of Korean literature.

Heartlessness is a sociocultural map of the problems that Korean society was facing in the middle of the first decade of the twentieth century. The novel deals with the uncomfortable coexistence of tradition and modernity and the conflict between social reality and traditional ethics. *Heartlessness* portrays everyday life in a period of confused values and of warring ideals and desires. The protagonist, Yi Hyŏngshik, and the supporting characters, Pak Yŏngch'ae, Kim Sŏnhyŏng, and Elder Kim of the church, all feel these clashing forces at some point in the story. Within the overall structure of conflict, Yi Kwangsu introduces the characters at various points in the story to show how individuals deal with the collapse of traditional society and the process of colonialism. However, at the end of the *Heartlessness,*

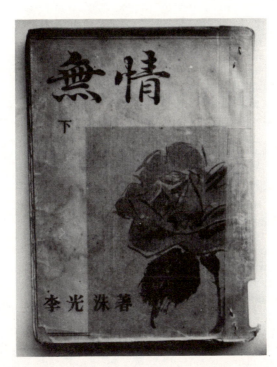

Cover of *Heartlessness* (Mujŏng), Korea's first modern novel

Yi falls victim to the same blind admiration for Westernization that dominated the new novel.

The following excerpt from *Heartlessness* shows Yi Kwangsu's deep insight into how people use the new culture to deceive each other. The scene is a description of the comic betrothal between Yi Hyŏngshik and Kim Sŏnhyŏng, with Elder Kim and the minister acting as intermediaries between the two.

> The elder looked at Hyŏngshik and Sŏnhyŏng and then turned to the minister and asked, "What should I do?" The elder wasn't familiar with Western weddings and had no idea of what to do next. The minister didn't know much either, but he had to pretend that if he knew what to do. . . .
>
> Not knowing what to say, the elder tapped his fingers on the table. He then thought that he should say something to Sŏnhyŏng first, so he began to speak in a soft voice, "Sŏnhyŏng, I asked Hyŏngshik if he would marry you, and he agreed. Now, do you want to be his wife?"

Pleased with his sensible and sophisticated speech, he looked at Sŏnhyŏng.

Sŏnhyŏng was too shy to bring up what they had just discussed or to ask questions. She didn't know much about Western weddings and though that it would be best to remain silent to save herself embarrassment. She bowed gently and said, "Thank you."

"Does this mean that you agree?" the elder asked.

"Yes." Sŏnhyŏng lifted her head and looked at a painting on the wall.

"Then I guess you're now engaged," said the elder. He turned to the minister of the church and then looked at the sky as if he were praying.

"Fine, now we have to hear what the parties concerned have to say," said the minister, trying to show that he knew more about Western weddings than the elder.

"Of course, the parties concerned have already agreed, but, well, I think that—we have to hear what they have to say," he said, turning to Hyŏngshik.

Sŏnhyŏn wondered if she had said something wrong. Hyŏngshik glanced at the minister and bowed his head.

The elder said, "Okay. Let's ask them what they want to do." He thought it would be best to take on the demeanor of a judge and ask Hyŏngshik what he wanted to do first and then ask Sŏnhyŏng the same question. "Mr. Hyŏngshik, do you agree to be engaged to Sŏnhyŏng?" the elder asked.

The minister thought that the elder's question was too simple. He turned to Hyŏngshik and said, "We need to know whether you want to marry Sŏnhyŏng, so please give us a direct answer—do you want to marry her?"

Hyŏngshik could barely manage to conceal his laughter. He was too embarrassed to speak. Thinking about the future, however, he raised his head with dignity and said, "Yes." His answer seemed somehow foolish.

From the March 1 Movement in 1919 (*samil undong*) to the mid-1920s, more and more modern novels were written as new authors such as Kim Tongin, Chŏn Yŏngt'aek, Yŏm Sangsŏp, Hyŏn Chingŏn, and Na Hyŏngbae dealt with the agony of the powerless individual under Japanese colonial rule. Kim Tongin's *Sadness of a Weak Man* (Yakhanja ŭi sŭlp'ŭm, 1919), Yŏm Sangsŏp's *A Green Frog in a Science Lab* (P'yobonshil ŭi ch'ŏnggaeguri, 1921) and *The Grave* (Myoji, 1923; changed to Mansejŏn in 1924), and Hyŏn Chingŏn's

Poor Wife (Pinch'ŏ, 1921) and *A Lucky Day* (Unsu choŭn nal, 1924) are works representative of this period. While maintaining a critical stance toward colonial society, novels from this period presented characters who could not turn their critical feelings into action and who were overwhelmed by sadness and a sense of helplessness.

In contrast, the proletarian movement, which emerged around 1924, challenged the contradictions in society. In works such as *The Death of Pak Tol* (Pak Tol ŭi chugŭm, 1925), *After a Heavy Rain* (K'ŭnmul chin twi, 1925), and *Bright Red Flames* (Hongyŏm, 1927), Ch'oe Haksong showed in stark detail how the oppression in colonial Korean society destroyed the lives of good people. Although proletarian literature was limited by its excessive adherence to ideology over literary form and style, it is important in the history of Korean literature as a window the internal conflicts and suffering of the common people under Japanese colonialism.

The modern novel, rooted in the late teens and the 1920s, developed in diverse directions from the 1930s onward as new writers and literary movements emerged in each era. Novels set in the countryside, such as Yi Kwangsu's *Soil* (Hŭk, 1932), Shim Hun's *An Evergreen* (Sangnoksu, 1935), and Yi Muyŏng's *Chapter 1, Part 1* (Che 1-chang che 1-kwa, 1939) focused on the details of village life, whereas works such as Yŏm Sangsŏp's *Three Generations* (Samdae, 1931) and Ch'ae Manshik's *Muddy Waters* (Tangnyu, 1937), and *Peace Under Heaven* (T'aep'yŏng ch'ŏnha, 1938) dealt with the dark side of colonial life in the strong vernacular of the common people. Works such as Yi Sang's *Wings* (Nalgae, 1936) and *Diary at the End of My Life* (Chongsaeng ki, 1936) dealt with the inner thoughts of a confused mind, whereas Hyŏn Chingŏn's *Shadowless Tower* (Muyŏngt'ap, 1938) presented characters who were trying to improve their lives. Some novels showed a delicate use of language and sensitive character development, whereas others, such as Kim Yŏnhan's *A Village Before the Temple* (Sahachon, 1936) and *Diary of Resistance* (Hangjin ki, 1937), criticized society by portraying the lives of oppressed people.

Despite this diversity, the modern novel deals with the distorted and ruined lives of people in the real world, themes closely connected to the tortured history of Korea in the twentieth century. The modern Korean novel thus focuses more on social and moral than metaphysical and aesthetic issues.

Since liberation from Japan in 1945, this interest in social and moral issues has endured. After a dearth of activity in the 1950s following the Korean War, the modern novel gained new vitality in the 1960s and has developed greatly since that time. The form still has to tackle the question it has dealt with since the 1920s and 1930s: how can one live a moral life in an immoral world? The problems that Korea has faced in the twentieth century—the social turmoil of industrialization, the search for the meaning of life amid social alienation, division into two opposing states, and political instability—are issues from which contemporary Korean literature cannot escape.

3. Dramatic Genres

Mask Dance

According to historical documents, early Korean drama and performance developed from indigenous sources and from Chinese and other cultural influences from west of the Korean Peninsula. The five dances that appeared in *Poems about Folk Music* (Hyangak chabyŏng, ca. 890 A.D.) by Ch'oe Ch'iwŏn (857–915), the Koryŏ dance referred to by the Chinese, and Koryŏ music, which influenced the development of performing arts in Japan, are all examples of early Korean drama. As the stern Confucian values of the Chosŏn period spread throughout Korean society, drama and performance were forced to develop under highly restrictive circumstances. By the middle of the Chosŏn period, this atmosphere had spread to the villages, where a rich variety of local theatrical forms had flourished until that time. The late development of commercial entertainment and the market economy in Korea also contributed to the stagnation of drama and performance in the Chosŏn period. Because of prevailing Chosŏn-period prejudices, much of the drama and performance of the Chosŏn period and earlier was not recorded and has thus been lost; since the end of the nineteenth century, much of what was recorded has been lost amid dramatic social and political change.

Among all the forms of traditional drama, the most important form surviving today is the mask dance (*t'alch'um*), sometimes referred to as *sandaenori, t'alnori, pyŏlshin kunnori, tŏtpoegi,* and *tŭlnorŭm*. The term *mask dance* originally referred to the form native to Hwanghae Province. Because it was transmitted by the common people, there were no scripts to follow, as there are in conventional drama, but the mask dance is considered a dramatic form of drama because the orally transmitted texts and performance practices adhered to clearly defined rules.

Mask dance can be divided into three main types. The first comprises comparatively simple mask dances, such as the Pukch'ŏng lion dance (Pukch'ŏng saja norŭm), the Kangnŭng mask dance (Kangnŭng kwanno t'alnori), and the Hahoe mask dance (Hahoe pyŏlshin kunnori), which were performed as part of local village festivals in particular regions of Korea. The second type is the more developed forms of mask dance that evolved in the Naktong River basin and along the south coast of South Kyŏngsang Province. Mask dances in this category originated east of the Naktong River in places such as Tongnae, Suyŏng, and Pusanjin and are called *tŭlnorŭm,* whereas those that developed west of the Naktong River in places such as T'ongyŏng, Kosŏng, Chinju, and Kasan are called *ogwangdae.* The third type is the complex forms of mask dance, such as the Yangju mask dance (Yangju pyŏlsandaenori), the Songp'a mask dance (Songp'a sandaenori), the Pongsan mask dance (Pongsan t'alch'um), and the Kŏnnyŏng Mask Dance (Kŏnnyŏng t'alch'um) that developed around Seoul and the coastal areas of Hwanghae Province.

Mask dances of the first type had close ties to local festivals; mask dances of the second and third types reflected the urban characteristics of the administrative and trading regions from which they emerged. This was especially true of the third type, which developed in trading regions and were more detailed in plot and presentation than those that emerged in rural areas. Many of the mask dances that developed in market towns near Seoul and in port villages along the west coast no longer exist. In addition to these three types of mask dance, there were many groups of performers who performed their own dances. Of these, only the *tŏtpoegi* performed by the namsadang group of performers has survived.

In rural villages, mask dances were performed at festivals such as the Lunar New Year and the Tano Festival (*tanoje*) in May; near Seoul and along the west coast they were performed on other special occasions as well. The performers were villagers who were familiar with the story and presentation. In certain regions, lower-level officials performed in their free time. Toward the end of the Chosŏn period, however, professional performers began to appear in market towns near Seoul.

Mask dances were performed in spaces wide enough for viewers to sit in a circle around the performance area. In certain places, they began at dusk and continued into the night, illuminated by torches. Depending on the region, masks were made from wood, gourds, paper, and other materials. Facial features were comic and exaggerated according to established patterns. The performers, however, gave the characters that they played originality and variety through individual variation in dancing, gestures, and lighting.

The overall structure of the mask dance was based on several loosely defined acts that were related to one another. In each act, characters with distinctive dancing styles and behavior made their appearance. Unlike actors in more realistic drama, the performers in mask dance were not restricted by time or by the configuration of the performance space; they concentrated on keeping things moving at a fast pace and on resolving the conflicts in the story. In the course of the dance, the performers often spoke to the audience or the musician (*sanbach'i*) and even brought these groups into the performance. The script consisted of a mixture of speech and song. At various points, gestures and dance movements carried the narrative, as in pantomime. The Kangnŭng mask dance is entirely silent, and certain characters in other dances, such as old monks and lepers, express themselves only through gestures and dance. Dance movements differed according to the type of character portrayed and the region.

The language of the mask dance was closely related to the oral language of the common people in whatever region the dance developed, but at times erudite Chinese expressions and refined Korean ones were used to enliven the narrative. The earthy culture of the common people was expressed in a lively and rich language of metaphors, repetition, and braggadocio in the mask dance. The following example is representative of the "yangban act" commonly found in many mask dances:

(Wearing a felt hat, the servant (malttugi) *enters to kut music. He guides the three yangban brothers onto the stage. The three yangban dance awkwardly to the music as they enter. The oldest is Saennim, followed by Sŏbangnim and Toryŏngnim. Saennim and Sŏbangnim are dressed in white clothes and wear the formal yangban horsehair hat. Toryŏngnim wears dark blue clothes. Saennim has a double cleft palate, and*

Sŏbangnim a single cleft palate. They carry fans and bamboo walking sticks. Toryŏngnim's nose and mouth are off center, and he carries only a fan. He has no lines of dialogue; he imitates exactly what his two elder brothers do, occasionally hitting them in the face by mistake with his fan.)

Servant: (Sarcastically, moving into the middle of the stage.) Hey! *(The kut music and dancing stop.)* Look, the yangban are coming! By "yangban," I don't mean retired yangban from the Noron or Soron factions, or officials who served on the State Council or in the Six Ministries. What I mean by "yangban" is yang for dog and pan for a small table with feet like a dog's paws.

Three yangban: Hey, you, what did you say?

Servant: Well, I guess they didn't hear what I said. I said that three yangban brothers named Yi Saengwŏn who've been members of the Noron and Soron factions and who have served on the State Council and in the Six Ministries have blessed us with their presence.

Three Yangban: (together) He called us Yi Saengwŏn!

(They dance together to the kut music. Toryŏngnim clumsily hits his two elder brothers in the face with his fan.)

Servant: Hey! *(The music and dancing stop as he faces the audience.)* Attention, everybody! Listen to what I have to say! Don't smoke with a short pipe. Go to a tobacconist's shop and buy some colored or bamboo-spotted pipes about one and a half times the length of your arm. Then decorate them with poulownia-tree engravings. After that, take them off the rack like fishing poles and smoke them one by one.

Three Yangban: What? What did you say?

Servant: I guess they didn't hear what I said again. I asked the audience not to smoke and fight in your honorable presence.

Three yangban: (together) He told them not to fight! *(They dance to the sound of kut music.)*

Servant: Hey! *(The music and dancing stop.)* Attention, musicians! Listen to me. Stop playing the five notes and six beats of Chinese music. Grab a willow twig and blow, and beat a dried gourd with chopsticks and a spoon.

Three yangban: Hey, you! What did you say?

Servant: Again? They still didn't hear what I said. I told them to play the lute, the drums, the flute, and the fife in harmony instead of jumping from one tune to another.

Three yangban: (together) Play in harmony! *(They dance to the sound of kut music.)*

—Pongsan mask dance, adapted by Yi Tuhyŏn

Mask dances vary according to region, but they can be divided into the following acts: the yangban act, which is developed around the conflict between a yangban(s) and a servant (*malttugi*); the grandmother act, which portrays an argument between an old woman and her husband about his concubine; and the old monk act, which deals with an argument between an old monk struggling to reconcile his worldly desires with Buddhist commandments, and with a troublemaker who hangs around markets. The conflicts in the mask dance are presented as a dramatic struggle expressed through wit and sarcasm. Intervals of music and dance between acts and between various sections of an act help to increase the audience's interest in the overall performance. Ultimately, the mask dance, a genre of drama based on the witty language of the common people, a variety of dances, and entertaining folk music, helped to expose the hypocrisy of the Confucian values that prevailed during the Chosŏn period.

Toward the end of the Chosŏn period, the mask dance entered a period of great activity. With the development of commerce, various groups of professional actors performed mask dances for profit in market towns. Mask dance has also been the source of contemporary developments in Korean drama, such as the outdoor *madanggŭk.*

Puppet Theater

Traditional Korean puppet theater is called *kkoktukkakshi norŭm* (also *kkoktukkakshi norŭm*). This term comes from the name of the only surviving puppet play in Korea. Several other works existed, but these have been lost over the years.

The namsadang group (*namsadangp'ae*) was a troupe of male actors who traveled around the countryside from spring until fall. They performed six types of music and drama: drumming and dancing (*p'ungmulnori*), bowl spinning (*pŏni*), acrobatics (*salp'an*), rope walk (*ŏrŭm*), mask dance (*tŏtpoegi*), and puppet theater (*tŏlmi*). Bowl spinning, acrobatics, and rope walk combine witty language and acrobatics with theatrics, whereas the mask dance and the puppet theater are considered folk theater.

Like mask dance, puppet theater could be performed in any open space in the market or village, but the audience sat facing the portable stage (*tŏlmi p'ojang*), rather than surrounding it as in mask dance. The covered stage was three meters by three meters and supported by posts in each corner, with a large opening in front where the puppets appeared. The puppeteers moved the puppets with their hands and provided narration for each character from within the covered space. The puppeteers did not use string or appear directly on stage as in other types of puppet theater.

The musician–narrator (*sanbach'i*) sat facing the stage from the outside, providing additional entertainment, particularly between acts. Puppet theater was traditionally performed at night and lit by torches placed on each side of the stage. The puppet appeared from the waist up, and the puppeteers used various interesting movements of the puppets' head, arms, and torso to bring it to life.

The story was told in the dialogue among the puppets and between a puppet and singer. The musician–narrator faced the audience and talked with the puppet in response to prompting from the crowd. This involved the audience in the drama and helped to overcome the physical limitations of the relatively small stage. Of all the forty or so human and animal characters that appeared in puppet theater, Pak Ch'ŏmji, the head of the village, was the most important character. Through conversations with the musician–narrator, Pak Ch'ŏmji provided background explanations and alluded to the future direction of the story. The importance of Pak Ch'ŏmji explains why puppet theater is also called the Pak Ch'ŏmji Puppet Play (Pak Ch'ŏmji norŭm) theater. Reaching out to the audience through music and speech is an important part of the mask dance, but in the case of puppet theater, it had a much more prominent role in exposition. Here is an example of a dialogue about a street vender taking place between the musician–narrator, the sanpatchi, and Pak Ch'ŏmji:

> *Pak Ch'ŏmji:* Aha, attention, everyone, something has just happened!
> *Sanbach'i:* Not again?
> *Pak Ch'ŏmji:* The governor of P'yŏngan's coming for a visit.
> *Sanbach'i:* Oh, what a big event that is!
> (*Pak Ch'ŏmji leaves the stage. The governor of P'yŏngan appears.*)
> *Governor:* Where is this fellow called Pak or Mang?
> *Pak Ch'ŏmji:* Hello, is someone looking for me?
> *Sanbach'i:* The governor is looking for you.
> *Pak Ch'ŏmji:* I present myself before you.
> *Governor:* So you're Pak?
> *Pak Ch'ŏmji:* You can call me Pak or Mang, whichever you like.

Governor: I'll call you Pak. Who helped clear the road? Go find him.

Pak Chŏmji: Oh, I have to tell you that something terrible has just happened.

Sanbach'i: Why do you say that?

Pak Chŏmji: He ordered me to find the helper, but I know something terrible will happen.

Sanbach'i: Go find him, and make sure you lash the wheels of the carriage with rope.

Pak Ch'ŏmji: Okay.

Sanbach'i: Hey, Chin Tonga!

Hong Tongji: (from inside the house) I'm eating.

Sanbach'i: You can eat later; something's up. Hurry!

Hong Tongji: (coming out of the house backward, bare buttocks first) What's up?

Sanbach'i: This guy comes out backward.

Hong Tongji: (turning to face forward) It's really late. What's up?

Sanbach'i: The governor said you did a good job clearing the road. He wants to give you a prize. Hurry, go see him.

Hong Tongji: Okay, I'll go, I'll go. *(Approaching the governor)* I present myself before you.

Governor: Are you the one who helped clear the road?

Hong Tongji: Yes sir.

Governor: Attendant.

Attendant: Yes sir.

Governor: Seize this fellow and flog him and tell him that he's being punished for doing a terrible job of clearing the road.

Hong Tongji: I'm sorry, I'm sorry! I apologize for doing a bad job! It won't happen again.

Governor: I forgive you this time. Now get out of here.

(Hong Tongji farts as he exists. The governor walks toward the front of the stage, but then moves back to the center.)

—adapted by Shim Usŏng

A performance of puppet theater is in two acts. In the four scenes of the first act, various family conflicts are presented. In the second act, which takes place in three scenes, the governor of P'yŏngan Province is satirized through jokes and humor. Pak Ch'ŏmji's nephew, Hong Tongji, plays a very important role throughout both acts. Hong Tongji humiliates the governor of P'yŏngan Province by stoically carrying a lady's coffin in the nude with his large red penis hanging down. The governor is offended by this sight and thus reveals his own insecurities about sex. Hong Tongji combines the function of the mask dance's servant (*malttugi*) and prodigal (*ch'wibari*), reflecting the sense of humor of the common people. The third scene of the first act, the puppet act, is similar to the grandmother act in the mask dance; in this scene, a group of professional entertainers represented by colorful puppets masterfully capture a pheasant and build a temple, both of which add interest to the action.

The origin of puppet theater remains unclear, but the *kkoktuk* part of kkoktukkakshi has been found in Mongolia, China, and Japan, suggesting that this form of drama entered Korea from central Asia before being transmitted to Japan. Because puppet theater contains a large number of Buddhist references and symbols and because the namsadang performers had close connections with temple life, it is thought possible that groups of Buddhist monks who had been expelled from their temples at the beginning of the Chosŏn period began entertaining the common people to survive in that Confucian-dominated era. In Korea, puppet theater did not develop into a form of high culture as it did in China and Japan; instead, it remained closely connected to the common people for whom it provided comic relief.

Ch'anggŭk

P'ansori, a strongly narrative form, gradually developed a number of features characteristic of drama, which contributed to the emergence of a new genre of performing art, *ch'anggŭk,* at the turn of the century. Ch'anggŭk is p'ansori adapted to a Western-style stage through the use of music and a team of actors.

Ch'anggŭk emerged from two groups of well-known performers of traditional folk songs at the turn of the century, Hyŏmnyulsa, active from 1902 to 1906, and Wŏngaksa, active from 1908 to 1909. These groups performed a variety of p'ansori and folk songs from Seoul and Kyŏnggi Province on the newly introduced Western-style stage; *Tale of Ch'unhyang* (Ch'unhyang chŏn) was first performed in 1903 and *Tale of Shim Ch'ŏng* (Shim Ch'ŏng chŏn) in 1904. Few records remain of these early ch'anggŭk performances, but it is clear that each actor played a different character, a practice which contrasts sharply with the solo narration of p'ansori. Because this change destroyed much of the traditional form of p'ansori dramatically, it is difficult to interpret it as a further development of that form. Ch'anggŭk is thus a new dramatic form that adopted the plots of p'ansori stories.

The use of existing p'ansori stories in ch'anggŭk pleased audiences at the time. The first newly composed ch'anggŭk was *The Ballad of Ch'oe Pyŏngdo* (Ch'oe Pyŏngdo t'aryŏng, 1908), which was based on the story of Ch'oe Pyŏngdo, an actual royal inspector of Kangwŏn Province, who died while in prison for robbery on a charge trumped up by the Japanese police. The work was well received by Korean audiences in this turbulent period and was the inspiration for the first half of the novel *Silver World* (Ŭnsegye, 1908) by Yi Injik. The treatment of issues of the day and the combination of p'ansori stories with Western-style staging contributed to the popularity of ch'anggŭk in the early twentieth century.

After the success of *The Ballad of Ch'oe Pyŏngdo,* the theater company Wŏngaksa tried to put on a similarly successful ch'anggŭk production, but nothing remains of their efforts. Wŏngaksa probably did not have time to put on such a performance because the company broke up in 1909, only a year after it had been formed. Ch'anggŭk gave way to the *shinp'agŭk* genre of drama soon after that.

After the demise of the popular ch'anggŭk, well-known singers in various regions of Korea joined together to form the Korean Vocal Music Research Group (Chosŏn songak yŏnguhoe), which was dedicated to composing new ch'anggŭk and adapting various p'ansori to the ch'anggŭk form. This group was successful in forming the basis for a national theater in Korea, but it was not successful in reviving the popularity of the ch'anggŭk. These singers also adapted classic novels, such as the *Tale of Yu Ch'ungnyŏl* (Yu Ch'ungnyŏl chŏn) and *Tale of Roses and Red Lotus Blossoms* (Changhwa hongyŏn chŏn), historical tales, such as *The Life of Hwang Chini* (Hwang Chini) and *The Life of Prince Maŭi* (Maŭi t'aeja), and new dramas such as *Reunion With the Spring* (Chebong ch'un, 1912) and *The Rich and the Poor* (Pinbu) to the ch'anggŭk form, but these were sentimental commercial productions with largely nostalgic appeal. After liberation from Japan in 1945, a women's theater company was formed by the women in the group, and they continued to perform sentimental dramas until the 1960s, when film began to become popular. Little research, however, has been done on the development of the ch'anggŭk after the breakup of Wŏngaksa in 1909, and this remains an important issue in the history of the form.

Shinp'agŭk

Shinp'agŭk refers to a form of commercial theater that began around 1915 and became popular in the 1920s and 1930s. The word shinp'a (Japanese: shimpa) was originally used in Japan to denote Western-style theater as opposed to kup'a (Japanese: kuha) or kabuki. The shin'pa emerged in the 1880s in Japan. Early shinp'agŭk dealt with themes related to the Meiji project of modernization, but as the form evolved, it took on the characteristics of melodrama in dealing with themes of family conflict and relations between men and women. Shinp'agŭk entered Korea in the second decade of the twentieth century under the strong influence of Japanese popular culture. By this time, Korea had lost its national sovereignty and with it, interest in modernization and Westernization. Under these conditions, shinp'agŭk was successful as a sentimental and melodramatic form of theater.

Shinp'agŭk was first performed by Hyŏkshindan, a theatrical company formed by Im Sŏnggu (1887–1921). The Hyŏkshindan started performing shinp'agŭk, such as Heaven Punishes the Unfilial (Pulhyo ch'ŏnbŏl, 1911) and Armed Robber (Yukhyŏlp'o Kangdo, 1912), which imitated existing Japanese shinp'agŭk, and moved on to plays with popular appeal, such as A Wanderer in the Rain (Ujung haengin, 1913), Dream of Lasting Resentment (Changhan mong, 1913), and Bitterness of a Faithful Wife (Chŏngbuwŏn, 1916), which were based on Korean New Novels and on popular Western novels. As shinp'agŭk grew in popularity, new theater companies such as Munsusŏng and Tanildan developed special forms of composition, dramatization, and production.

Although these works and theater companies differed from one another, they had much in common because they needed to attract and please a paying audience. The most popular themes—family conflicts and relationships between men and women—were presented melodramatically, to move the audience emotionally, usually to tears. This pedestrian sentimentality not only kept shinp'agŭk from developing into a meaningful dramatic form, it also distracted audiences from the problems of Korean society under Japanese colonialism. Several more sophisticated versions of shinp'agŭk emerged in the 1920s and 1930s, but although these works included more references to social problems of the time and were performed in a more realistic manner, they could not overcome the limitations imposed by the inherent commercialism of the form.

Modern Drama

A new form of theater began to emerge at the time shinp'agŭk was dominating the stage, represented by such works as *Sad Days* (Kyuhan, 1917) by Yi Kwangsu, *Fate* (Unmyŏng, ca. 1915; first performed in 1921) by Yun Paengnam, and *Twilight* (Hwang Hon, 1919) by Ch'oe Sŭngman. Although these writers failed to overcome their blind worship of modernization and the melodramatic characteristics of shinp'agŭk, they are important in the history of modern Korean drama because they attempted to go beyond simple commercialism by bringing the ethical and social conflicts of the time to the stage.

Modern drama (*hyŏndaegŭk*) began to develop in earnest in Korea in the 1920s with the creation of the Drama Research Society (Kŭgyaesul Yŏnguhoe) by Korean students in Tokyo and the Kyŏngsŏng High School theater company, Kaldophoe. The Drama Research Society went on tour in Korea, performing works such as Cho Myŏnghŭi's *The Death of Kim Yŏngil* (Kim Yŏngil ŭi sa, 1921) and a dramatization of Hong Nanp'a's *The Last Handshake* (Ch'oehu ŭi aksu). Kaldophoe went on tour in 1921, performing works such as Yun Paengnam's *Fate* and the anonymous *Overworking the Poor* (Pingonja ŭi muri) and *A Dying Wish* (Yuŏn). The group extended their tour to all corners of Korea in 1922, with a different reperatory. In 1922, some members of the Drama Research Society founded a new company, Sawŏlhoe, in Tokyo. Sawŏlhoe visited Korea during the summer of 1922, performing works by George Bernard Shaw and Pak Sŭnghŭi's *Kilshik,* 1923). [Kilshik is a man's given name. —Trans.] The emergence of other theater companies in the schools contributed to the development of modern drama in Korea through translations of well-known Western works and composition of new works by Korean writers.

Despite this activity, the works performed remained underdeveloped, particularly the comedies, because audiences were not prepared to accept a style of theater that had been imported directly from the West without adequate adaptation to Korean sensibilities. In addition, colonial oppression and the lack of adequate cultural facilities restricted the development of modern drama. The greatest problem, however, was the excessive attachment to imitations of Western drama on the part of the leaders of the modern drama movement. As companies such as Sawŏlhoe placed increasing importance on direct translations of Western works, interest in creating truly Korean modern drama that dealt with the realities of Korean life under colonialism waned. These problems continued to affect Korean drama into the 1930s, and after liberation, into the 1950s.

Realism dominated Korean modern drama from the early 1920s on, as is clear from the work of Kim Ujin (1897–1926), the dominant playwright of the 1920s, and Yu Ch'ijin (1905–1974), the dominant playwright of the 1930s. Although Kim Ujin experimented with expressionism and realism in his work, he was more interested in showing how people attempted to escape from the pressures of everyday life under Japanese colonial rule in the early 1920s. In works such as *Mud Wall* (T'omak, 1932), *Scenes of a Town Surrounded by Willow Trees* (Pŏdunamu sŏn tongni p'unggyŏng), and *The Water Buffalo* (So, 1934), Yun Ch'ijin dealt with various conflicts among weak and impoverished characters living under Japanese colonial rule. Ch'ae Manshik and Kim Chinsu also used realism in their comedies.

The rise of realism in modern Korean drama resulted from a desire to investigate the problems of Korean society under Japanese colonialism. In the various branches of the arts in modern Korea, however, realism remains a matter of the appropriate form of artistic expression, because it entails the question that has remained at the center of the arts in Korea since the 1920s and 1930s: how are Korean authors to deal with the experience of everyday life, given the various forms of artistic expression available to them?

4. Didactic Genres

Akchang

Throughout Korean history, kings have used music in ceremonies designed to assert their legitimacy as rulers. *Akchang* are the lyrics and chants that accompany court music. Akchang from the ancient Korean kingdoms have been lost, but some scholars speculate that "Song of Tuṣita Heaven" (Tosol ka, A.D. 28) was the first akchang because the lyrics express the ruler's desire to promote the welfare of his subjects. In the Koryŏ period, *hyangak,* indigenous Korean court music, was used along with Chinese court music, or *Tangak*. Original akchang were composed for the court, and some folk songs were adapted to the akchang form for use at court, but few of these works survive in their original form because they were altered significantly or lost when court music was catalogued at the beginning of the Chosŏn period. What is referred to as akchang nowadays is court music written in the fifteenth century to glorify the newly founded Chosŏn Dynasty.

Composed to extol Confucian ideology in court ceremonies, the akchang of the Chosŏn period had a grave tone. Human feelings were ignored in favor of ethical solemnness and praise for the virtuous rule of the Chosŏn kings. For these reasons, akchang are considered a didactic genre of literature.

Despite these characteristics, some scholars question whether akchang should be classified as a unified genre of literature at all because they are so diverse in length, form, and language. Akchang range from works written in classical Chinese to works written in hangŭl on Chinese models, such as "Upon Receiving This Auspicious Diagram" (Suborok, 1393) "Song of Nayacu" (Nap ssi ka, 1393), "Song of Bringing Peace to the East" (Chŏng tongbang kok, 1393), and "Song of Cultivating Virtue Through Literature" (Mundŏk kok, 1395); and works such as "Song of the New Capital" (Shindo ka, 1394) and *Songs of Flying Dragons* (Yongbi ŏch'ŏn ka, 1445–1447) written on indigenous Korean models. Some akchang, such as "Song of the Censor" (Sangdae pyŏlgok, 1419) and "Song of Hwasan" (Hwasan pyŏlgok, 1425), were based on the form of the *kyŏnggich'ega*, whereas others, such as "Song of the New Capital" had a *Koryŏ kayo* chorus between seven uniform verses. *Songs of Flying Dragons* and its Buddhist derivative, *Songs of the Moon Reflecting a Thousand Rivers* (Wŏrin ch'ŏngang chi kok, 1447) are continuous songs without a chorus or repeating verse.

Normally such varied works would not be classified as one literary genre, but because these works have a common social function that transcends their diversity, they are grouped together to create the unique genre of akchang.

Akchang portrayed the founders of the Chosŏn Dynasty as heroes who restored virtuous rule to Korea and were thus entitled to the "mandate of heaven." Praise for the military prowess of the founder of the Chosŏn Dynasty, Yi Sŏnggye, appears in works such as "Song of Nayacu" and "Song of Bringing Peace to the East," while "Song of Cultivating Virtue Through Literature" and *Songs of Flying Dragons* praised in a rich poetic language Yi Sŏnggye's virtuous behavior and the moral authority on which he based his rule. *Songs of Flying Dragons* praised not only the rule of Yi Sŏnggye, but also many of the early leaders of the Chosŏn Dynasty. These akchang were statements of political idealism by Confucian scholars such as Chŏng Tojŏn (b. 1398), Kwŏn Kŭn (1352–1409), and Chŏng Inji (1396–1478), who were instrumental in making Confucianism the ruling ideology of the Chosŏn Dynasty.

The composition of the akchang declined as the Chosŏn Dynasty established its rule in the fifteenth century because the number of official ceremonies was limited, making new compositions unnecessary since Confucianism had spread throughout Korean society, and was no longer challenged openly by competing ideologies.

Because *Songs of the Moon Reflecting a Thousand Rivers* is a long narrative poem on the life of Buddha, it cannot be considered court music; it is considered an akchang, however, because it is a long chant and because the language and form of composition are similar to those of *Songs of Flying Dragons*.

Ch'angga

Ch'angga, a genre of songs in tetrameter, originated in the mid-1890s as songs for school children. The National Anthem (Aeguk ka, 1896) by Yun Ch'imin, first sung at the cornerstone-laying ceremony for the Independence Gate in 1896, is an example of ch'angga. The lyrics, some of which had first appeared in *The Independent* (Tongnip shinmun) as an ode to independence, were typical of Korean patriotic songs of the period.

From the mid 1890s to the early years of the twentieth century, the number of Western-style schools expanded rapidly in Korea, and most schools adopted Western-style music in the curriculum, a fact which contributed to the dramatic growth of ch'angga. Leaders of Westernization in the arts, Ch'oe Namsŏn for example, promoted ch'angga by printing a great many of them in early literary magazines such as *Youth* (Sonyŏn) and *Bloom of Youth* (Ch'ŏngch'un). In addition to short ch'angga, Ch'oe promoted long ch'angga such as "Song of the Kyongbu Railroad" (Kyŏngbu ch'ŏldo norae) and "Song of a Trip Around the World" (Segye ilju ka), which praised the material benefits of modernization.

Although some ch'angga are characteristic of the lyric genres, they were composed to extol the virtues of modernization in the school system and thus belonged more to didactic genres of literature, until around 1910. This optimistic view of modernization gave way to a more critical outlook as the oppression of Japanese imperialism weighed more heavily on Korean society in the 1920s. The following ch'angga, entitled "Song of Hanyang" (Hanyang ka ["Hanyang" refers to Seoul. —Trans.]), was written by Ch'oe Namsŏn:

> Just as we once stood proud,
> Independence Gate, once grand and bright,
> has losts its glow for now, but
> will soon glitter like the sun once more.
>
> The Changch'ung Altar near the foot of Namsan,
> holds the souls of those who died for the nation,
> those heroes whom we hold dear, like a feather aloft
> for their everlasting loyalty to the nation.

Prose Literature

Essays, random thoughts, biographies, diaries, and travelogues all differ greatly from each other, but they are all records, either objective or subjective, of actual events and persons. All types of prose writing in classical Chinese and hangŭl will be dealt with in this section.

Writing in Korea began with official documents that recorded the historical evolution of a people from their emergence in ancient times to the establishment of the three kingdoms of Koguryŏ, Shilla, and Paekche. The historical records of the Koguryŏ kingdom, the Yugi (ca. 600 A.D.), and the records of the Paekche kingdom, the Shinjip (ca. 600 A.D.), have been lost. The works on which *The History of the Three Kingdoms* (Samguk sagi, 1145) and *Memorabilia of the Three Kingdoms* (Samguk yusa, ca. 1285) were based, *The Old History of the Three Kingdoms* (Ku samguk sa), *Chronicles of the Hwarang* (Hwarang segi, ca. 730), and *Tales of Eminent Monks* (Kosŭng chŏn, ca. 730), have been lost, but most scholars believe that the lost works comprised prose biographies and stories of individuals mixed with official history. In particular, *Tales of Eminent Monks* influenced Hyech'o (704–787), one of the greatest monks of the Shilla kingdom, in his prose journal, *Record of a Journey to Five Indian Kingdoms* (Wang o ch'ŏnch'ukkuk chŏn, 727). This was the first collection of essays in Korean literature; the form remains vibrant today. All of these early works were written in classical Chinese, the *hyangch'al* system being used for the *hyangga* and for textual notes.

Prose literature in classical Chinese spread throughout the Koryŏ period, and a wide variety of works were produced according to Chinese conventions of rhetoric. In keeping with Chinese tradition, poetry was preferred to prose, but public officials at various levels of government were required to use prose in carrying out the business of state and in presenting their own views to others in the government. Much detailed literary prose can be found in Koryŏ period historical sources, such as *The Eastern Literary Anthology* (Tongmun sŏn, 1478) and other collections. [The words "East," "Eastern," or "Easterners" refer to Korea. —Trans.]

Another important trend of the period was the composition of collections of random thoughts on life, such as *Jottings to Relieve Idleness* (P'ahan chip, 1214) by Yi Illo (1152–1220), *Jottings in Idleness* (Pohan chip, 1254) by Ch'oe Cha (1188–1260), and *Tales of Yŏgong* (Yŏgong p'aesŏl, 1342) by Yi Chehyŏn (1287–1367). Consisting of various short notes and stories about events and people in the author's life, such collections combined the factual writing style of public records with the more poetic language of essays. *Essays on Poetry by Easterners* (Tongin shihwa, 1474) by Sŏ Kŏjŏng (1420–1489) is an example of the more factual style of writing that was dominant in the early Chosŏn period, and *Peaceful and Humorous Stories for Leisure* (T'aep'yŏng hanhwa kolgye chŏn, 1477) of the poetic style of essay writing that was popular from the middle of the Chosŏn period on.

Unlike the aristocratic writers of the Koryŏ period, the yangban of the Chosŏn period emphasized real-life experience and Confucian ideology over metaphysical themes. Together with the social and cultural changes in Korean society that began to occur in the middle of the Chosŏn period, this resulted in a shift from a terse poetic style of writing to a more lucid and realistic one better suited to detailed descriptions of everyday life. Related to this change was the proliferation of diaries, travelogues, random notes, and essays of the period. Lengthy works such as the 72–volume *Popular History of the Great East* (Taedong yasŭng, early seventeenth century) and the 266–volume *Forest of Stories* (P'aerim, late nineteenth century) are typical of mid-Chosŏn period prose collections. Works by eminent scholars of the period such as Chŏng Yagyong and Pak Chiwŏn, who called for change in response to worsening social problems, also belong in this category.

With the development of hangŭl, an indigenous writing system, in the seventeenth century, prose writing grew tremendously. Hangŭl had been popular with woman and children of the yangban class during the sixteenth century, but most of their writings remained private. Travelogues and random notes such as *Record of an Official Visit to China* (Tyot'yŏn nok, 1620), "Song of an Uprising" (Nalli ka, ca. 1730), Yu Ŭiyang's *Record of the Sights Across the South Sea* (Namăe mungyŏn nok, 1771), Yi Hŭip'yŏn's *Diary from Hwasŏng* (Hwasŏng ilgi, 1795), and diaries and records such as *Diary of the Year Kyech'uk* (Kyech'uk ilgi, 1613), *Record From the Bottom of Sadness* (Hanjung nok, 1805), and *Record of Sad Days* (Kyuhan nok, mid-nineteenth century) are examples of the diversity of prose written exclusively in hangŭl. Many essays and autobiographies written by women belong to this category. Because women of the yangban class wrote in hangŭl from an early age, unlike the men, who wrote primarily in classical Chinese, yangban women describe their experiences in particularly sensitive and detailed written language.

5. Mixed Genres

The Kyŏnggich'ega

The *kyŏnggich'ega* is a form of song composed prolifically from the beginning of the thirteenth century to the early Chosŏn period and sporadically from then until the nineteenth century. Some scholars refer to kyŏnggiche'ga as "*pyŏlgokch'e.*" Although kyŏnggiche'ga were composed for over six hundred years—the first, "Song of the Confucian Scholars" (Hallim pyŏlgok, ca. 1215–1216), was written by various Confucian scholars in the mid-Koryŏ period, and the last, "Song of Filial Piety" (Ch'unghyo ka), was written by Min Kyu in 1860—only about twenty are extant.

The strict formulaic limitations on the composition of kyŏnggich'ega inhibited its wide acceptance. Until the early part of the Chosŏn period, the kyŏnggich'ega adhered to strict formulaic rules by which the narrative link in the structure was dependent on nouns or phrases in classical Chinese. At the middle and end of each stanza was an emphatic sentence that expressed the feelings of the composer. The following example is taken from three stanzas of "Song of the Confucian Scholars," a kyŏnggich'ega of eight lines:

Kyŏnggich'ega, "Song of the Confucian Scholars" (Hallim pyŏlgok)

The prose of Yun Wŏnsun, the poetry of Yi Illo, the four-six rhythmic prose of Yi Kongno, the lucid poetry of Yi Kyubo and Chin Hwa, the commentaries of Yu Ch'unggi, the interpretations of Min Kwangjo, and the lyricism of Kim Yanggyŏng—

Oh, seeing them gathered together for an examination is a truly magnificent scene.

> The outstanding disciples of Scholar Kŭm Ŭi,
> the outstanding disciples of Scholar Kŭm Ŭi.
> Oh, including me, how many could there be?

The History of the Han and *The History of the Tang,* the works of Zhuang Zi and Lao Zi, the works of Han Yu and Liu Zongyuan, the poetry of Li Bai and Du Fu, *Collection of the Orchid Terrace,* the poetry of Bai Juyi, *The Book of Songs, The Book of Documents, The Book of Changes, The Spring and Autumn Annals, The Book of Rites*—

Oh, memorizing these books, including children's notes, is truly a magnificent scene.

> The *Broad Record of the Taiping Era* in four hundred scrolls,

the *Broad Record of the Taiping Era* in four hundred scrolls.
Oh, reading these books is truly a magnificent scene.
The handwriting of Yan Chenqing, the black-and-white script, half-running and running script, small and large seal script, tadpole script, the handwriting of Yu Shinan, the goat-hair brushes and the rat-hair brushes—
Oh, dipping these brushes into ink is a magnificent scene.
Master O and Master Yu,
Master O and Master Yu
Oh, watching them write is truly a magnificent scene.

The emotive first section of each stanza is distinguished from the second section by a different meter: the first section is in trimeter and the second in tetrameter. This distinction broke down in the sixteenth century as the rules governing the use of nouns and classical Chinese phrases broke down.

Before the changes of the sixteenth century, the poetic structure of the kyŏnggich'ega differed from other forms of Korean poetry in that it used material things as metaphors for reality and a fixed form of emotive phrases in the first section of each stanza. Instead of emphasizing ephemeral emotions and feelings that emerge from a particular time, the kyŏnggich'ega dealt with real events and things through metaphors. Because they make normative comments on the world, kyŏnggich'ega have, according to some scholars, more in common with didactic genres of poetry than with lyric genres such as shijo.

Although the above analysis has merit, kyŏnggich'ega also include an emotional and lyric element in the last line of the first section of each stanza, which helps to depict the real-world events discussed in the first section. The emphasis on actual events in kyŏnggich'ega represented an attempt to achieve a better balance between the real world and the closed world of the author's inner thoughts, rather than an attempt to present factual information about those events. This reflects the need of literate aristocrats in the Koryŏ and Chosŏn periods to add emotional richness to their lives. Despite their factual tone, the kyŏnggich'ega contain a strongly emotional and lyric element. Because kyŏnggich'ega combines elements of poetic and narrative genres, it is classified as an intermediate genre. The balance between poetic and narrative elements in kyŏnggich'ega varies with the author and the work; in this regard the form has a great degree of flexibility.

Kyŏnggich'ega were composed by an emerging group of Confucian literati at the end of the Koryŏ period. The authors of "Song of the Confucian Scholars" were members of this group, as was An Ch'uk (1287–1348), the author of "Song of a Path in a Bamboo Forest" (Chukkye pyŏlgok, ca. 1330) and "Song of Kangwŏn Province" (Kwandong pyŏlgok, ca. 1330). Although the authors of "Song of the Confucian Scholars" were trained to write in classical Chinese and composed according to its patterns, kyŏnggich'ega emerged from their desire to express themselves freely in Korean.

The desire on the part of yangban literati to express themselves in Korean contributed to the development of akchang-style kyŏnggich'ega such as "Song of the Censor" (Sangdae pyŏlgok), "Song of a Banquet for My Brothers" (Yŏn hyŏnje kok), and "Song of the Five Morals" (Oryun ka) in the early years of the Chosŏn period. Works devoted to neo-Confucian themes in the sixteenth century, such as Chu Sebong's (1495–1554) "Song of Todong" (Todong kok, 1541), "Song of Majesty" (Ŏmyŏn kok, 1541), and "Song of Six Sages" (Yukhyŏn ka, 1541) and Kwŏn Homun's (1532–1587) "Songs of Lonely Pleasure" (Tongnak p'algok, ca. 1580), express the thoughts of yangban literati in vivid Korean vernacular. Buddhist monks also composed kyŏnggich'ega at the beginning of the Chosŏn period. The monk Kihwa's (1376–1433) "Song in Praise of Amitābha" (Mit'a ch'an), "Song in Praise of Anyang" (Anyang ch'an), and "Song in Praise of Amitābha's Teachings" (Mit'a kyŏng ch'an), are examples of this type of work, as is "Song of the Western Paradise" (Sŏbang ka) by the monk Ŭisang. Because these works dealt with Buddhist themes, they are denser and more esoteric than the kyŏnggich'ega written by yangban literati.

Kyŏnggich'ega fell out of favor in the middle of the Chosŏn period but continued to be composed sporadically until the nineteenth century. Its decline resulted from the rigidity of the form, which prevented it from absorbing influences from other genres. Kyŏnggich'ega was restrictive not only structurally, but also regarding the types of subjects that could be dealt with, which further limited its appeal. This restrictiveness reflects the austere aesthetics of the early Confucian literati in Korea, a group that sought ideological purity as a means of legitimatizing its role in Korean society. In his "Twelve Songs of Tosan" (Tosan shibi kok, 1565), Yi Hwang (1501–1570), one of the great Confucian scholars of the Chosŏn period, noted that he had turned away from kyŏnggich'ega because it was too restrictive.

Kasa

Although *kasa* is a form of verse of an indefinite number of lines, its content differs dramatically from other genres of Korean poetry. Kasa range from works in language with a strongly lyric quality to those that deal with real events in a style more akin to prose, and from works that attempt to impart Confucian ethics to those that describe fictional events for entertainment.

Kasa is united as a genre, however, by a form that is composed of a varying number of tetrameter. Some folk songs have the same tetrameter form, and some of the *chapka, shibi kasa,* and *hŏduga* that make extensive use of tetrameter are difficult to distinguish from kasa. Some scholars place the last three genres and kasa within a larger genre. In this framework, chapka, shibi kasa, and hŏduga are referred to as *kach'ang kasa,* and kasa as *ŭmyŏng kasa,* or "sung kasa."

Except for the use of tetrameter and the lack of stanzaic divisions, kasa were not restricted as to subject, organization, or type of language. The great diversity of kasa continues to cause debate among scholars of Korean literature. Cho Yunje has argued that kasa are a mixture of poetry and prose and Yi Nŭng'u that kasa are essays in verse; Chang Tŏksun has divided kasa into works that have an affinity with poetry and those that have an affinity with prose, and Cho Dong-il [Cho Tongil] has argued that kasa are a form of didactic literature written in verse. Although most extant kasa have come under close scrutiny, scholars have yet to agree on how to define the genre. Our discussion here will focus on the diversity of kasa and on illustrating its varied characteristics, rather than on the debate about how to define kasa as a genre of Korean literature. Rather than trying to classify into a particular genre lyric verse such as Chŏng Kugin's (1441–1481) "Song to Welcome Spring" (Sang ch'un kok, 1481) and Chŏng Ch'ŏl's (1536–1593) "Song to My Love" (Sa miin kok, 1585) and "Second Song to My Love" (Sok miin kok, 1585), travelogue verse such as *Song of a Journey to Yanjing* (Yŏn haeng ka, 1866 ["Yanjing" refers to Beijing. —Trans.] and the long *Song of a Journey to the East* (Ildong changyu ka, ca. 1763 [in this case "East" refers to Japan], narrative verse such as "Song of a Spinster" (Noch'ŏnyŏ ka) and "Song of a Market Bard" (Kŏsa ka), and didactic verse such as "Song of the Way to Virtue" (Kŭnsŏn chiro ka), "Song in Praise of God" (Ch'ŏnju konggyŏng ka), and "Song to Cultivate Virture" (Tosu sa), we will focus on the diversity and contradictions within a single work.

In addition to its great diversity, kasa was not restricted in length. This contributed to its rise in popularity because authors could deal extensively with ideas and feelings that could not be dealt with in the three-line shijo or the slightly longer narrative sasŏl shijo. Although kasa lacked the succinct emotive power of shijo, the form was better suited to deal with lengthy expressions of feeling and the explanation of ideas.

Some scholars argue that kasa emerged as a literary genre toward the end of the Koryŏ period; others that it did so at the beginning of the period. The former cite "Song of a Journey West" (Sŏwang ka, 1741) by Naong Hwasang (1320–1376), a monk of the late Koryŏ period. The latter group, however, argue that the gap of almost four hundred years between Naong's time and the publication of "Song of a Journey West" (Sŏwang ka, 1741) makes it impossible to prove that he was the author. The existence of an early kasa by Chŏng Kugin, "Song to Welcome Spring," supports the argument that kasa emerged in the late Koryŏ period. Although this may be the case, it is considered a Chosŏn-period poetic genre because it became popular at that time.

The history of kasa is similar to that of shijo in that it can be divided into three periods: the early Chosŏn period (from the fifteenth to the mid-seventeenth century), the late Chosŏn period (from the mid-seventeenth to the mid-nineteenth century), and the period of reform at the end of the nineteenth century. Kasa of the early Chosŏn period were composed mainly by yangban such as Song Sun (1493–1584), Chŏng Ch'ŏl (1536–1593), Pak Illo (1561–1642), and Cho Yuin (1561–1625). These authors were all proficient in classical Chinese and wrote poetry and shijo in that language, but turned to kasa because the lack of restriction on length allowed them to express themselves more freely. In particular, retired yangban composed kasa devoted to subjects found in nature, attempting to get close to nature in order to escape from the worldly power struggles in Seoul. This type of kasa tends to go beyond the personal experience of the author, seeking to put the individual in harmony with an idyllic natural world through compelling poetry. Kasa from the early Chosŏn period are thus more poetic than those of later eras. The following example is from "Songs of Sŏngsan" (Sŏngsan pyŏlgok, 1587) by Chŏng Ch'ŏl:

> People's minds are like their faces, changing with each passing
>   glance.
> The world is like the clouds, moving farther and farther away.
> Wondering if the rice wine I made a few days ago has fermented,
> I pour some into my cup and take a sip;
> The clinched worries in my heart lessen.
> I tune my zither and play the song "P'ungipsong"
> As I play, I forget who is the host and who is the guest.

More women and common people began composing kasa in the middle of the Chosŏn period, causing the form to diversify in several directions. The inclusion of themes rooted in the daily lives of women and the common people was the most important such change. Kasa composed by yangban also underwent a significant change in this period, as poetic descriptions of an idyllic and benevolent nature declined in favor of stronger, harsher descriptions of everyday experience. Long kasa describing journeys, such as *Song of a Journey to the East* by Kim Ingyŏm (b. 1707) and *Song of a Journey to Yanjing* by Hong Sunhak (b. 1842); kasa written during exile, such as *Song of Repentence* (Manŏn sa, late eighteenth century by An Chohwan (late eighteenth century), and Kim Chinhyŏng's (1801–1865) *Song of an Exile in the North* (Pukch'ŏn ka, 1853); and kasa that describe everyday life in a particular place, such as the anonymous *Song of Hanyang* (Hanyang ka, 1844 ["Hanyang" refers to Seoul. —Trans.]), exemplify the diversity of late–Chosŏn period kasa. The change in theme and language reflects the gradual collapse of the idealistic view of the world that grew out of the political and ideological stability of the first half of the Chosŏn period.

Kasa that were composed mainly by women and yangban children are referred to as *kyubang kasa,* or "women's kasa." This type of kasa was most popular in southeastern Korea, but it was found throughout Korea. Kyubang kasa was diverse and included works on subjects such as moral advice on everyday issues relating to women and interesting experiences in the lives of individuals, as well as expressive lyric verse. Most kyubang kasa were read within a family, and brides often took several collections with them when they got married.

Kasa composed by the common people are somewhat more diverse and can be divided into three types. The first is kasa that describe the suffering of the common people during the Chosŏn period; "Song of the Peasant Army" (Kammin ka, late eighteenth century), "Song of the Peasant Uprising in Chŏngŭp County" (Chŏngŭp-kun millanshi yohang ch'ongyo, ca. 1836), and "Song of Kŏch'ang" (Kŏch'ang ka) are examples. These kasa were composed by various kinds of the common people, often collectively, and they contributed to group solidarity because the themes grew out of the frustrations of everyday life. "Song of Bitterness Toward the King" (Hapkangjŏng ka, ca. 1792) follows these themes, but from its style, it is difficult to determine whether it was written by a disgruntled yangban who chose to remain anonymous or by a commoner or commoners who later passed it on to a yangban for editing.

The second type of commoner-kasa consisted of works such as the anonymous "Song of Three Foolish Men" (Ubu ka) and "Song of a Foolish Wife" (Yongbu ka), which described the insecurity and change in Chosŏn society in great detail through the lives of indecent and greedy characters. Parts of works of this type show great similarity to sections of the p'ansori. The following example from "Song of Three Foolish Men" shows how a selfish and greedy character is portrayed in this type of kasa. In addition to preaching against selfishness and greed, this type of kasa indirectly criticizes injustice in Chosŏn society.

> The man standing over there, Kkom Saengwŏn, got a lot of money
>   from his father.
> He never took his friends out for a drink or a meal.
> He went to a fortuneteller, pretending to be somebody important.
> He spent his whole life seeking money, a good grave site, and a safe
>   place to live.
> He abandoned his wife and children as he wandered.
> He spent money like water, but none of his relatives are rich.
> He accomplished a few useless things and wandered around Seoul
>   and the countryside.
> He worked as the prime minister's chief attendant, but blundered
>   and resigned.
>
> —anonymous

The third type of kasa by commoners dealt with various aspects of relations between men and women. "Song of a Spinster," "Tale of a Young Widow" (Ch'ŏngch'un kwabu chŏn), and "Song of a Market Bard" (Kŏsa ka) are examples of this type of kasa. Because these works were printed and sold commercially, several versions of many of them exist; for example, "Song of a Spinster" is found in the novel *Samsŏlgi*. These kasa are interesting because they contain a great deal of fictitious narrative that adds interest to the story. The narrative in these works cannot match the classic novel for plot and realism, but kasa by commoners expanded the literary range of the form beyond simple literary description to include narrative resolution of a conflict. If kasa by yangban are considered restrained and reflective, those composed by commoners are active and passionate. "Song of a Spinster" was later published as a novel entitled *Tale of a Puppet* (Kkoktukkakshi chŏn).

These three types of kasa, along with "Song of Contemplation" (Sangsa pyŏlgok), "Song of a Broken Heart" (Tanjang ka), and "Song for a Lucky Day" (Yangshin hwadap ka), are referred to as "love kasa." Love kasa include not only works written by commoners, but also some of written by the wives and children of yangban. Except for perfunctory references to love for the king, the kasa of yangban men made no reference to love or relations between men and women. The common people and the wives and children of yangban were freer to deal with such issues because they were under less pressure to uphold Confucian decorum.

Buddhist monks and lay people composed kasa dealing with Buddhist themes throughout the Chosŏn period; more and more of such works were written toward the end of the Chosŏn period as the power of the dynasty weakened. Kasa devoted to Roman Catholic themes appeared in the late eighteenth century as Catholicism spread among the yangban class. "Song in Praise of God" (Ch'ŏnju konggyŏng ka) by Yi Pyŏk and "Song to the Ten Commandments" (Ship kyemyŏng ka) by Chŏng Yakchŏng are examples of such Catholic kasa; "Song of the Dragon's Lotus Pond" (Yongdam kasa) by Ch'oe Cheu (1824– 1864) is a late Chosŏn Buddhist kasa. Kasa devoted to religious themes have played an important role in the growth of religion by presenting religious teachings in simple, clear language in order to inspire believers or convert nonbelievers.

As kasa spread to various groups in society and became more diverse toward the end of the Chosŏn period, the genre grew more open and flexible. The development of kasa in various directions—detailed narratives of experience, great relevance to social problems, fictional narratives, lyricism in love kasa, and strong belief and ideology in religious kasa—resulted from the diversification of authors during the Chosŏn period.

The diversity of the form declined, however, after the Treaty of Kanghwa of 1876 forced Korea to open itself to the outside world. The introduction of foreign culture and the struggle to maintain national sovereignty imbued the kasa of the late nineteenth and early twentieth centuries with nationalistic themes; this marked the third period in the history of kasa. Traditional kasa did not die out completely, as shown by "Song to Soothe Officer Shin" (Shin ŭigwan ch'angŭi ka) of the 1920s, but most kasa composed at this time, which appeared in publications such as *The Independent* (Tongnip shinmun) and *The Korea Daily News* (Taehan maeil shinbo, 1904–1910), expressed nationalistic themes.

Kasa of this period are referred to as *kaehwagi kasa* or *kaehwa kasa;* "opening-period kasa" and "opening kasa," respectively. They were short so that they could be recited without difficulty. They also included distinct verses divided by a repeated refrain. These characteristics placed these kasa between traditional kasa and the ch'angga. In terms of form, all of these kasa follow a meter based on feet, but the patriotic kasa that appeared in *The Independent* are structurally closer to ch'angga than are those that were printed in *The Korea Daily News*.

The patriotic kasa published in *The Independent* first appeared in a column by Ch'oe Tonsŏng. The newspaper continued to publish kasa submitted by readers in a column entitled "Aeguk Ka," or "patriotic songs." These kasa were relatively simple in content and form, most of which were composed in tetrameter and about ten lines long. Some had a refrain at the end. The following example, "Song to Independence" (Tongnip ka) by Ch'oe Pyŏnghŏn, appeared in *The Independent* on October 3, 1896:

> After creating all things in the world,
> Heaven gave all of the nations boundaries.
> In East Asia,
> an independent Chosŏn is natural.
> Independence comes from
> cooperation between the king and the people.
>
> Glorious day, oh, glorious day.
> The day Chosŏn is independent.
> Glorious day, oh glorious day.
> The day Chosŏn is independent.

Some of these kasa resemble Western-style religious songs of the 1890s because they follow Western musical rhythm. As shown in the above example, they focused optimistically on the need for national self-reliance during modernization. This optimistic attitude toward modernization was possible before the Japanese takeover of Korea in 1910, but at a more basic level, it reflected the ideas of the leaders of the Independence Club (Tongnip hyŏphoe), who argued that creation of a Western-style constitutional monarchy was the way to reform Korea.

The patriotic kasa in *The Korea Daily News,* which first appeared in 1907, presented a darker picture of society by dealing with the issue of corruption through irony and criticism and the need for survival in a hostile world. Thus, the energetic feeling of the patriotic kasa in *The Independent* gave way to sharp, satiric comment on issues of the day. The patriotic kasa in *The Korea Daily News* were longer and more lucid than those in *The Independent.* The following example is entitled "Opening a New Laundry" (Set'ak shinsŏl):

> Looking around Seoul, I don't know who's Korean and who's
>   foreign;
> there are many laundries, but nobody is really clean.
> Seeking the secrets of the trade, I open a laundry
> with a washtub of loyalty and a stick of civilization.
> One by one, I will wash all the filthy-hearted people for free.
>
> All of the local inspectors and military officers
> and corrupt mining officials who massacre innocent civilians.
> With foreigners lending a land, they take people's money, paddies,
>   and fields,
> killing their fellow Koreans, and denying them an education and
>   learning.
> One by one, I want to tie up all the filthy-hearted ringleaders.
>
> Visit a wealthy family and you will see a stingy man
> and his relatives living well while others die of starvation.
> The schools and public facilities have no money,
> yet they won't give a cent to charity, treating us like enemies.
> One by one, I want to tie up all the filthy-hearted ringleaders.
>
> I will plunge all the ringleaders in a washtub of loyalty, putting soap
> in the water to wash their eyes out. And after that I will boil it all
> to sterilize it. I want to wring them into a bucket of freedom,
> pound them dry with a stick of civilization, hang them out on a

clothesline behind a building of independence, and dry them in
the air of reform.
Let's save all the other filthy things for another day.

The above example is in tetrameter, but strictly adheres to a pattern of
four syllables to each foot. Unlike traditional forms of kasa, which
emphasized the continuous flow of verse, this form allowed a more
concentrated focus on a particular problem. Scholars believe that most
of the kasa in *The Korea Daily News* were composed by progressive
Confucian scholars who lamented the decline of Confucian values that
accompanied the deepening of Japanese influence in Korea. About 700
patriotic kasa were composed between the end of the nineteenth century and 1910, when the Japanese authorities prohibited their publication and that of other forms of literature that threatened to stir up
national feeling among the Korean people.

Kajŏn

Kajŏn, or "fictitious biography," is a special genre of works composed periodically by aristocrats, beginning in the middle of the
Koryŏ period. They are also referred to as *kajŏnch'e,* fictitious biographical writings, or *ŭinjŏngich'e,* personified biographical tales,
by some scholars. Works in this genre turn everyday objects into
historical fictitious characters, and present a biography of those
characters and their families. This form originated in the works of
Han Yu (768–824) in Tang Dynasty China and in works such as *The
Flowers' Warning to the King* (Hwawanggye) by the seventh-cen-
tury Shilla scholar Sŏl Ch'ong. The use of personification with biographies has much in common with the animal fables found in oral
literature. It is difficult to argue in favor of a common origin, however, because most such fables focus on an event that involves various animals, whereas kajŏn intensely investigate the life of one
person.

The form developed in the middle Koryŏ period because it appealed to the strict form of neo-Confucianism that had entered
Korea at the time. In contrast to previous elite groups, the late-Koryŏ
elite tried to understand worldly affairs so that they could interpret events
logically; as a genre, kajŏn appealed to the elite because it related an
event to an abstract concept. The emphasis on detailed analysis of an

event and of a character's experience according to Confucian ideology made kajŏn a didactic genre. The kajŏn reflect the characteristics of narrative genres by presenting a moral discussion through the detailed descriptions of the life of fictitious characters and their families. Kajŏn thus represents a unique combination of elements both of the didactic and the narrative genres. The following example is a summary of the plot of *Tale of Sir Malt* (Kuksun chŏn, ca. 1160) (by Im Ch'un (d. 1170). [The story is set in China. —Trans.]

> Pure Malt was also known by the title of respect Zihou, and his ancestors were from Longxi. His ancestor of ninety generations ago, Barley, was a great hero because he helped save thousands from starvation. Barley became a loyal vassal of the king and was granted lordship over the village of Zhongshanhou and its surrounding areas. He then took the surname Malt.
>
> Pure was mature and had an excellent personality. He was pure, but not overly clear, although he didn't become muddy when shaken. He often visited a monk called Ye, and they usually ended up drinking all night. Other people present at these drinking sessions were enchanted by Pure. As Pure became known far and wide, people started to call him Sir Malt. People from all over—court nobles, military officers, Daoist immortals, scholars, barbarians, and foreigners—longed to have a chance to enjoy Sir Malt's wonderful aroma. He was so beloved that people felt disappointed, even depressed, if he did not appear.
>
> One of the emperor's retainers, Shandao, was worried that Pure's popularity might cause social chaos and so banished him. Pure later became an official messenger in Pingyuan but was distraught over his bad luck. He went to a fortuneteller, who said,
>
> "Your face is flushed with color, so you will gain popularity again. Don't worry, and wait patiently for your time to come."
>
> Pure became very popular during the reign of Emperor Hou in Chen but was blamed for bringing disaster on the nation and was relieved of his position. He later died of depression.
>
> Pure had no children, but the descendants of his younger brother Clear prospered.

As is clear from the above example, *Tale of Sir Malt* is about the history of alcohol. The author describes the characteristics, the history, and the advantages and disadvantages of alcohol, as well as the social perception of it, in biographical form. Kajŏn are thus allegorical fables that imbue everyday objects with ethical and moral significance in order to instruct the reader. They are close to didactic genres because the plot is based on the judgment that the writer passes on the characteristics of the fictionalized object.

The kajŏn, however, used the narrative power inherent in the biographical format to develop a narrative style that went beyond simple descriptions of persons and events. In *Tale of Sir Malt*, "malt" (*kuksun*) is a person, one who has a full range of human experience. Thus, rather than being given a moralistic treatise on the advantages and disadvantages of alcohol, readers are presented with these issues in a fictional biography of a particular character.

This pattern reappears in other kajŏn. Money is personified in *Tale of Mr. Coin* (Kongbang chŏn, ca. 1163) by Im Ch'un; a tortoise in *Tale of the Turtle in Clear Water* (Ch'ŏnggang saja hyŏnbu chŏn, ca. 1220) by Yi Kyubo (1168–1241); bamboo in *Tale of Madame Bamboo* (Chuk puin chŏn, ca. 1340) by Yi Kok (1298–1351); paper in *Tale of Master Paper* (Chŏ saeng chŏn, ca. 1380) by Yi Ch'ŏm (1345–1405), and a walking stick in *Tale of Mr. Walking Stick* (Chŏngshija chŏn) by Shik Yŏngam. In *Tale of Master Malt* (Kuk sŏnsaeng chŏn, ca. 1210), Yi Kyubo also personifies alcohol, but the character and events portrayed differ significantly from those in *Tale of Sir Malt* by Im Ch'un. This shows that the form was flexible enough to incorporate various ideas and views on morality, a fact that further supports the argument that kajŏn combines elements of the narrative and didactic genres.

Kajŏn began to decline in the Chosŏn period as personification became common in various other forms of writing. Works such as *Record of Victory Over Worry* (Susŏng chi) and *History of Flowers* (Hwasa) by Im Che (1549–1587), *Tale of the King of Heaven* (Ch'ŏngun chŏn) by Kim Uong (1540–1603), *A Banquet with the King of Heaven* (Ch'ŏngun yŏnŭi) by Chŏng T'aejae (1612–1669), and *History of the King of Heaven* (Ch'ŏngun pongi) by Chŏng Kihwa (1786–1840) reflect the characteristics of kajŏn. Except for *History of Flowers*, in which flowers are personified, a person's mind is personified in all of these works. For this reason, they are often referred to as *shimsŏng kajŏn*, or "kajŏn of the mind."

Although kajŏn were written over a long period of time, the genre remained popular with only a few people proficient in classical Chinese. This was not only because a great deal of background knowledge was required in order to read kajŏn, but also because they emphasized esoteric themes through the creation of an artificial reality.

Dream Records

Dream records (*mongyurok*) emerged in the middle of the fifteenth century and became popular among the yangban class. The basic structure of dream records follows that of *A Dream of Nine Clouds* (Kuun mong, ca. 1687–88), a fifteenth-century fantasy novel, but in terms of content and style they differ greatly. In the fantasy novel, the main character is reborn in a dream as a heroic figure whose death destroys the dream, bringing the main character back to reality; this story is told from the omniscient, third-person viewpoint. In dream records, however, the narrative is in the first person, as the main character reflects on how a dream relates to events that preceded it. In addition, the dream segment in a fantasy novel discusses events that are directly related to the overall plot; in dream stories, the main character in the dream segment meets various people who do not reappear or have any relation to the real-life segments of the story.

Dream records thus differ from Korean legends and classic novels, which develop around a central incident or event, because they express ideas through the interaction of various characters in the artificial environment of the dream segment. In *Record of a Dream Visit to Taegwanjae* (Taegwanjae mongyurok) Shim Ŭi (b. 1475) presents the great Shilla period poet Ch'oe Ch'iwŏn as the emperor of an ideal kingdom. Other historical figures, such as Ulji Mundŏk, Yi Kyubo, Chŏng Tojŏn, and Kim Chongjik, are presented along with Shim himself in various official roles according to their particular talents. In the story, Shim gains wisdom from his interaction with these illustrious figures from Korea's past. In Im Che's *Record of Yangban Wŏn's Dream Adventure* (Wŏn saeng mongyurok), a yangban full of remorse, Wŏn Chahŏ, drinks with famous military leaders from the past, such as Sŏjong and the Sayukhŏn heroes. In the middle of drinking and singing, the main character suddenly feels depressed and is awakened from the dream, reflecting a critical view of King Sejo's usurpation of power. *Record of a Dream Visit to Kŭmhwa Temple* (Kŭmhwasa mongyurok), *Record of a Dream Visit to Sasu* (Sasu mongyurok), *Record of a Visit to Talch'ŏn* (Talch'ŏn mongyurok), *Record of Yangban P'i's Dream Adventure* (P'i saeng mongyurok), and *Record of a Dream Visit to Kangdo* (Kangdo mongyurok) all similarly present dreams in which the main character, whether famous or obscure, mingles with famous figures from history in a dream.

Because of these characteristics, scholars disagree on whether to classify dream stories as a didactic genre or a narrative genre. Scholars who argue that dream stories belong to the former base the claim on the moralistic evaluation of historical events in the dream stories. Those who argue that dream stories belong to the latter base their claim on the depiction of fictitious elements created by the conflict between the subjectivity of the author and historical reality. If we dispense with rigid definitions of genre, we see that this disagreement is natural because scholars emphasize either didactic or narrative aspects of dream stories.

Dream stories originated in romantic dream stories such as *Account of the Southern Continent of Jambūdvīpa* (Namyŏmbuju chi) and "Record of a Banquet in the Dragon Palace" (Yonggung puyŏn nok) in *Tales of Kŭmo* (Kŭmo shinhwa). The transformation was closely connected with the deepening contradictions between Confucian ideals and social reality in the mid-Chosŏn period. While attempting to maintain ideal virtue in the face of ever increasing social contradictions, literate yangban, who could not air their frustrations openly, expressed their hopes for a better world through their interaction with historical figures in the artificial space of the dream segment. Dream stories can be divided into two main types: those expressing pessimism about the world, such as *Record of Yangban Wŏn's Dream Adventure, Record of a Dream Visit to Talch'ŏn,* and *Record of Yangban P'i's Dream Adventure* (P'i saeng mongyurok); and those that portray the world optimistically by fictionalizing ideology, such as *Record of a Dream Visit to Taegwanjae, Record of a Dream Visit to Sasu,* and *Record of a Dream Visit to Kŭmhwa Temple.* The first type of dream story expresses a rigid view of ethical behavior, whereas the second, which has a lighter quality, presents temporary happiness and satisfaction through fantasy.

As a genre that emerged from the tension between Confucian ideals and social reality, dream stories lost their raison d'être in the late Chosŏn period because the basic order of Chosŏn society had collapsed by then. Dream stories were succeeded by classic novels such as *Record of a Dream Visit to the Heavenly Palace* (Ch'ŏngung mongyurok) and *Record of the War between Chu and Han China* (Monggyŏl Ch'o-Han song). Features from dream stories were adapted in these novels only to add interest and not as a basic element of the plot. Late-nineteenth-century novels such as *Dreams in the Sky* (Kkum hanŭl) by Shin Ch'aeho (1812–1884) and *Dream of a Meeting With Che Kallyang* (Monggyŏn Che Kallyang) by Yŏm Wŏnp'yo (n.d.) adopted the dream segment to comment on society in this period of change. Among the many contemporary authors, Ch'oe Inhun uses dream segments in his works.

Yadam

Yadam is a genre of simple, short stories written in classical Chinese; it is extremely difficult to define the genre in more detail because it comprises works of such diverse content and formal characteristics. Some yadam, known as *sashildam,* present the biography of one person, some comment on various historical and current events, and some depict social conditions and problems with irony that may or may not have been directed at real people. Yadam thus range from biographies of actual people to works that focus on the social issues of a particular time by means of fictional events and characters.

Because yadam is such a diverse genre, it includes both factual and fictional narrative and various prose styles that mix fact and fiction. Thus, yadam is a mixed genre, drawing in varying degrees on narrative and didactic genres.

The three-volume *Anthology of Short Stories in Classical Chinese of the Chosŏn Period* (Yijo hanmun tanp'yon chip [sang, chung, ha], 1973–78), edited by Yi Usŏng, and Im Yŏngt'aek, stimulated interest in yadam. By referring to them as "short stories," Yi and Im implied that the yadam had a close affinity with narrative genres. Many, however, are written versions of orally transmitted stories, which makes it difficult to argue that yadam originated as a written form of literature. Some yadam originated in oral literature, whereas others were composed as written works in classical Chinese. As described in the beginning of *A Collection of Kyesŏ Yadam* (Kyesŏ yadam), the yadam, both fictional and non-fictional, are based on interesting and stimulating observations of events and people, a feature which allowed them to combine features from the narrative and didactic genres to create a new genre marked by openness and flexibility.

The period during which yadam emerged as a genre remains unclear, but most scholars agree that the basic form of the yadam developed from collections of miscellaneous stories and anecdotes such as *Tales of Yŏgong* (Yŏgong p'aesŏl 1342) by Yi Chehyŏn (1287–1367), and the more developed *Peaceful and Humorous Stories for Leisure* (T'aep'yŏng hanhwa kolgye chŏn, 1477). The first works that can be called yadam are those in *A Collection of Ŏu Yadam* (Ŏu yadam, 1622) by Yu Mongin (1559–1623). The diversity of stories from everyday life, many of them orally transmitted, in this collection shows the influence of *Humorous Stories From the Country* (Ch'ondam hae'i) by Kang Hŭimaeng (1424–1483) and *A Collection of Humorous Stories* (Ŏmyŏnsun) by Song Saerim (b. 1479).

The yadam spread rapidly in the last half of the Chosŏn period, resulting in a wide variety of collections of yadam. Among these many works, *A Collection of Kyesŏ Yadam* (Kyesŏ yadam), *A Collection of Yadam from Green Hill* (Ch'ŏnggu yadam), and *A Collection of Yadam from the Eastern Field* (Tongya hwijip) are the most important. Other important collections of yadam are *Random Notes from Haksan* (Haksan hanŏn), *A Collection of Strange Stories* (Kimun ch'onghwa), *Writings from This Mountain* (Chasan p'ildam), *Humorous Tales from Sŏlgyo* (Sŏlgyo mannok), and *Strange Stories from the Great East* (Taedong kimun ["Great East" refers to Korea. —Trans.]), a collection of biographical yadam. General collections such as *Popular History of the Great East* (Taedong yasŭng) and *Forest of Stories* (P'aerim) also included many yadam.

The authors and compilers of most collections of yadam came from the yangban class, but some yadam were written by members of the chungin class of merchants and artisans. Despite the dominance of the yangban class, yadam—in contrast to other forms of literature written in classical Chinese—dealt with social problems and included detailed descriptions of the everyday life of a variety of people, not just the yangban class. This reflects the fact that many yadam were based on orally transmitted stories popular with the common people, and that the yangban class was becoming increasingly critical of Chosŏn society in the midst of the social upheavals that marked the middle of the Chosŏn period. Some members of the yangban class longed for the social order of the early Chosŏn period.

Themes common in yadam were the accumulation of wealth, basic human desires, worldly relationships, the collapse of aging aristocratic orders, conflicts between owner and servant, thieves and swindlers, the daily life of merchants in the market, the lives of entertainers and other social outcasts, and witty and ironic views of the life of common people. These themes show that yadam was able to express the concerns of the yangban class as the Chosŏn social order collapsed in the eighteenth and nineteenth centuries. Well-known classic novels written in classical Chinese, such as Pak Chiwŏn's (1737–1805) *Tale of Yangban Hŏ* (Hŏ saeng chŏn) and *A Tiger's Rebuke* (Hojil), and those by yangban such as Yi Ok and Kim Yŏ were probably influenced by yadam.

Although the form flourished as the social order of the Chosŏn period collapsed, authors of yadam could not escape from the yangban—or, in certain cases, the chungin—worldview. Yadam was not rebellious literature; for example, many yadam that are based on orally transmitted stories of the common people include references to Confucian morality at the end, so as to appeal to a yangban audience. Most oral versions of such stories lack these references. More research on yadam is needed to establish how they relate to Chosŏn society and to other genres of Korean literature.

The following two examples show the diversity of this genre. The first is from a short realistic story in *A Collection of Ŏu Yadam*. The second is from a well-known story in *A Collection of Humorous Tales* (Ŏsu shinhwa) about the suffering of a fallen yangban and his family after the loss of their wealth and prestige.

1.

Prince Iksŏng and Hong Yŏn were discussing how to repel the Japanese invaders. Hong Yŏn said, "If they haven't landed yet, we could probably stop them at sea, but if they've already landed, we probably won't be able to mount a good defense."

"I don't agree," replied Prince Iksŏng. "If they've already come ashore, they'll be like fish out of water, which will make them easier to push back. Why are our strategies so different? I think you're wrong."

In general, people learn from hindsight, and in the case of the Imjin Wars with Japan, Korea gained impressive victories at sea but lost the land war. Hong Yŏn was right about the Japanese invasion. People usually think of him as a Confucian sage, but without that reputation, he would probably be known as a great military leader.

—translated by Yi Minsu

2.

Hong Saengwŏn lived the life of a widower with his two daughters in a house on the other side of Soŭimun (also known as Sŏsomun), the western gate to Seoul. Poor and hungry, he always begged for food at the section of the tribute tax office in charge of soybean products. The officials there always gave him food, which he wrapped up in mustard leaves to take back to his daughters.

One day, when he came to beg for food, an official, who was drunk at the time, scolded Hong Saengwŏn.

"Hong Saengwŏn, do you think this office is at your beck and call? Do you think that we are your servants? Why do you come begging for food every day?"

Hong Saengwŏn burst into tears and returned home. At home, he did not eat for six days.

When one of the official from the tribute tax office came to check on Hong Saengwŏn and his daughters, he found them crying hysterically. Feeling a sense of urgency, the official went out and brought back some rice porridge for them.

Hong Saengwŏn looked at his elder daughter, who was thirteen, and said,

"Ah, do you want to eat porridge? We learned how to endure hunger for six days. We almost died. We still have our pride, don't we? Now eat this bowl of porridge. I know it would be nice if that person always brought us porridge, but do you want to suffer embarrassment day in and day out?"

As Hong Saengwŏn spoke, his younger daughter, who was six, smelled the porridge and moved her head as if she were going to stand up. The older daughter said to her younger sister, "Let's go to bed, let's go to bed." She soothed her younger sister to sleep.

Two days later, the official came to check on them, but found all of them dead.

No one can finish this story dry-eyed. How must the official who discovered them have felt at the time?

How terrible poverty is. I'm depressed about how poor I am, but compared to Hong Saengwŏn, I have nothing to be depressed about.

—translated by Yi Usŏng and Im Yŏngt'aek

5

Literary Criticism

Preliminary Principles

If literary criticism is defined as discussion of general literary trends and of the characteristics of specific works, it can only occur following those trends or after a particular work has been published. As literature developed from a way of dealing with basic human emotions and with the experiences of a particular group of people to a way of dealing with the inner workings of the human mind and society, critical views of this literary activity emerged. It is natural that critical views appear wherever literary activity takes place. Thus, in order to understand the literature of any ethnic group, we need to examine not only the historical development of literary creation, but also the critical views that emerged in response to and in turn influenced the development of literary trends.

Despite the importance of literary criticism, it has been largely over-looked in research and scholarship on Korean literature, a tendency that is particularly acute with regard to traditional Korean literature before the end of the nineteenth century.

Of course, several external factors have exacerbated this tendency. Very few original sources of literary criticism prior to the eleventh century are extant, which makes it difficult to get an overall view. Most extant sources that date from after the eleventh century deal mainly with literature in classical Chinese; as a result, much literature in hangŭl is excluded from the discussion. These facts, however, fail to account for the deeper reason behind this lack, which lies in the nega-tive views of traditional Korean philosophy and culture that prevailed at the end of the nineteenth century. Thirty-six years of Japanese colo-nial rule, from 1910 to 1945, made the situation worse, because Ko-reans were forced to negate the value of traditional Korean culture, which further limited the possibility of research on the nation's tradi-tional literature.

This negative view of traditional Korean culture and literature contributed to significant distortions regarding any understanding of the history and development of Korean literary criticism. It also hindered the development of an independent and objective view of modern literary history in the twentieth century. These distortions are the source of the sharp distinction between traditional and modern Korean literature that plagues Korean literary criticism. Another serious problem is the emphasis on Chinese literature's influence and its "transmission," in traditional Korean literature, and on that of Western literature in modern Korean literature.

We cannot deny that Korean literary criticism faced a crisis in the early years of the twentieth century. Recognizing the close relationship that traditional Korean literature had with other literatures of East Asia and that modern Korean literature has with Western literature, we must look deeper to investigate the meaning of these relationships. Changes in literary criticism inevitably follow upheavals in literary creation, such as those experienced in Korea in the early twentieth century, and the range of literary criticism evolves and expands with contact and exchange with foreign literature and literary criticism. Literary criticism that ignores internal conditions in favor of external influences imposes explanations that remove literature from its historical and cultural context. As a debate on the reason for literature, literary criticism is an essential part of all literary activity. Seen from this perspective, a detailed investigation of the historical reality of Korean literary criticism is in order.

A great deal of specialized research and revision is necessary if we are to gain a more balanced, comprehensive understanding of Korean literary theory and criticism. The following discussion is too limited to achieve this goal; it is rather a historical overview that provides a tentative outline of such an understanding.

Ancient Views of Language and Literature

Research on ancient views of Korean literature is hampered by the dearth of original sources. This forces scholars to deduce what such views might have been like from the extant ancient songs, or *kodae kayo,* and myths. In the oldest extant Korean songs, "Song for My Drowned Husband" (Kongmu toha ka) and "Song of Nightingales" (Hwangjo ka, 17 B.C.), we can see that people had a basic understanding of the function of poetry because these songs include background information describing why they were composed and what they express. In the respective stories of a woman who sang of her lost husband through the voice of another woman and of a king (King Yuri) who found it difficult to express the loneliness he felt after his lover's death, we can see that poetry was not yet understood as the expression of inner emotions.

The myths described in "Song of the Turtle" (Kuji ka, A.D. 42) reveal that ancient Koreans had great faith in the power of incantation in religious and public ceremonies. All of the above ancient songs contain a strong element of legend, and of a simple literary awareness developed in the formative stages of the ancient Korean kingdoms.

Beginning with the hyangga of the Shilla period, Korean literature developed into genres diverse in content and form. Various views of Korean literature at this time are recorded in *Memorabilia of the Three Kingdoms* (Samguk yusa, ca. 1285). The most prominent of these views is expressed in references to the power of song and poetry to move heaven and spirits in nature. This is reflected in a scene from "Song to the Sea" (Hae ka) in which Haeyong steals Prince Sunji's wife, Suro. The people rise up and sing, giving Prince Sunji the power to rescue Suro. The story is similar to that of "Song to the Turtle." Other examples are "Song of the Comet" (Hyesŏng ka, ca. 599) by Great Monk Yungch'ŏn, which was said to repel invading Japanese soldiers when it was sung; "Song of Regret" (Wŏn ka, ca. 737) by Shinch'ung, in which passionate lyrics of resentment cause pine trees to wilt and King Hyosŏng to repent his unethical behavior; "Song of Ch'ŏyong" (Ch'ŏyong ka, 879), in which the shaman Ch'ŏyong admonishes the god of disease for abducting his wife; and the story of King Kŏin, in which the king brings about changes in the weather by singing of his unjust imprisonment. All of these songs and the legends contained in them refer to the mystical power of song and poetry, which is expressed in the supernatural power ascribed to basic emotions such as hope, rage, and affection.

In reading the great many original sources on ancient Korean literature in *Memorabilia of the Three Kingdoms,* we also need to consider the development and awareness of the lyric function and the political and social uses of song and poetry. Works such as "Song of Tuṣita Heaven" (Tosol ka, 760), which describes how society improved after Yuri, the third king of Shilla, instituted just rule, and "Song of Virtuous Rule" (Anmin ka, 742–765), which reveals the political idealism of King Kyŏngdŏk, show that song and poetry were viewed as being closely related to the promotion of ethical rule and social order. The view of the function of song and poetry in hyangga such as "Song of Nightingales" and "Song for My Drowned Husband" centers on their power to express personal anguish and religious faith, in the attempt to invoke a supernatural response, as expressed in "Requiem for My Sister" (Che mangmae ka, ca. 742–765). The recognition of people's need to express their inner feelings and desires verbally gave rise to symbolic myths such as the myth of the headband maker (*poktujang shinhwa*) in the section of *Memorabilia of the Three Kingdoms* that deals with King Kyŏngmun (r. 861–875) of Shilla.

As more and more literature in classical Chinese was composed, its quality improved, and criticism of ancient songs and hyangga appeared. Literature in classical Chinese flourished particularly in the late Shilla period among the erudite yuktup'um scholars. By using allegory to praise the king's virtuous rule in his "The Flowers' Warning to the King" (Hwawanggye, ca. 681–691), Sŏl Ch'ong connected writing and literary creation with moral and political ideology. Ch'oe Ch'iwŏn (b. 857) stated that "poetry represents one's mind, whereas prose represents one's body." From this we can clearly see that Ch'oe viewed literary training as being closely related to moral training. Thus, literary criticism in the Three Kingdoms developed as literacy in classical Chinese and Confucian views of literature spread among the literate classes of society.

Literary Criticism in the Koryŏ Period

With the establishment of the Koryŏ Dynasty in 918, the biggest change in Korean literature was the flourishing of literary activity in classical Chinese. The founders of the Koryŏ Dynasty abolished the Shilla system of hereditary aristocracy (the bone-rank system), and adopted a merit-based civil service examination in order to concentrate political power in a centralized bureaucracy. The adoption of a Chinese-style civil service examination contributed greatly to the development of literacy in classical Chinese in Korea. The examination was divided into two sections: the composition section (*chesurŏp*) and the reading comprehension section (*myŏnggyŏngŏp*). Of these two sections, the composition section was of greater importance in determining the success or failure of the applicant, and this meant that training in classical Chinese poetry was required of every civil servant. Thus, classical Chinese, which had been the esoteric pursuit of a few scholars, such as the yuktup'um scholars in the Shilla period, became the norm of written expression among the aristocracy and government officials.

The introduction of the examination system at the beginning of the Koryŏ period, however, did not mean that classical Chinese was universally adopted overnight. In his introduction to the classical Chinese translation of the eleven hyangga of Kyunyŏ (923–973) from "Songs of the Ten Vows of Samantabhadra" (Pohyŏn shipchong wŏnwangsaeng ka, 973), one section of *Memorabilia of the Three Kingdoms,* Ch'oe Haenggwi noted that, although the form and language differ, the power of expression and depth of feeling are the same in the hyangch'al and classical Chinese versions of these eleven works. This shows us that Ch'oe, a scholar steeped in the classical Chinese tradition, viewed vernacular Korean as being the equal of classical Chinese. Ilyŏn (1206–1289), the compiler of *Memorabilia of the Three Kingdoms,* noted that hyangga were as beautiful and expressive as classical Chinese forms of poetry and songs of praise. Despite these positive views of vernacular Korean literature, literary criticism in the Koryŏ period came to reflect the influence of classical Chinese literature. The dominance of classical Chinese in Korea reflects its spread throughout East Asia from the fourth to seventh centuries A.D., and literary criticism was no exception to this trend.

Although literary criticism developed in tandem with the spread of literary activity in classical Chinese, very few works from the first half of the Koryŏ period survive, which makes it difficult to trace the development of literary criticism throughout the period. The work of Kim Pushik (1075–1151), compiler of *The History of the Three Kingdoms* (Samguk sagi, 1145), reflects the belief that works of literary value should contain discussions of Confucian ethics by containing references to ancient Chinese texts. As mentioned above, literary criticism from the time of Ch'oe Ch'iwŏn was deeply influenced by the Confucian ideas that emerged from the Tang-period Ancient Literature Movement, but this influence had become more powerful by the time Kim Pushik was writing. Although ancient Confucian texts were revered at this time and aesthetics were rejected in an attempt to conform to Confucian ideals, such literary views were not supported by a strong

Confucian philosophical base. For Kim Pushik, ancient texts served as models of good writing style rather than as sources of philosophical authority. Chŏng Chidang (d. 1135), a major political and literary opponent of Kim's, probably held different views of literature, but unfortunately, there are no extant sources on them.

These literary sensibilities—reverence for ancient works with a focus on an elegant writing style—began to change after the army coup d'état in 1170. The first important development to consider is the diversification of literary activity that resulted from the expansion of the ruling elite after the expulsion of the privileged aristocracy, who viewed sophisticated prose and poetry as a necessary component of an aristocratic cultural sensibility.

The development of literary sensibility was inevitably limited before the coup d'état because political power was concentrated in the hands of the aristocracy, who used literature to maintain its hold on the bureaucracy. Thus literacy and political power were interrelated, and any challenge to or deviation from this system threatened the social position of the writer. The coup d'état of 1170 changed this drastically by breaking up the old aristocracy's monopoly on power, allowing new groups to engage in literary activity. This weakened dominant views of literature and permitted new ones to come to the fore. Much more literary criticism survives from the last half of the Koryŏ period than from the first half. This is not only because there are more extant sources, but also because of the diversity of views of literature in the last half of the period.

The growth of literary criticism is evident in the number of collections of prose in classical Chinese (*shihwa*), which included many essays on individual works of literature. Collections such as *Jottings to Relieve Idleness* (P'ahan chip, 1214), *Jottings in Idleness* (Pohan chip, 1254), and *Tales of Yŏgong* (Yŏgong p'aesŏl, 1342), which included discussions on the composition, rhetoric, character, and value of poetry, are valuable references on the trends and tastes in literature of the times.

The elements of literary criticism of the last half of the Koryŏ period are very diverse, but two views of literature are of particular importance in its history. The first is the discussion of syllabification in the composition of poetry in classical Chinese; the second is the discussion of the relationship between established tradition and individual creativity. The first type of criticism was concerned with the creation of more detailed and richer poetic language by means of the grammatical and tonal organization of Chinese characters. The ultimate aim of this criticism was to improve the aesthetic appeal of poetry. The second type of criticism arose from a critical view of the extreme emphasis on grammatical and tonal organization in the first type, and was mainly concerned with the question of the basic meaning of poetry itself. The debate over the importance of form (*yongsa*) and creativity (*shinŭi*) is a representative conflict of these two strands of late Koryŏ-period criticism.

Yi Illo (1152–1220) and Yi Kyubo (1168–1241) were the two most important critics concerned with the conflict between the form theory (*yongsa ron*) and the creative theory (*shinŭi ron*), on which they had divergent views. This does not mean that Yi Illo denied the importance of individual creativity in poetry or that Yi Kyubo was concerned with the use of elegant and refined language. Both men held broadly similar literary views, but they focused on different aspects of literary criticism. Yi Illo was conservative, emphasizing the importance of elegant meter and language, a focus that was closely related to classical Chinese forms of poetry. Yi Kyubo, however, was more innovative and appealed to the needs of the more diverse post-coup aristocracy; his view of the importance of sincerity and creativity in poetry was expressed in such statements as "Material force (*ki;* Chinese: *qi*), which is the basis of all things in the universe, is impossible to learn through study."

Im Ch'un (d. 1170), a contemporary of Yi Kyubo's, also emphasized the subjective basis of elegant tonal and grammatical organization in poetry. Ch'oe Cha (1188–1260) took Yi Kyubo's ideas and developed a compromise theory, but in his discussion of the importance of material force (*ki*) and meaning (*ŭi;* Chinese: *yi*) in poetry, he began to focus on the poetry's essential character. His interest in the essential character of poetry shows that he was influenced by neo-Confucianism, which had begun to spread in Korean society at the time.

Toward the end of the Koryŏ period, neo-Confucianism had a powerful affect on literary criticism; Taoism also began to exert influence on views of literature at this time. While viewing ancient forms of classical Chinese, Yi Chehyŏn (1287–1367) also believed that literature gained its legitimacy from helping people find Dao. He stated that "virtue is the essence of life." These views of literature became dominant as neo-Confucianism spread in society, and became the basis of late-Koryŏ and early-Chosŏn period literary theory under the influence of Yi Saek (1328–1396) and his followers.

Literary Criticism in the First Half
of the Chosŏn Period

Neo-Confucian literary theory became even more prevalent after neo-Confucianism was established as the ruling ideology of the Chosŏn Dynasty in 1392. Chŏng Tojŏn (d. 1398) was largely responsible for the official adoption of neo-Confucianism in the early years of the Chosŏn period. Basing his views on those of Yi Chehyŏn and Yi Saek, he stated that literature was "a tool for perfecting virtue" and believed that didactic poetry and prose were of the greatest literary value. He believed that people need to perfect virtue in whatever they do, that they are born with an inner morality that can be drawn out though virtuous thought and action. Thus literature must play a part in bringing about proper order in society and the universe by remaining true to these principles. According to this theory, literature is part of an overall value system that attempts to forge a unity between human society and the metaphysical principles of the universe.

Although this theory of literature was dominant throughout the Chosŏn period, classical Chinese poetic formalism was also respected. Kwŏn Kŭn (1352–1409) was one of the first to establish a connection between the perfection of virtue and classical Chinese poetic formalism, but after the establishment of the Chosŏn Dynasty, the division between the literati officials in the central government and the neo-Confucian literati grew as some of the ruling literati were attracted to the formal theory of poetry. Adherents of this view of literature were all supporters of neo-Confucian doctrine and the accompanying view that literature was "a tool for perfecting virtue." Their views of literary form and aesthetic value brought new ideas to literary criticism of the times.

Sŏ Kŏjŏng (1420–1488), an exponent of these views, set literary trends throughout his twenty years of writing official histories. He also edited the *Eastern Literary Anthology* (Tongmun sŏn, 1478 ["Eastern" refers to "Korean." —Trans.]) of Koryŏ-period writing and completed his own collection of prose in classical Chinese, *Essays on Poetry by Easterners* (Tongin shihwa, 1474). Although Sŏ agreed with the traditional virtue-dominated view of literature, he believed literature plays an important role in successful government and that it should pass wisdom on to future generations. According to this interpretation, a work must be well written if virtue is to be conveyed properly. The focus on form comes from the emphasis on linguistic sophistication and proficiency in classical Chinese literature.

These views are rooted in the literary values and aesthetics of the literati officials. Because of their strong interest in political philosophy, and the neo-Confucian interest in the relationship between principle and material energy (*i-ki;* Chinese: *li-qi*) and the mind and human essence (*shim-sŏng;* Chinese: *xin-xing*), the neo-Confucian literati focused on ethical theories of literature. Yi Hwang (1501–1570) and Yi I (1536–1584) are representative of this group. Emphasizing the imperative need to inculcate virtue, they had much in common with early–Chosŏn period writers, but they were more interested in the essence of virtue than in the social uses of literature. Yi Hwang asked, "Is it possible to ignore literature? No, learning to write is necessary to develop proper values." Yi I stated, "We learn poetry for much more than pleasure. Through the peace and harmony that poetry brings, we can expunge our impure thoughts, an action which leads toward mindfulness."

Yi I's *Revised Version of Ch'oe Ip's Treatise* (Chŭng Ch'oe Ip chi sŏl) epitomizes this view of literature clearly. By linking the neo-Confucian theory of the origin of the universe with human values and existence, Yi I placed literature clearly within neo-Confucian thought. In this view, idealistic literature was an important means of demonstrating how the Eternal Great Ultimate (*mugŭk t'aegŭk*), the basis of the universe, is embodied in the human mind.

Hŏ Kyun (1569–1618) took literary criticism in a new direction, away from these sixteenth-century traditions. To Hŏ, poetry was the truest expression of our inner feeling, whereas the established view was that poetry was a means of cultivating ethics. Hŏ also criticized the dominant idea that form and language were more important in poetry than depth of experience. His criticism of the reverence for ancient Chinese forms of poetry paved the way for greater use of vernacular Korean. In his literary essays "Composition" (Munsŏl) and "Different Types of Poetry" (Shibyŏn), Hŏ argued that each period of history has unique literary trends and that poets and writers should not copy styles from previous eras but should write in a unique style, and from their own experience. This view of literature forms part of a tradition that extends from Yi Kyubo in the mid-Koryŏ period and Pak Chiwŏn and Yi Ok in the eighteenth century.

Literary Criticism in the Last Half
of the Chosŏn Period

As the contradictions in Chosŏn society came to the surface in the seventeenth century, negative views of traditional forms of literature began to take hold. Much more research is needed in this field, but the trend away from strict neo-Confucianism and toward an interest in society probably affected literary criticism at this time as well. Chang Yu (1587–1638) and Hong Manjong (1643–1725) were very interested in the neo-Confucian and Daoist philosophy of Wang Yang-ming (Wang Yangmyŏng) and developed views of literature critical of neo-Confucianism.

Chang Yu not only placed greater emphasis on aesthetics, but also argued that beauty in literature resided in the content of a work, rather than being a property of the language used. Hong Manjong emphasized the need to go beyond discussions of ethical rules and external form. In editing *A Comprehensive Collection of Essays on Poetry* (Shihwa ch'ongnim, ca. 1710), a collection of important prose in classical Chinese from the Koryŏ and early Chosŏn periods, he chose only works on forms of poetry based on aesthetically pleasing language, presenting as well his own critical views on the history of Korean poetry in classical Chinese.

Kim Manjung (1635–1720) extended literary criticism to discussions of native Korean forms of literature in hyangch'al and hangŭl. This stimulated an interest in native Korean forms among many yangban literati. By comparing Korean poets' attempts to express their inner feelings in classical Chinese to a parrot's attempt to imitate human speech, Kim Manjung admonished the yangban literati to pay more attention to native Korean forms of poetry. His work contributed greatly to the development of literary criticism that dealt with native Korean literary forms.

As literary activity spread among those common people who had contact with the elite, collections of shijo and poetry in classical Chinese by *Wihangin* poets (members of the chungin class) began to appear. The emergence of new literature based on the native Korean literature of the market towns is an important development in literary criticism of the last half of the seventeenth century. In the early eighteenth century, authors such as Kim Ch'ŏnt'aek, compiler of *Songs from Green Hill* (Chŏnggu yŏngŏn, 1728), a collection of shijo; Chŏng Yungyŏng and Maok Noch'u, who wrote the introduction to *Songs From Green Hill;* Kim Sujang (b. 1690), compiler of *Songs from Haedong* (Haedong kayo, 1763 ["Haedong" refers to Korea. —Trans.]), a collection of shijo; and Hong Taeyong (1731–1783), author of *Collected Poems from the East* (Taedong p'ungyo sŏl, ca. 1780), compared shijo to the ancient Chinese anthology *The Book of Songs* (Korean: *Shi kyŏng;* Chinese: *Shi jing*), arguing that shijo was an honest form of literature that allowed Koreans to express themselves in the simple language of the common people. These views reflect the shift in literary criticism, away from the classical Chinese literature of the elite and toward the native Korean literature of the common people. On the subject of what motivated them, wihangin poets such as Hong Set'ae (1653–1725) and Ko Shiŏn (1671–1734) noted that some literati had encouraged them to write because their writing was more sincere than that of the literati. With their focus on the natural expression of feeling rather than on ethical restrictions and sophisticated literary form, the works of the wihangin poets represent the first major rebellion against established literary forms and values.

Some progressive literati associated with the shilhak reform movement attempted to reject the philosophical emphasis on virtue and reactionary classicism and adopt an approach that permitted the honest expression of everyday experience. Pak Chiwŏn (1737–1783) and Yi Ok (1681–1763) are two of the most important figures in this movement. In rejecting the reverence for ancient Chinese forms of literature, which strictly limited form and content, Pak argued for change, and for greater realism and individuality in literature. To Pak, honest literature did not come from fossilized language and the experience of previous eras expressed in old forms, but from a close relationship with the everyday experience of the present combined with a respect for the wisdom of the past. He criticized mindless imitation of Chinese forms and praised poetry that was rooted in Korean history and culture. He also valued fiction that dealt with the complexities of contemporary life with irony and subtlety, rather than in strictly rhetorical language.

In the revolutionary literary treatise he wrote for his *Introductory Essays on Songs From Everyday Life* (Yiŏn in), Yi Ok extended these arguments by rejecting the Confucian-based universalism and classicism that dominated Korean thought at the time. He argued that because nothing in nature is exactly the same, literature also must reflect the diverse character of different places and periods in history. In his literary works and criticism, Yi rejected traditional yangban literati views and focused on the everyday lives of common people in markets. He placed people at the center of his writing, arguing that they are the key to understanding society and that love between men and women is the key to understanding people. Rejecting the formalism and tradition of literature in classical Chinese in favor of a new literature, he expressed some of the sharpest criticism of the established literary views of the last half of the Chosŏn period.

The great shilhak scholar Chŏng Yagyong (1762–1836) sought to overcome the inward characteristics of early-Chosŏn literary theory by other means. Although he based his own theory on the primacy of the development of virtue, he interpreted that development to be the promotion of political and social justice rather than the cultivation of individual virtue, as the sixteenth-century neo-Confucianists had argued. He wrote many poems about social problems, and he analyzed *The Book of Songs* as social commentary on troubled times. He argued that literature is a social record that shows the authors' sincerity through their relationship with the outside world.

The preceding discussion is only an overview of the general trends in literary criticism in the late Chosŏn period; more research is needed if we are to gain a better understanding of these diverse trends.

Literary Criticism in the Late Nineteenth Century

The overall direction of literary criticism in the late Chosŏn period was part of a larger trend in the arts against the ruling neo-Confucian values of the time. This critical tendency, however, was not strong enough to encourage a positive response to the new forms of language and literature that emerged in the late nineteenth and early twentieth centuries. The literary criticism that emerged in the first decade of the twentieth century in response to the collapse of the old order and the increasing influence of Western culture is known as "modern literary criticism." Seen in this light, modern Korean literary criticism is burdened by internal contradictions as a result of the difficult historical conditions under which it developed. Many aspects of Japanese colonial rule—rejection of the importance of traditional Korean culture, admiration of Western culture, conflicts between advocates of universal beauty in art and advocates of realism and historicity—seriously impaired any objective understanding of the relationship among literature, society, and people in literary criticism of this period. To understand the genesis of modern Korean literary criticism, we need to understand how these problems came together through conflict and compromise to create a new way of thinking, one that was a mixture of Korean and foreign thought. Simple descriptions of modern literary criticism as "development" should be avoided because such descriptions place an excessive emphasis on the reception of Western literary criticism.

The first stage in the development of modern literary criticism began with the opening of Korea to Western and Japanese culture in 1876. Writers of new novels and progressive Confucian scholars argued for a literature that responded to the needs of these times. Writings about literature, such as "Theory of a Literature for National Development" (Nonguk ungwan munhak), the introduction to Pak Ŭnshik's translation of *Record of Swiss Independence* (Sŏsa kŏnguk chi, 1907); Shin Ch'aeho's "Essay from Chŏn Mŭidang" (Chŏn Mŭidang shihwa), the introduction to Yi Haejo's *Blood from Flowers* (Hwa ŭi hyŏl, 1911), the postscript to An Kuksŏn's *National Welfare Society* (Kongjinhoe), and an editorial in *The Korea Daily News* (Taehan maeil shinbo), called for literature that was socially, politically, and ethically helpful to the cause of modernization. These authors argued that literature, especially novels, should move the reader emotionally as in stories taken from everyday life. This would, they argued, help readers realize the need for change and modernization and encourage them to change their personal habits in the interest of broader social change. This approach combined traditional neo-Confucian views of the ethical imperative of literature with calls for a new literature for a new age. This debate occurred mostly in relation to prose with few references to the ch'angga, or New Poetry, but these genres emerged from similar literary views.

As a result of Japanese suppression of various strains of literary thought after the loss of national sovereignty in 1910, the above theories gave way to sentimental ones. In his "What Is Literature?" (Munhak iran ha o, 1916), Yi Kwangsu (b. 1882), the leading exponent of the latter, argued that the human mind is composed of intellect, emotion, and intention, and that literature fulfilled the need to express emotion. In his sharp rejection of traditional Confucian culture, Yi argued that traditional Korean literature was misguided because it dealt only with the intellect, at the expense of emotion, and that a new theory of literature based on human feelings was necessary to counter the negative influence of neo-Confucian moralism. The literary theory of the early years of Japanese colonial rule denied the social and moral efficacy of literature in favor of individuality, freedom, and sentimentality (Yi's changed view of literature after the mid-1920s should be considered separately).

Shin Ch'aeho (1880–1936), then a noted literary critic, took the opposite point of view. He emphasized the social value of literature and criticized the obsession with inward escapism of the literature of the time. In his "Essay from Ch'ŏnhŭidang," he called for unity between patriotic political consciousness and a strong sense of poetic feeling with the slogan, "For a Revolution in Eastern Poetry" (Tongguk shigye hyŏngmyŏng ["Eastern" refers to "Korean." —Trans.]). In writings on poetry such as "Recommendations for Writers of Contemporary Novels" (Kŭngŭm sosŏl chŏja ŭi chuŭi) and "Random New Year's Notes by a Wanderer" (Nanggaek ŭi shinnyŏn manp'il), he argued that the meaning of art, whether based on aesthetic ideals or on human need, was found in the social relevance of that art to the time in which it appeared. Shin thus called for a socially relevant literature that forged a unity between traditional neo-Confucian views of literature and the social reality of the time.

Literary Criticism of the 1920s and 1930s

The opposition between the sentimental and social views of literature discussed above was at the root of the conflict between the romantic view of literature and the socialist criticism that appeared at the beginning of the 1920s. The sentimental view of literature that emerged from the early writings of Yi Kwangsu became the romantic movement in the mid-1920s under the leadership of authors such as Pak Yŏnghŭi (b. 1901), Hwang Sŏgu (1895–1959), Kim Ŏk (b. 1896), and Pak Chonghwa (1901–1981). Opposing this movement were the "new wave" group of writers (shingyŏnghyangp'a) and the KAPF group of proletarian writers who stressed the importance of social relevance and political struggle in literature.

The proletarian literary critics, first led by Kim Kijin (1903–1985) and Pak Yŏnghŭi, and by Im Hwa (b. 1908) in the late 1920s, criticized all previous literature as the product of false consciousness and bourgeois deception. Arguing that all forms of art must express the class struggle, they focused on the use of literature to liberate oppressed groups in society. Taking the opposite point of view, Yi Kwangsu, Yŏm Sangsŏp (1897–1963), and Kim Ŏk called for artistic autonomy in literature and focused on national rather than class consciousness. Yang Chudong (1903–1977) proposed a theory that unified these two opposing ones, but it did not gain many followers. Through debate between these opposing schools over the meaning and function of literature and literary criticism, modern Korean literary criticism developed the beginnings of modern critical consciousness. Many works of literary criticism on both sides, however, were dominated by superficial idealism at the expense of any detailed analysis of literary works.

The close relationship between content and form in Kim Kijin's *Art and Poetic Criticism* (Munye ship'yŏng, 1926) reflects the conflicts in literary criticism of this period. Kim Kijin argued that the class conflict should be embedded in an aesthetic structure that fits the content of the work; Pak Yŏnghŭi, on the other hand, argued that content and consciousness in literature need to be independent of each other in a period of transition and turmoil, thus legitimizing literature expressing the class struggle. Historical circumstances resolved this issue, as Pak's ideas became the guiding literary ideology of the KAPF group of writers. Literary debate in the 1930s continued to center on socialist realism.

As Japanese censorship and control over publishing increased in the late 1930s, proletarian criticism began to decline. Critics who emphasized aesthetics, internal sophistication, and artistic autonomy, such as Pak Yongch'ŏl 1904–1938), Kim Hwant'ae 1909–1942), and Kim Munjip (b. 1909), began to emerge at this time. They were interested in developing a new approach to literature in opposition to both the romantic literary criticism of the early 1920s and the ideological dogma of proletarian criticism. They argued that literature is a spiritual activity that is independent of other arts and society, and that it is thus inappropriate to force the interpretation of a literary work to conform to an external standard of judgment. These critics emphasized instead the individuality of the poet or writer, the mystery of literary creation, the beauty of language, and the beauty of experience. Although they drew heavily on aesthetic literary criticism and stressed the importance of individual experience and response in evaluating a particular work, they viewed other forms of literary criticism in the aesthetic tradition as impressionistic. Their approach was subjective, in contrast to the doctrinaire objectivity of the proletarian critics.

Ch'oe Chaesŏ (1908–1964) and Kim Kirim (b. 1908), critics who emerged slightly later, in the mid-1930s, introduced contemporary British and American criticism to Korea in an attempt to overcome the dichotomy between proletarian critics and subjective of critics such as Kim Hwant'ae. In particular, Ch'oe believed that literary composition is an attempt to understand social reality and values. In emphasizing the need for judgment in literary criticism, he developed a theory that united aesthetic values in literature with social and ethical values. As a poet and poetry critic, Kim Kirim was more interested in poetry criticism and in developing a modernist movement in Korean poetry than in the construction of a comprehensive literary theory.

After the KAPF movement was disbanded by the Japanese authorities in the early 1930s, Im Hwa and Kim Namch'ŏn (b. 1911) carried on the tradition of proletarian criticism by extending the range of dogmatic ideological criticism. This growth included Im Hwa's combination of romanticism and realism, new approaches to the history of Korean literature, Kim Namch'ŏn's theory of the novel, and various debates on the value of commercial literature. Further study of literary criticism in the 1930s is needed, as some of these issues remain difficult to research because of the continuing ideological conflict on the Korean Peninsula. Regardless of the controversies, the 1930s were a decade marked by the most diverse literary debate in the history of modern Korean literary criticism.

Literary Criticism After the Liberation From Japan

In the years following the liberation from Japanese colonial rule, which was particularly oppressive during World War II, Korean literary criticism became entangled in the strong ideological conflict that affected all areas of Korean life at the time. As an integral part of ideological debate, literary criticism was at the center of this conflict.

The most significant point of contention at this time was the debate on how to establish an independent national literature that fulfilled the hopes of the Korean people after liberation from Japan. Most scholars place views of the meaning of national literature into two opposing groups: the nationalistic view on the right and the Marxist view of the left. This is an oversimplification, however, because these groups were not united among themselves. Within the nationalistic group, for example, some critics argued that only pure literature that embraced universal values qualified as national literature, whereas others argued that a Korean national literature needed to be rooted in the social reality of the times so that it could offer a way of solving internal and external social problems. The Marxist critics were divided over the relationship between class struggle and national liberation. Some critics argued that a national literature should be based on the class struggle, whereas others argued that national liberation should be given priority. The intensity of this debate laid the ground for the development of a new literary criticism, but it was cut short by the hardening of the political and social division of Korea into North and South. As a result, the pure-literature faction of right-wing nationalist critics came to dominate literary criticism in the South. In the North, those who favored national liberation over the class struggle as the basis of a national literature were purged early on, ensuring the dominance of those who argued for the class struggle.

Literary circles lost much of their vitality after the division of the country in 1948 and, with a few notable exceptions, literary criticism made little progress in the years immediately after the Korean War. After President Syngman Rhee resigned under pressure during the revolution of April 19, 1960, literary criticism became more active as critics reflected on the causes of the revolution and the state of contemporary Korea. British and American criticism and formalistic criticism focused attention on the social meaning and function of literature, giving rise to a heated debate between the advocates of pure and participatory literature. Toward the end of the 1960s, doubts about the applicability of Western literary theory emerged. Questions regarding the legitimacy of literary criticism at the time came to the fore as the debate surrounding the place of traditional literature in the history of Korean literature continued.

As social and political tension grew in the 1970s, literary criticism dealt increasingly with differences in critical approach and theoretical structure. The controversy over whether to view literature as a closed system of independent aesthetics or as an open system of meanings closely related to social reality was not new, but new interpretations of literature as an open system emerged at this time. Two quarterly literary journals, *Creation and Criticism* (Changjak kwa pip'yŏng) and *Literature and Intelligence* (Munhak kwa chisŏng), played an important role in the literary debate of the 1970s. Many approaches to literary criticism that continue to influence literary debate today emerged at this time: literature for the common people (*shimin munhak ron*), popular literature (*soshimin munhak ron*), debate on literary realism (*riŏllijŭm nonjaeng*), national literature (*minjok munhak ron*), and people's literature (*minjung munhak ron*). A detailed description of these theories is beyond the purview of this chapter. What is important to remember about literary criticism in the 1970s is that the sudden burst of activity resulted from the need to analyze the relationship between literature and social conditions in a period of tension and rapid change. These forces continue to influence Korean literary criticism to this day.

6

The Trade in Literary Works

Regardless of its complexity, a work must have readers as well as a writer to be considered a work of literature. The transmission and diffusion of literary works have not received much attention in the history of Korean literature, but such works are influenced greatly by material culture and social environment over time. With this in mind, we will look at the transmission of literary works by studying the rise of commercial publishing and the trade in works of literature in hangŭl during the last half of the Chosŏn period. Other phenomena of the trade and dissemination of works of Korean literature will be mentioned only in passing; by focusing on commercial publishing in the late Chosŏn period, we can gain a better understanding of the social background of literature and of the relationship between external and internal factors in the development of a literary work.

The transmission and dissemination of literature are historically diverse, as shown in the following chart.

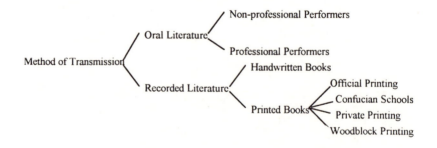

The Performance and Transmission of Oral Literature

Dependent on performance and the strength of the human memory, oral transmission is the most basic of all forms of literary transmission. Oral literature continued to exist as a popular form of literature long after written literature emerged. The following genres of Korean literature had their origins in oral literature: ancient epic poems, chants, lyric songs, Koryŏ sogyo, folk songs and myths from various eras, chapka, shaman chants, p'ansori, and various forms of folk theater. Most scholars believe that the four-line hyangga originated orally. Shijo and kasa were transmitted both orally and in written form. Although yadam is a highly diverse genre, many of the works within it are written versions of stories orally transmitted in the marketplace. We will focus here on the performance and mobility of oral literature.

Oral literature is presented in words or in song by a storyteller or group of storytellers before an audience; thus a work of literature is composed as it comes out of the mouth of the storyteller but disappears immediately after that. The presenter and audience have the chance to hear the same story again, but it may not necessarily be told in the same way. The contents of the work are flexible and dependent on the will of the storyteller. The time, place, occasion, atmosphere, and type of audience all affect the performance, as do the tone, facial expressions, and gestures of the storyteller. Because the influence of these variables is strong, it is impossible for each performance of a particular work to be exactly the same. The environment surrounding a performance is thus critical to an understanding of oral literature.

Oral literature is fluid because it is changed consciously and unconsciously with each performance. The concept of an "original" text for a work thus does not apply to it. Original texts for works such as "The Fisherman's Calendar" (Ŏbu sashi sa, 1651) by Yun Sŏndo (1587–1671) and *Peace Under Heaven* (T'aep'yŏng ch'ŏnha, 1938) by Ch'ae Manshik (1902–1950) exist, but various versions of legends such as "Hang in There, Big Brother" (Onui changsa himneagi) and folk songs such as "My Dear Husband from Chinju" (Chinju nanggun) are considered one work. Storytellers can change the content of a work depending on their own whims and on the type of audience. At times, the storyteller may shorten or cut a section of the story. The song "Monorae," which is traditionally sung while planting rice in the spring, underwent extensive oral transmission, and new verses could be added or new lyrics composed impromptu depending on the talent of the lead singer and the atmosphere surrounding the performance. In this process of constant change and adaptation, new elements were added to oral literature all the time.

The amount of change and adaptation that takes place during the transmission of oral literature depends on the genre of the work and the social background of those who perform it. To explain these differences accurately, we need to divide the performers of oral literature into professional and nonprofessional.

Nonprofessional performers were ordinary people who made a living by other means and who sang songs or told stories in their everyday lives. In each village some people were considered better storytellers than others, but nonprofessional performers were united by the fact that they gained no social or financial benefit from singing or storytelling, regardless of how good they may have been. Most folk songs and myths were performed by common people who were nonprofessional singers or storytellers.

Professional performers were persons who made their living from singing or storytelling and whose body of work included many oral literary performance. Shamans who sang chants in ceremonies (*kut*), p'ansori singers, and chapka singers are examples of professional performers of oral literature; traveling storytellers who depended on their talent belong to this group as well. Some of these storytellers also read literature such as classic novels to the public in marketplaces, thus placing themselves between oral and written literature. Koryŏ sogyo were performed as court music; Kisaeng who included song and poetry in their repertoires were also professional performers. Although we have no recorded evidence, it is likely that those who recited epic foundation myths during the ceremonies of the ancient Korean kingdoms and in the era of the Three Kingdoms received special treatment or recognition.

Although professional performers of oral literature faced many restrictions, the extent and type of such restrictions varied greatly according to the type of performance. Nonprofessional performers were affected by indirect restrictions—such as limited memory or lack of knowledge of erudite literary expressions—that were as important as the type of performance. Professionals, however, rarely encountered these problems because they were constantly performing their repertoire. This allowed them to concentrate on more theatrical aspects of the performance, such as developing a unique style and adapting their repertoire to a particular audience for maximum effect.

Two divergent trends, however, should be kept in mind. Some forms of oral literature were, depending on their character and function, expected to be transmitted faithfully, whereas others allowed for a significant amount of flexibility and individual adaptation in performance. Liturgical songs and songs sung at royal ceremonies and parties are examples of the first type of oral literature; the hypothetical foundation epics of the ancient Korean kingdoms also belong to this category. Rather than entertainment, these songs were solemn expressions of prayer and sacred beliefs. Because performers were trained specifically to execute these works faithfully and not as autonomous artists, they were not free to alter the original form of the song. This type of oral literature did not change significantly unless there was a major change in the structure of society.

P'ansori singers and storytellers, on the other hand, were free to make creative changes in the stories they presented because interesting and creative approaches to the performance were valued by the audience. They were not required to adhere to strict rules or a set original form. Unlike official performers of oral literature at court, p'ansori singers and storytellers depended on audience satisfaction for their livelihood. P'ansori singers and storytellers made a greater effort to develop a rich repertoire and to give their performances individuality, both of which stimulated the development of the text and of performance technique.

The performance of narrative shaman chants is somewhat complicated. Most shaman chants from the southern half of the Korean Peninsula followed the original pattern of official ceremonial chants, which had more in common with official oral literature than with forms like p'ansori. With the increase in folk and theatrical elements in shamanistic ceremonies in the last half of the Chosŏn period, however, shamans began to be more creative, becoming more like p'ansori singers and storytellers.

As discussed in the brief summary above, the oral transmission and dissemination of literature were diverse and constantly changing. An understanding of the differences between the transmission and dissemination of oral and recorded literature is essential to any understanding of oral literature itself.

The Diffusion of Literature in Hyangch'al and in Classical Chinese

Recorded literature is disseminated though the diverse processes of writing, editing, producing, and distributing of books. Of the two varieties of books—handwritten and printed—printed books were the most popular in traditional Korean society. Because hangǔl was invented hundreds of years after Chinese characters and classical Chinese writing came to Korea, the earliest recorded literature is in classical Chinese. Because for the first several centuries after Chinese characters were introduced to Korea, only very few people could read this literature, serious literary activity in this medium did not begin until the yuktup'um scholars emerged at the end of the seventh century with the establishment of the Kukhak, a national Confucian college, during the reign of the Shilla king Shinmun (A.D. 681–692). Works by esteemed scholars such as Kangsu (seventh century A.D.), Sǒl Ch'ong (seventh century A.D.), and Kim Inmun (629–694) have been lost over time. *Writings from the Cinnamon Garden* (Kyewǒn p'ilgyǒng chip, ca. 885) by Ch'oe Ch'iwǒn (b. 857), written in honor of King Hǒngang, together with the other works of this writer reflect the sophistication of literature written in classical Chinese in the late Unified Shilla period. This literary activity, however, was still confined to a few persons in society. Literature in classical Chinese had also taken hold in Palhae, as is evident from the poems in classical Chinese that were given to Japan in diplomatic exchanges and that were presented as tribute to the court of the Tang Dynasty.

Regrettably *The Collection from the Three Kingdoms* (Samdaemok), a collection of hyangga compiled by Wihǔng and Taegu Hwasang at the order of Queen Chinsǒng in A.D. 888, has been lost. We know, however, that hyangga developed from the four-line form based on folk songs to the ten-line form that reflected individual creativity in composition. It is difficult, however, to argue that all of the ten-line hyangga were originally composed and transmitted as recorded literature. The case of shijo and kasa shows that the oral transmission of literature remained predominant even after the development of basic printing techniques. Most genres developed from oral to written forms. These differed from purely oral forms of literature in that they were based on an original written text by an individual writer, which worked to limit distortion in the process of transmission. The original work may not have had many readers, but it did serve as a point of reference for performers of oral literature.

As hyangga declined in the Koryǒ period and literature in classical Chinese spread among the elite, recorded literature was written in or translated into classical Chinese. In the aristocratic society that dominated the Koryǒ period, familiarity with and proficiency in literature were a means not only of maintaining social position, but also of demonstrating the power and prestige of the ruling class. This meant that the elite in Koryŏ were more proficient in classical Chinese and in classical Chinese literary forms than the elite of the Shilla period. Although about 30 collections of works in classical Chinese survive from the Koryŏ period, at least 350 collections are known to have existed, from historical records. Most literature was handwritten for private use in the early Koryŏ period, but works started being published for other readers in the late thirteenth century. *The Collected Works of Minister Yi of Korea* (Tongguk Yi sangguk chip, 1251) by Yi Kyubo (1168–1241) and *A Collection of Humble Writings* (Cholgo ch'ŏnbaek, 1354) by Ch'oe Hae (1287–1340) were published under official sponsorship, whereas *A Collection From the Silver Pavilion* (Ŭndae chip, published sometime between 1220 and 1260) by Yi Illo (1152–1220) was published privately. Because printing was a complicated and time-consuming process, most literary activity took place at gatherings dedicated to song and poetry, and most literature was handwritten. In this context, the number of collections published at this time not only reflected the considerable literary activity but also stimulated it.

The publication and editing, both public and private, of collections of literature of various lengths expanded considerably in the early Chosŏn period. *An Eastern Literary Anthology* (Tongmun sŏn, 1478 ["Eastern" refers to Korean. —Trans.]) by Sŏ Kŏjŏng, a collection of various works written from the Shilla period to the early Chosŏn period, is one of the most important collections of the early Chosŏn period. It comprises 154 books in 45 volumes. About six thousand handwritten and printed collections of literature and essays from the Chosŏn period exist today, reflecting the high level of interest on the part of the learned classes of that period in preserving ideas on paper.

In Confucian societies such as Korea's was at the time, literary scholarship was a necessary part of every writer's cultural development; it was also one of the most important things that a writer could leave to posterity. Writers started training in poetry after learning how to read Confucian classics using basic texts, such as *Selected Readings for Children* (Tongmong sŏnsŭp), and *Lesser Learning* (Korean: Sohak; Chinese: Xiaoxue). The purpose of this training was to enable them to write prose and poetry in classical Chinese for the rest of their lives. A writer became used to collecting and exchanging his writings with other writers and family members because he had to practice a great deal to become proficient enough to write socially acceptable messages to his teacher or parents. Through this active exchange of works by famous writers, both living and dead, literature spread rapidly among the elite. Because most collections of literature were published after the death of the writer, information about works by living writers was spread by word of mouth or by the direct exchange of works. This, however, did not work against the dissemination of works by living writers because many works were discussed and exchanged among the literati and their students. In many cases, students and descendants collected the writings of famous literati and, when the financial situation allowed, published them as collected works.

The Trade in and Commercial Lending of Handwritten Works in Hangŭl

Literature in vernacular Korean after the development of hangŭl in 1446 was, except for a few officially sponsored works, handwritten. The trade in handwritten literature depended on many copies being made of a single work and began with friends and relatives copying each other's books. As the number of people who could read hangŭl and the number of interesting works written in it increased, the trade and distribution of literature written in hangŭl entered a new phase, with the emergence of professional readers and book lenders in, it is believed by most scholars, the seventeenth century.

Like professional readers, book traders, also known as book lenders, began as amateurs who bought books to lend to readers for a fee. Book traders would wander from house to house, like other peddlers, reading interesting sections of books to the children of yangban and chungin families. They would then lend or sell several works to the family. *Record of Twenty Days* (Isun nok) by Ku Suhun relates an incident in which a lower class book trader raped the wife of a yangban after reading a story to her. Because many children of the yangban and chungin families were literate in hangŭl, they did not need someone else to read stories to them, and they bought or borrowed books from book traders without a reading. It is believed that Kim Manjung (1637–1692) wrote *A Dream of Nine Clouds* (Kuun mong, ca. 1689) for his mother after he had been banished to the countryside. If this is true, it is probable that his mother had acquired an interest in novels from having read novels she had borrowed or purchased.

Page from a handwritten (*p'ilsabon*) classic novel

The commercial trade in books was based on wandering book traders for a long time, but with increased urbanization and the rise in
readers at the end of the eighteenth and the beginning of the nineteenth
centuries, some of these book traders established bookstores. This is
important because it reflects two changes in society: improvements in
book production stimulated the production of and trade in literary
works; and with the development of market towns, more people, particularly men, came into contact with works of literature. This stimulated the creation of works that appealed to male readers. In addition,
bookstore owners needed to expand their markets, a need which contributed to the development of and trade in woodblock-printed novels.
This development will be discussed in the next section. The following
quotation from the introduction to *Bibliographie Coréenne* (*Hanguk
sŏji,* 1894); by Maurice Courant, a French diplomat who lived in Korea

from 1890 to 1892, gives a late but useful account of bookstores in the late Chosŏn period:

> Books are sold in many places other than the bookstores in the center of Seoul, which are known for selling important books. There are many book lenders who generally sell novels, either printed or handwritten copies. Most of these books are written in hangŭl. Most are printed on better paper and in clearer printing than that of books sold in bookstores. The charge to borrow these books is relatively low, usually about ten to twenty percent of the cost of buying the same book new. Sometimes books can be borrowed in exchange for certain household goods. Apparently, this type of business used to flourish in Seoul but it has declined in recent years. Koreans tell me that they have not heard of such lenders operating in provincial centers such as Songdo, Taegu, and P'yŏngyang. The profits from lending books are relatively low, but it is recognized as a respectable occupation, even to the point of attracting some fallen yangbans into the business.
>
> —translation by Pak Sanggyu

As this quotation indicates, books other than novels written in hangŭl—memoirs and collections of song, kasa, and yadam—may have been sold at bookstores, but we have no proof of this.

Professional novel readers emerged from the ranks of those who traveled with book traders from house to house. Those who became noted for their reading skills moved to marketplaces, where they would read on the street and collect money from the crowd. This type of professional reader, known as *chŏngisu,* had unique talents that helped them attract and hold audiences. According to a mid-eighteenth-century source, a man became so excited by a reading that he killed another reader at the market with a knife. From this, we can see that the content of the novel and the skill of the reader had a powerful influence over some members of the audience. The following passage from *Strange Stories of Ch'uje* (Ch'uje ki'i) by Cho Susam (1762–1849) describes well the life of a professional reader. The audience referred to was composed largely of men in the marketplace.

> Professional novel readers live outside Tongdaemun, the eastern gate of Seoul. They read popular novels such as *Tale of Sukhyang, Tale of So Taesŏng, Tale of Shim Ch'ŏng,* and *Tale of Sŏl Ingwi.* They rotate regularly throughout the city in a monthly cycle: under the first bridge

on the first day; under the second bridge on the second day; at Paeogae on the third day; at the well in Kyodong on the fourth day; at the well in Taesadong on the fifth day; in front of Chonggak on the sixth day. Because they bring the novels to life, they attract a large crowd. They pause before the climax of the story, waiting for donations before continuing. This is how they make their living.

The Development of Woodblock Printing and Publishing

As a result of the book trade and professional reading, the readership for novels grew, and the more and better-quality works were written. This increased demand caused the development of woodblock printing, a more efficient way of producing a large number of books than copying them by hand. Books printed with engraved woodblocks are called *panggakpon,* "woodblock-printed books." Woodblock-printed books, which were published and sold for profit by private book publishers, fell into the following three categories: (1) basic texts of Confucian philosophy, such as the *Thousand-Character Classic* (Ch'ŏnjamun; Chinese: Qianziwen), dictionaries (*ŏkp'yŏn*), *Selected Readings for Children* (Tongmong sŏnsŭp), histories (*sayak*), records (*t'onggam*), and Confucian classics (sa sŏ sam kyŏng; Chinese: san shu shi jing); (2) books with a practical application; and (3) novels written in hangŭl and classical Chinese. Before discussing woodblock-printed novels, we will explore the development of woodblock-printed books generally.

Although some scholars argue that woodblock-printed books were first produced during the Koryŏ period during the reign of King Sukchong (1095–1105) or in the early Chosŏn period during the reign of King Chungjong (1506–1544), they did not appear in wide circulation until the beginning of the seventeenth century, after the Imjin Wars and the Manchu invasions. The circulation of woodblock-printed books increased at this time for the following three reasons: (1) the demand for books had reached a level sufficient to sustain a publishing industry; (2) traders had enough capital to invest in such projects; and (3) artisans were freed from required service in official handicraft industries.

Of these three developments, the first reflects the weakening of the rigid social structure of the Chosŏn Dynasty and the growing social and economic clout of the commoner class. The loss of a large number of books during the Imjin Wars and the Manchu invasions also contributed to the demand for books in the period of recovery that followed. Official publication projects were launched as part of recovery measures, but they were not enough to make up for the losses. Many influential yangban in the countryside distributed privately published versions of important Confucian texts to meet the demand for books, and many of these books ended up in the hands of merchants, who then made woodblocks of them and printed large numbers for commercial sale. Several examples of woodblock-printed books from this time are the Chŏnju Sŏgye kae version of the *A Collection of Important Historical Writings* (Sayo ch'wisŏn, 1638), the Chŏnju version of *Selected Readings for Children* (Tongmong sŏnsŭp, 1654), the T'aein version of *A Handbook for Cultivation of the Mind* (Myŏngshim pogam, 1686) published by Sŏ Kijo, the Musŏng version of *Accurate Versions of Ancient Writing* (Komun chinbo, 1676) published by Chŏn Ich'ae, and *Handbook for Farmers* (Nongga chipsŏng, 1686) published by Chŏn Ich'ae and Pak Ch'iyu. Chŏn Ich'ae and Pak Ch'iyu are considered to be the first commercial publishers of woodblock-printed books. Chŏn and Pak were successful in commercial publishing because they had sufficient background to print and sell books from their experiences in trade and government service.

The second development has not been investigated in detail, but the general outlines are clear. According to the results of research on Korean economic history, the number of independent retail and wholesale merchants grew rapidly in the seventeenth century, and with the enactment of the Uniform Land Tax Law (*taedongbŏp*) in the middle of the seventeenth century, merchant activity increased greatly because it allowed government purchasing agents to accumulate capital. As a market economy based on money and commodities developed, some merchants thus entered the publishing business to meet the demands of an expanding readership.

After the collapse of official handicraft industries, artisans were free to apply their talents to other types of economic activity, which stimulated the growth of the commercial woodblock-printed-book industry. These artisans began to work as self-proprietary handicraft producers or as employees of other merchants; because the production of woodblock-printed books was complicated, and a considerable amount of skilled labor and time was required before a return could be realized a return on the initial investment, many artisans worked as employees for publishers, who had more capital than they did.

Beginning with this combination of demand, capital, and technical skill, the woodblock-printed-book industry spread throughout the country, Seoul, Chŏnju, Ansŏng, T'aein, and Naju becoming important publishing centers. Publishing of woodblock-printed books continued uninterrupted until the late nineteenth century in Seoul, Chŏnju, and Ansŏng. These centers of publication depended on a steady supply of wood and paper, a positive commercial environment, and a sufficient number of readers who were willing to buy books. All of the above areas met these conditions.

The quality of woodblock-printed books was not as high as that of official publications, publications by Confucian schools, and privately published books. The central government and wealthy yangban were able to spend large sums of money to purchase the best printing technology, but commercial publishers had to keep costs down to make a profit. Thus the size (based on the amount of paper needed), the clarity of the print, and the quality of the paper were usually not the best. Despite these limitations, woodblock-printed books were key in the history of Korean literature from the seventeenth to the nineteenth century. These books allowed written literature, which had been exclusively controlled by a small ruling elite, to reach a much larger reading public. The growth of the reading public eventually stimulated demands for change in the rigid social structure of the Chosŏn period. In particular, novels published as woodblock-printed books played an important role in the development of a critical approach to social issues in the late Chosŏn period.

The Development of Woodblock-Printed Novels

Most scholars believe that woodblock-printed novels were first produced in the early eighteenth century. The earliest written reference to a woodblock-printed novel is the Ŭlsa version (written in classical Chinese) of *A Dream of Nine Clouds,* which states that the book was printed by a commercial publisher near Nammun in Naju, South Chŏlla Province, in 1725. Because novels appeared later than Chinese classics or practical books, if the Ŭlsa version of *A Dream of Nine Clouds* was not the first, the earliest woodblock-printed novel was probably published sometime between the end of the seventeenth century and 1725.

Woodblock-printed novels in hangŭl first appeared later than this, but it is difficult to know exactly when. Most woodblock-printed novels, particularly novels written in hangŭl, contain little information about date and place of publication. Even when one is recorded, it is difficult to determine the date of publication for novels because most dates followed the *yukkap* system in which each year is designated by a combination of two Chinese characters that repeat themselves every 60 years. Most scholars believe that the oldest woodblock-printed novels in hangŭl are the Pyŏl version of *Tale of Ch'unhyang* (Pyŏl Ch'unhyang chŏn), published in 1846, and *Samsŏlgi* published in 1848. Assuming that woodblock-printed novels in classical Chinese appeared in the early eighteenth century, woodblock-printed novels in hangŭl probably appeared about a half century later, because they were more marketable. In an essay sharply criticizing the novel as a genre, Yi Tŏngmu (1741–1793) mentioned that some teachers at Confucian schools (*sŏdang*) in the countryside made woodblocks to sell to publishing houses. This is further evidence of the existence of woodblock-printed novels in the eighteenth century.

Woodblock-printed novels became commonplace and were printed in large numbers in the nineteenth century. Because many original woodblock-printed books were lost in the early years of the twentieth century, it is difficult to determine the exact number of woodblock-printed novels, but 179 were reprinted in *A Complete Collection of Woodblock-Printed Classic Novels* (Kososŏl panggakpon chŏnjip), edited by Kim Tonguk. Given this number, the total number was probably much larger. Most of the novels in this collection were written in hangŭl and published in the major publishing centers of Seoul, Chŏnju, and Ansŏng. Books published in Seoul, which were known as Kyŏngp'an, were mostly printed in cursive print. Many of Kyŏngp'an were abridged versions of the originals, elegant in content and style. Books published in Chŏnju, known as Wanp'an, were printed in easy-to-read block letters, and the content was more detailed than that of Kyŏngp'an. Ansŏngp'an, books published in Ansŏng, were similar to Kyŏngp'an regarding typeface and content but were generally considered to be inferior versions of them.

Despite regional differences, most readers of woodblock-printed books were probably women and children of the yangban and chungin class and men of the commoner class. Book distribution was diverse because most of these readers exchanged books with each other to copy or to read to each other, rather than buying books outright. In this process, deliberate and unconscious changes in wording and content create different versions of the same work that, in some cases, altered the work significantly. Not only were woodblock-printed books themselves based on a particular version of a work that may or may not have been the original, but various versions of works continued to develop even after a woodblock-printed version was published. This explains why seventy to eighty percent of extant versions of popular works, such as *Tale of Ch'unhyang, Tale of Hong Kildong, Tale of Shim Ch'ŏng,* and *Tale of Cho Ung,* are woodblock-printed books.

In the eighteenth and nineteenth centuries, professional writers who wrote and produced novels for profit emerged. As commercial publishing and the book trade developed in the nineteenth century, these professional book producers became very active. Except for a few yangban who particularly liked to write, most of these professional writers were yangban who had lost their family fortune or members of the chungin class.

Professional book producers at this time, however, differed greatly from professional writers of today. Because literature in hangŭl was open to anybody who could sell his or her work in the marketplace, writing and producing novels was not considered the creation of an autonomous artist. This was particularly true of woodblock-printed novels written exclusively for profit. Professional book producers could not escape the need to make money and when reprinting novels would abridge, expand, or embellish the original to fit the commercial demands of book production. In addition, book producers from the yangban class eschewed fame and would not sign their work because Confucian philosophy did not hold commercial activity in high esteem. Because writing and producing books is—despite some writers' assertion to the contrary—a projection of the writer's worldview through the plot and the characters while considering the needs of readers, more research on professional book producers of the yangban class in this period is needed.

While contributing greatly to the development of the novel in the late Chosŏn period, some professional book producers and writers successfully made the transition from the classic novel to the New Novel in the last years of the nineteenth century. The most prominent example is Yi Haejo, who built on his experience as a writer of classic novels to become one of the most skillful writers in the latter genre.

Profits from increased sales of novels in the late Chosŏn period were not equally divided between book producers and lenders of woodblock-printed books. Because the work was different, the type of influence that these industries exerted on the development of the novel was also different. Printing many copies of a limited number of works gave publishers the chance to make a steady profit from a set of woodblocks. It was easier to make a profit from five hundred copies of a single book than from five hundred total copies of three different books. Rather than seeking to expand their line of books, publishers of woodblock-printed books focused their efforts on publishing works that were highly marketable. Long novels were more expensive to produce and thus had a more limited readership, which meant that commercial publishers preferred short novels to long ones. These conditions worked against the publication of long novels, and long novels that were published were often abridged or otherwise shortened.

Book lenders, on the contrary, made more money by offering a wide list of books for loan. They also preferred long novels to short ones. Most readers who borrowed books would look for another interesting work to read after returning a book, and book lenders needed to have a wide selection of books available to satisfy their customers. In addition, long novels of several volumes brought book lenders great profits because they could charge separately for each volume, furthering the development of long novels. Book lenders thus had to acquire a great number of books, both handwritten and woodblock-printed, to compete with other book lenders, a fact which stimulated the lengthening of existing books. Of the extant versions of *Tale of Ch'unhyang,* the four-volume *Old Song From Namwŏn* (*Namwŏn kosa*) was a handwritten book in the collection of a book lender. The novels in the Naksŏnje collection, which range from works of a dozen or so volumes to some of a hundred-odd volumes, were distributed to the royal court through book lenders in the Seoul area.

Modern Printing Technology and the Diffusion of Literature

The introduction of modern Western printing technology toward the end of the nineteenth century suddenly and dramatically transformed the diffusion of literary works in Korean society. Because printing with lead type was faster and more economical, it quickly replaced woodblock printing. In addition, the trade in books expanded rapidly with modern transportation, more efficient distribution systems, and a surge in the number of readers. The "six-chŏn novel," which appeared in large numbers from 1900 onward, was a product of these changes. [A *chŏn* is a hundredth of a *wŏn*, the Korean unit of currency. —Trans.] Six-chŏn novels drew on the following four sources: woodblock-printed novels; lengthy handwritten novels, such as *Dream in a Royal Pavilion* (Wangnu mong); new versions of classical novels; and New Novels.

Newspapers, academic journals, and magazines, products of the new printing technology, opened the way for the broader transmission of traditional culture and stimulated the development of new types of literature that were in keeping with the needs of the times. Newspapers, which strongly favored Westernization; socially critical kasa and shijo; and genres such as changga, New Poetry, the New Novel, and historical and biographical novels all gained strength from improvements in printing technology. Stemming from the collapse of Chosŏn society, the decline of literature in classical Chinese and the rapid spread of hangŭl influenced the development of these forms, but the new printing technology allowed books to reach all levels of society for the first time in Korean history.

From this period until the present day, the printed form has had a near monopoly on the diffusion of literary works. Oral literature persisted, however, even after the development of modern printing technology. During the harsh years of Japanese rule, poor people in Korean society expressed their frustration and sense of hopelessness in folk songs and folk tales. Despite this, the collapse of traditional Korean society and ways of life combined with the growth of written literature meant that from this period onward literature was diffused primarily by means of printed forms. With the rise of contemporary visual media and attempts to transform literature into an interactive group process as opposed to solitary reading, the relationship between literature and books will no doubt change considerably in the future. But regardless of how it changes, literature, the art of language, will continue to be based on reading.

Looking at the forms of literary diffusion since the beginning of the twentieth century, we need to consider how books—regardless of the quality of the content were sold to the majority of readers. As unofficial publications, works of literature today are consumer products, because publishers produce books to sell to readers for a profit.

Obviously, this means that books that sell well realize a high profit for the publisher and the writer, a fact which itself is not negative. The question is, what benefit does this profit bring to readers? Through detailed description and lonely composition, poets and writers can present important issues in everyday life through creative form, or they can provide cheap sympathy and skillful deception in order to reach a wide readership. We thus need to realize that the structure of the diffusion of a literary work not only depends on the method and technology of diffusion, but is also closely connected to the popular appeal of the content of the work itself.

7

Phases of Korean Literature

People base their views of the future on their knowlege of past and present events. It is inevitable that they base their actions on a recognition of the world around them. This self-understanding, which is necessary for an individual or a group, manifests itself in introspective writing that examines the totality of temporal and spatial relationships. Seen from this perspective, Korean literature today is the product of all linguistic phenomena created by Koreans from the ancient past to the present. It also includes various related subjects that are close to and distant from literature.

In this discussion, if everything other than the self is referred to as "the other," then literature from the past is "the other" with regard to literature of today, and foreign literature is "the other" with regard to Korean literature. Without a thorough self-examination of the relationship between oneself and "the other," it is impossible to achive real self-understanding. Except for a few sections, this book has not yet paid much attention to the relationship between Korean literature and world literature. For a more complete understanding of Korean literature in the contemporary world, it is necessary to gain an understanding of one of the major debates concerning Korean literature today: the debate over the role of traditional Korean literature in the development of modern Korean literature.

Traditional and Modern Korean Literature

Korean literature written before the end of the nineteenth century is referred to as "traditional Korean literature" and literature written after that time as "modern Korean literature." The dichotamy between "traditional" and "modern" is not based on a detailed study of the history of Korean literature, but on common perceptions of the difference. Because this distinction is widely accepted for convenience in research on Korean literature, these two terms will be used in the following discussion. In looking at how the dichotomous view of Korean literary history has prevailed and at how this view affects our perspective today, we need to remain critical of the philosophical basis of this dichotomy.

Transcending the Dichotomous View of Korean Literature

The dichotomous view of Korean literary history is a problem not only in literature but also in the analysis of Korean history and culture. In the twentieth century, Korean society and culture underwent the most traumatic changes in all of Korean history. Amid these traumatic changes, it is natural to describe the period of change and the eras preceeding these changes with different terminology. Describing the differences between traditional and modern literature with different terminology does not mean a denial of the continuity between traditional and modern literature. Although significant qualitative and quanitative differences exist between various eras of history, these differences are based on the continuity of the history of the Korean people.

The danger of dividing Korean literature into traditional and modern is that it reflects the colonial view of Korean history which denied the significance of historical continuity through the value of traditional Korean culture. This view of Korean literary history is reflected in statements made by Yi Kwangsu (b. 1892) around 1915, such as the following: "We are a new people, without ancestors, without parents, that came from Heaven in the present." This view is also expressed by Ch'oe Chaesŏ (1908–1964) in the 1930s: "In terms of contemporary culture, our attitudes are dominated by those of Western culture and not by those from the Chosŏn period and before. . . . This will and must continue in the future."

From this point of view, traditional and modern Korean literature are two completely different types of literature that are foreign to each other. Traditional literature, the argument continues, is a dead literature that lost its vitality during the traumatic changes of the late nineteenth and early twentieth centuries. Imported from the West, modern literature is a completely new literature introduced to fill this void; traditional and modern literature are viewed as oil and water in the same bowl. This view of the Korean literary history was dominant until the end of the 1950s, when modern research on Korean literature emerged. Two representative histories of Korean literature based on this dichotomous view are *A Complete History of Korean Literature* (Kungmunhak chŏnsa, 1957) by Yi Pyŏnggi and Paek Ch'ŏl and the revised version of *The History of Korean Literature* (Kungmunhak sa, 1949; rev. ed. 1963) by Cho Yunje, which includes modern literature.

A reaction against this dichotomous view emerged in the early 1960s. At first this reaction centered on the debate over continuity and the discontinuity of traditional Korean culture. The rush toward economic development in the Third Republic (1962–1979), as exemplified by the phrase "modernization of the homeland," emphasized rapid industrial development, exacerbating negative views of traditional values and culture. In this atmosphere, the problem of traditional culture, which had perviously been mentioned intermittently, developed into a critique of the rapid changes in Korean society. This varied greatly from field to field but was based on a rejection of the negative view of Korean tradition and an affirmation of those positive aspects of traditional culture that could be applied creatively to the needs of modern society. Attempts to transcend colonial views of Korean history in modern Korean historiography also stimulated the reaction against the dichotomous view of the history of Korean literature.

Problems with Theories of Visible Continuity

The rapid growth of interest in "our culture" since the late 1960s, along with a reevaluation of traditional art and culture, was a natural outcome of the critique of modernization and industrialization that emerged in Korea in the 1960s. Researchers and literatry critics responded to this trend by focusing on the continuity of tradition in ancient and modern Korean literature in an attempt to overcome the limitations of the dichotomous view of the history of Korean literature.

In general, research was focused on finding traditional themes, plots, styles, narratives, rhythms, and meters in Korean literature written from the late nineteenth century to the present. It yielded many examples of how modern korean literature absorbed and appropriated various aspects of traditional Korean literature. This research contributed greatly to correcting the distortions in the history of Korean literature that emerged from the emphasis on the foreignness and newness of modern Korean literature, that was dominant in the blind acceptance of Western culture and the colonial view of Korean culture. This re-evaluation will no doubt continue as future research elucidates more examples of continuity between traditional and modern literature.

It is also naive to suggest that all previous distortion of Korean literatry history can be corrected by proof that continuity between traditional and modern literature exists. Korean literature has gone through dramatic changes and experienced numerous shocks from the late nineteenth century to the present and has been preoccupied with a creation of the self of which continuity with the past is only one major facet. Of course, revealing the weaknesses of the dichotomous view of it by discovering continuity of form, writer, and genre between traditional and modern literature contributes much to our understanding of the history of Korean literature. This should not, however, become an excuse for glossing over the dramatic changes in Korean literature that occured at the end of the nineteenth century and the beginning of the twentieth century.

What is needed urgently today is a multifaceted point of view that focuses on the change from traditional to modern literature by looking at continuity and discontinuity and appropriation and rejection in the relationship between the two. Attempts to define the life of a group of people in terms of a rigid dichotomy between continuity and discontinuity end up being a distortion. As long as we try to understand culture, which is abstract and intangible, we cannot unilaterally deny either continuity or discontinuity. Because of the limitations of language, we are forced to divide continuity and discontinuity, which are actually part of the same thing. Continuity without change means death, and change that is not rooted in continuity amounts only to a change of surface decoration.

We need to escape from the belief that continuity can only be understood in terms of visible continuity throughout various literary periods and between traditional and modern literature. Of course, continuity of form is an important part of continuity in Korean literature, and it is useful as a proof of deeper kinds of continuity regarding style, rhythm, structure, and theme. We need to be aware that a meaningful continuity exists among literary themes and concepts that appear to conflict with one another. The struggle between negation and affirmation is another form of historical continuity. Although it may seem an extreme example, Nietzsche's declaration that "God is dead" is an extension of the

Christian belief in the existence of one omnipotent god. It is therefore necessary to understand the role of Christianity in Western culture to understand Nietzsche's statement. Lu Xun's *The True Story of Ah Q* (A Q chŏngjŏn; Chinese: A Q zhengzhuan, 1921) and Baudelaire's *Les fleurs du mal* (Ak ŭi kkot; (English: Flowers of Evil, 1857) are clearly connected with the past but are not considered to have much continuity with previous forms of Chinese and French literature.

Toward Problematic Continuity: An Example

What does essential continuity that includes the issues discussed above mean? We will call this type of continuity *problematic continuity,* defined as "continuity that emerged from historical problems of everyday life regardless of surface conflicts or similarities."

When we understand the importance of problematic continuity in terms of the historical connection between traditional and modern literature, we are able to escape from the simplistic logic that divides continuity from discontinuity and rejection from affirmation. The relationship between traditional and modern Korean literature can be defined neither in terms of abrupt discontinuity, as those who deny the existence of intrinsic continuity argue, nor in terms of simple continuity of literary themes and devices, as those who attempt to refute this argument contend. Historical continuity, which continuously expands and brings about change, is one aspect of problematic continuity dominated by ways of expression that go beyond surviving themes and forms easily identifiable as "traditional."

The work of Yi Sang (1910–1937), the most "modern" poet of the 1930s, provides us with a good example of problematic continuity. In writings such as the narrative poem *A Crow's-Eye View* (Ogamdo, 1934) and the short stories "Wings" (Nalgae, 1936) and "Diary at the End of My Life" (Chongsaeng ki, 1937), Yi Sang established himself as an experimental avant-garde writer in modern and contemporary Korean literature. The influence of Western literary trends is clear in Yi's work because it contains many elements of Dadaism, surrealism, psychological references, and self-reflection, all of which were popular in the West at the time. On the surface, it is difficult to find themes, motifs, forms, and styles from traditional literature in Yi's work, which has none of the obvious elements from traditional literature that are found in the references to folk songs in the poetry of Kim Sowŏl and the p'ansori-style prose that appears in Ch'ae Manshik's *Peace Under Heaven* (T'aep'yǒng ch'ǒnha, 1938). Rather than dealing with the issue of tradition, Yi Sang attempts to flout the conventions of contemporary modern Korean literature. Does this mean that Yi Sang's work is an abberation that came out of nowhere? Does it mean that Yi Sang is an extraordinary individual who appeared by chance and who was strongly influenced by the Westernized Japanese avant-garde? The answer to both questions is clearly "no."

This does not mean, however, that Yi Sang's work reflects the language, narrative, and motifs of traditional Korean literature in ways that have gone unnoticed by scholars. *Ogamdo* is different not only from traditional narrative shijo such as *Twelve Songs of Tosan* (Tosan shibi kok, 1565) and "The Fisherman's Calendar" (Ŏbu sashi sa, 1651), but also from other modern poems, such as "Azaleas" (Chindallae kkot, 1925) and "To My Bedroom" (Na ŭi chimshil ro, 1923). Though it is admirable to look for traditional Korean literary characteristics in works that are different, we need to focus on problematic continuity—differences and similarities—when looking at works that are fundamentally different from an objective historical perspective.

Seen from this perspective, Yi Sang's work represents, in the broad context of Korean culture, the most extreme example of the rejection of Korean tradition in the process of modernization that sought to replace defunct traditional attitudes and morality with something entirely new.

In the foreword to the short story "Wings," Yi gave readers the following stern warning: "In any era, people are in despair. Despair gives birth to artistic talent, which, in turn, leads to more despair." As the second sentence shows, Yi's work is about the despair resulting from the failure to overcome general despair during the colonial period, that is, the failure of the movement to create a new society and culture in the wake of the collapse of traditional society in the late nineteenth century. Yi Sang's works thus express disgust for old customs that have lost their vitality, and contempt for superficial cultural forms and styles that have little connection with reality, and the self trapped in subjectivity and isolated from a world devoid of moral principle. These themes, which run through all of Yi's work, are not mere imitations of Western and Japanese avant-garde literature of the time. Rather, they are the products of self-examination stimulated by a distorted way of life, which was nurtured by the colonial urban environment that emerged after the collapse in the early twentieth century of traditional values that had dominated Korean culture for hundreds of years. Researching this topic and thematic changes in Korean literature from the sixteenth century to the twentieth century is a major project in its own right.

What is important here is not whether the above analysis of Yi Sang's work is valid or not, but rather the need for a new look at continuity and similarity in the history of Korean literature. Without an understanding of how literature relates to history, literary history amounts only to a detailed chronology of various periods. To transcend this simple approach, we need to go beyond the search for superficial resemblance to see how adaptation, change, reaction, and succession in the literature of each period in the history of Korean literature interrelate.

An understanding of traditional literature is necessary to gain a complete understanding of the place of modern literature in the overall history of literature. Thus, discussions of modern literature devoid of any understanding of what came before it are limited to a simplistic focus on modern features; research on traditional literature without adequate consideration of important debates in literary theory from the beginning of the twentieth century to the present is not relevant to contemporary debate. Investigating the problematic continuity between traditional and modern Korean literature will help us construct a complete picture of the overall development of Korean literature without falling into the traps of oversimplification and superficiality.

Glossary

Aeguk ka 愛國歌 National Anthem

Agi changsu chŏnsŏl 아기 장수 전설 Legend of the Boy General

Aidŭl poi 아이들 보이 Readings for Children

Ak ŭi kkot 惡의 꽃 Les fleurs du mal

Akchang kasa 樂章歌辭 A Collection of Courtly Songs

Akhak kwebŏm 樂學軌範 Canon of Music

An ŭi sŏng 雁의 聲 Cry of a Wild Goose

Anmin ka 安民歌 Song of Virtuous Rule

Anyang ch'an 安養讚 Song in Praise of Anyang

Arirang 아리랑 Arirang

Chagyŏngji Hamhŭng ilgi 慈慶志咸興日記 Diary of a Journey to Hamhŭng Province

Ch'an Kip'a rang ka 讚耆婆郎歌 Ode to the Hwarang Kip'a

Chang P'ung chŏn 張風傳 Tale of Chang P'ung

Changhan mong 長恨夢 Dream of Lasting Resentment

Changhwa hongyŏn chŏn 薔花紅蓮傳 Tale of Roses and Red Lotus Blossoms

Ch'angjak kwa pip'yŏng 創作과 批評 Creation and Criticism

Ch'angjo 創造 Creation

Changkki t'aryŏng 장끼타령 Ballad of a Male Pheasant

Changmich'on 薔薇村 Rose Village

Ch'asan p'ildam 此山筆談 Writings From this Mountain

Chayujong 自由鍾 Liberty Bell

Che 1-chang che 1-kwa 第1章 第1課 Chapter 1, Part 1

Che mangmae ka 祭亡妹歌 Requiem for My Sister

Chebong ch'un 再逢春 Reunion With Spring

Chindallae kkot 진달래꽃 Azaleas

Chinguk myŏngsan 鎭國名山 Songs of Famous Mountains

Chinju nanggun 晋州郎君 My Dear Husband From Chinju

Cho Ung chŏn 趙雄傳 Tale of Cho Ung

Choch'im mun 弔針文 Requiem for My Dead Needle

Ch'oe Pyŏngdo t'aryŏng 최병도 타령 Ballad of Ch'oe Pyŏngdo

Ch'oehu ŭi aksu 最後의 握手 The Last Handshake

Chŏkpyŏk ka 赤壁歌 Song of the Red Cliff

Cholgo ch'ŏnbaek 拙藁千百 Collection of Humble Writings

Ch'ondam hae'i 村談解이 Humorous Stories From the Country

Chŏngan kisa 田間記事 The State of the Fields

Chŏngbuwŏn 貞婦怨 Bitterness of a Faithful Wife

Ch'ŏngch'un 青春 Bloom of Youth

Ch'ŏngch'un kwabu chŏn 青春寡婦傳 Tale of a Young Widow

Ch'ŏnggang saja hyŏngbu chŏn 清江使者玄夫傳 Tale of the Turtle in Clear Water

Ch'ŏnggu yadam 青邱野談 A Collection of Yadam From Green Hill

Ch'ŏnggu yŏngŏn 青邱永言 Songs From Green Hill

Chŏng Kwajŏng kok 鄭瓜亭曲 Song of Chŏng Kwajŏng

Ch'ŏn Hŭidang shihwa 天喜堂詩話 Essays by Ch'ŏn Hŭidang

Chongsaeng ki 終生記 Diary at the End of My Life

Ch'ŏngsan pyŏlgok 青山別曲 Song of the Green Mountains

Ch'ŏngun chŏn 天君傳 Tales of the King of Heaven

Ch'ŏngun pongi 天君本紀 History of the King of Heaven

Ch'ŏngun yŏnŭi 天君演義 Record of the King of Heaven

Ch'ŏngung mongyurok 天宮夢遊錄 Record of a Dream Visit to the Heavenly Palace

Chŏngŭp-kun millanshi yŏhang ch'ŏngyo 井邑郡民亂時閭巷聽謠 Song of the Peasant Uprising in Chŏngŭp County

Chŏngŭp sa 井邑詞 Song of Chŏngŭp

Ch'ŏnjamun 千字文 Thousand-Character Classic

Ch'ŏnju konggyŏng ka 天主恭敬歌 Song in Praise of God

Chŏnshija chŏn 丁侍者傳 Tale of Mr. Walking Stick

Ch'ŏnsusŏk 泉水石 Ch'ŏngsusŏk

Chŏ saeng chŏn 楮生傳 Tale of Master Paper

Choshin mong 調信夢 Dream of Chosin

Chosŏn ch'anggŭk sa 朝鮮唱劇史 The History of Korean Dramatic Songs

Chosŏn mundan 朝鮮文壇 Chosŏn Literary World

Chosŏn munhak ŭi kaenyŏm 朝鮮文學의 概念 Concepts of Korean Literature

Chosŏn p'ung 朝鮮風 Chosŏn-style Poems

Chosŏnshi 朝鮮詩 Chosŏn Poems

Ch'ŏyong ka 處容歌 Song of Ch'ŏyong

Ch'uje ki'i 秋齊奇異 Strange Stories of Ch'uje

Chukkye pyŏlgok 竹溪別曲 Song of a Path in a Bamboo Forest

Chuk puin chŏn 竹夫人傳 Tale of Madame Bamboo

Chŭngbo munhŏn pigo 增補文獻備考 The New Reference Compilation of Documents on Korea

Ch'unghyo ka 忠孝歌 Song of Filial Piety

Chungyong 中庸 Doctrine of the Mean

Ch'unhyang chŏn 春香傳 Tale of Ch'unhyang

Ch'unmang 春望 Hoping for Spring

Ch'uwŏlsaek 秋月色 Color of an Autumn Moon

Hae 해 Sun

Hae egesŏ sonyŏn ege 海에게서 少年에게 From the Sea to Boys

Hae ka 海歌 Song to the Sea

Haedong kayo 海東歌謠 Songs From the East

Hak chi kwang 學之光 The Light of Scholarship

Haksan hanŏn 鶴山閑言 Random Notes From Haksan

Hallim pyŏlgok 翰林別曲 Song of the Confucian Scholars

Hangjin ki 亢進記 Diary of Resistance

Hanjung nok 閑中錄 Record From the Bottom of Sadness

Hanyang ka 漢陽歌 Song of Hanyang

Hapkangjŏng ka 合江亭歌 Song of Bitterness Toward the King

Hojil 虎叱 A Tiger's Rebuke

Hong Kildong chŏn 洪吉童傳 Tale of Hong Kildong

Hŏnhwa ka 獻花歌 Song of Offering Flowers

Hŏ saeng chŏn 許生傳 Tale of Yangban Hŏ

Hongyŏm 紅焰 Bright Red Flames

Hujŏn chinjak 後殿眞勺 Secret Lives at Court

Hŭk 흙 Soil

Hŭngbu chŏn 興甫傳 Tale of Hŭngbu

Hunmin chŏngŭm 訓民正音 Correct Sounds to Instruct the People

Hwajŏn ka 花煎歌 Song of Flower Cakes

Hwang Chini 黃眞伊 The Life of Hwang Chini

Hwanggye sa 黃鷄詞 Song of the Yellow Rooster

Hwanghon 黃昏 Twilight

Hwangjo ka 黃鳥歌 Song of Nightingales

Hwarang segi 花郎世紀 Chronicles of the Hwarang

Hwasan pyŏlgok 華山別曲 Song of Hwasan

Hwasa 花史 History of Flowers
Hwasŏng ilgi 華城日記 Diary From Hwasŏng
Hwawanggye 花王戒 The Flowers' Warning to the King
Hwa ŭi hyŏl 花의 血 Blood From Flowers
Hyangak chabyŏng 鄉樂雜詠 Poems About Folk Music
Hyesŏng ka 彗星歌 Song of the Comet
Hyo kyŏng 孝經 The Book of Filial Piety
Hyŏl ŭi nu 血의 淚 Tears of Blood
Hyŏn Sumun chŏn 玄壽文傳 Tale of Hyŏn Sumun
Hyŏn-ssi yangung ssangnin ki 玄氏兩雄雙麟記 History of the Two
    Branches of the Hyun Family
Ikchae chip 益齊集 The Collected Works of Ikchae
Ildong changyu ka 日東壯遊歌 Song of a Journey to the East
Illyŏmhong 一念紅 Tale of Strong Will
Im Kyŏngŏp chŏn 林慶業傳 Tale of Im Kyŏngŏp
Imjin nok 壬辰錄 Record of the Imjin Wars With Japan
Inhyŏn wanghu chŏn 仁顯王后傳 Tale of Queen Inhyŏn
Isun nok 二旬錄 Record of Twenty Days
Kaebyŏk 開闢 Genesis
Kammin ka 甲民歌 Song of the Peasant Army
Kangdo mongyurok 江道夢遊錄 Record of a Dream Visit to Kangdo
Kangnŭng maehwa t'aryŏng 강릉매화타령 Tale of Maehwa of Kangnŭng
Kangsang p'ungwŏl 江上風月 Song of Moon Watching
Karujigi t'aryŏng 가루지기 타령 Ballad of a Ghost's Revenge
Kashiri 가시리 Are You Leaving Now?
Katcha shinsŏn t'aryŏng 가짜 神仙 타령 Tale of a Fake Daoist Immortal
Kilshik 길식 Kilshik
Kim Pangul chŏn 金방울傳 Tale of Kim Pangul
Kim Yŏngil ŭi sa 金英一의 死 The Death of Kim Yŏngil
Kimun ch'onghwa 奇聞叢話 A Collection of Strange Stories
Kkoktukkakshi chŏn 꼭둑각시전 Tale of a Puppet
Kkot tugo 꽃두고 On Flowers
Kkŭt ŏmnŭn kangmul i hŭrŭne 끝없는 강물이 흐르네 The Endless River
Kkum hanŭl 꿈하늘 Sky of Dreams
Kŏch'ang ka 居昌歌 Song of Kŏchang
Koguryŏ pongi 高句麗本紀 The History of Koguryŏ
Komun chinbo 古文眞寶 Accurate Versions of Ancient Writing

Konghuin 공후인 Song of the Konghu Zither

Kongjinhoe 共進會 National Welfare Society

Kongmu toha ka 公無渡河歌 Song for My Drowned Husband

Kongbang chŏn 孔方傳 Tale of Mr. Coin

Koryŏ sa 高麗史 The History of Koryŏ

Kŏsa ka 居士歌 Song of a Market Bard

Kososŏl panggakpon chŏnjip 古小說 坊刻本全集 A Complete Collection of Woodblock-Printed Classic Fiction

Kosŭng chŏn 高僧傳 Tales of Eminent Monks

Kuji ka 龜旨歌 Song for the Turtle

Kuksun chŏn 麴醇傳 Tale of Sir Malt

Kuk sŏnsaeng chŏn 麴先生傳 Tale of Master Malt

Kumagŏm 驅魔劍 The Magic Sword

Kŭmgang kyŏng 金剛經 Diamond Sutra

Kŭmhwasa mongyurok 金華寺夢遊錄 Record of a Dream Visit to Kŭmhwa Temple

Kŭmo shinhwa 金鰲神話 Tales of Kŭmo

Kŭmsu hoeŭi rok 禽獸會議錄 Minutes From a Meeting of Animals

Kungmunhak chŏnsa 國文學全史 A Complete History of Korean Literature

Kungmunhak sa 國文學史 The History of Korean Literature

Kungmunhak t'ongnon 國文學通論 An Introduction to Korean Literature

Kŭngŭm sosŏl chŏja ŭi chuŭi 近今 小說著者의 注意 Recommendations for Writers of Contemporary Novels

Kunma taewang 軍馬大王 The Great King Kunma

Kŭnmul chin twi 큰물 진 뒤 After a Heavy Rain

Kŭnsŏn chiro ka 勸善指路歌 Song of the Way to Virtue

Kusamguk sa 舊三國史 The Old History of the Three Kingdoms

Kuun mong 九雲夢 A Dream of Nine Clouds

Kwandong pyŏlgok 關東別曲 Song of Kangwŏn Province

Kwanŭm ch'an 觀音讚 Song in Praise of Guanyin

Kwi ŭi sŏng 鬼의 聲 Voice of the Devil

Kyech'uk ilgi 癸丑日記 Diary of the Year Kyech'uk

Kyesŏ yadam 溪西野談 A Collection of Kyesŏ Yadam

Kyewŏn p'ilgyŏng chip 桂苑筆耕集 Writings From the Cinnamon Garden

Kyoyuk i pulhŭng imyŏn saengjon ŭl puldŭk 教育이 不興이면 生存을 不得 Education is Essential for Life

Kyuhan nok 閨恨錄 Record of Sad Days

Kyuhan　閨恨　Sad Days

Kyujung ch'iru chaengnon ki　閨中七友爭論記　A Debate Among a Woman's
　　Seven Best Friends

Kyunyŏ chŏn　均如傳　The Life of the Great Monk Kyunyŏ

Kyuwŏn ka　閨怨歌　Song of Resentment

Kyŏngbu ch'ŏldo norae　京釜鐵道 노래　Song of the Kyŏngbu Railway

Maehwa sa　梅花詞　Song of Plum Blossoms

Maengja　孟子　Mencius

Mango kangsan　萬古江山　Old Rivers and Mountains

Manjŏnch'un pyŏlsa　滿殿春 別詞　Spring Overflows the Pavilion

Manŏn sa　만언사　Song of Repentence

Mansebo　萬歲報　Independence News

Maŭi t'aeja　麻衣太子　Prince Maŭi

Mit'a ch'an　彌陀讚　Song in Praise of Amitābha

Mit'a kyŏng ch'an　彌陀經讚　Song in Praise of Amitābha's Teachings

Mo Chukchi rang ka　慕竹旨郎歌　Ode to the Hwarang Chukchi

Monggyŏl Ch'o-Han song　夢決楚漢訟　Song of War Between Chu and Han
　　China

Monggyŏn Che Kallyang　夢見諸葛亮　Dream of a Meeting With Che Kallyang

Muae　무애　Muae

Mujŏng　無情　Heartlessness

Mundŏk kok　文德曲　Song of Cultivating Virtue Through Literature

Munhak iran ha o　文學이란 何오　What is Literature?

Munhak kwa chisŏng　文學과 知性　Literature and Intelligence

Munye ship'yŏng　文藝時評　Critical Views on Literary Issues

Muo Yŏn haeng nok　戊午燕行錄　Record of a Journey to Yanjing in the
　　Year Muo

Musuk i t'aryŏng　武叔이타령　Ballad for Musuk

Muyŏngt'ap　無影塔　Shadowless Tower

Myŏji　墓地　The Grave

Myŏngju powŏlbing　明珠寶月聘　Treasure of Bright Pearls in the Moonlight

Myŏngshim pogam　明心寶鑑　A Handbook for Cultivation of the Mind

Nakchŏn tŭngun　落泉登雲　Falling Spring and Rising Clouds

Nakhwa　落花　Falling Blossoms

Nalgae t'aryŏng　날개타령　Ballad of Wings

Nalgae　날개　Wings

Nalli ka　날리가　Song of an Uprising

Namga ki　南柯記　Account of the Southern Branch

Namhae mungyŏn nok 南海聞見錄 Record of the Sights Across the South Sea

Namhun t'aep'yŏng ka 南薰太平歌 Song of the Peaceful Scent From the South

Namwŏn kosa 南原古詞 Old Song From Namwŏn

Namyŏmbuju chi 南炎浮州志 Account of the Southern Continent of Jambūdvīpa

Nanggaek ŭi shinnyŏn manp'il 浪客의 新年漫筆 Random New Year's Notes by a Wanderer

Na ŭi ch'imshil ro 나의 寢室로 To My Bedroom

Nap ssi ka 納氏歌 Song of Nayacu

Noch'ŏnyŏ ka 노처녀가 Song of a Spinster

Nongga chipsŏng 農家集成 Handbook for Farmers

Nongmu 농무 Farmers' Dances

Nonguk ungwan munhak 論國運關文學 Treatise on the Relationship Between Literature and the Future of the Nation

Nuhang sa 陋巷詞 In Praise of Poverty

Nŭngŏm kyŏng 能嚴經 Sūrāmàma-sūtra

O Yuran chŏn 烏有蘭傳 Tale of O Yuran

Ŏbu sashi sa 漁父四時詞 The Fisherman's Calendar

Ogamdo 烏瞰圖 Crows-Eye View

Ŏmyŏn kok 儼然曲 Song of Majesty

Ŏmyŏnsun 禦眠楯 A Collection of Humorous Stories

Ong Kojip chŏn 雍固執傳 Tale of Stubborn Mr. Ong

Ongnu mong 玉樓夢 Dream in a Royal Pavilion

Oryun ka 五倫歌 Song of the Five Morals

Ŏsu shinhwa 禦睡新話 A Collection of Humorous Tales

Ŏu yadam 於于野談 A Collection of Ŏu Yadam

Paekcho 白潮 White Tide

Paekku sa 白鷗詞 Song of the Gull

Pae pijang t'aryŏng 裵裨將타령 The Ballad of General Pae

P'aerim 稗林 Forest of Stories

P'ahan chip 破閑集 Jottings to Relieve Idleness

Pak Ch'ŏmji norŭm 박첨지 노름 Pak Ch'ŏmji Puppet Play

Pak ssi chŏn 朴氏傳 Tale of Lady Pak

Pak Tol ŭi chugŭm 朴돌의 죽음 The Death of Pak Tol

Panyu ka 般遊歌 Song of Making Merry

Pari kongju 바리公主 Princes Pari

Pinbu 貧富 The Rich and the Poor

Pinch'ŏ 貧妻 Poor Wife

Pingonja ŭi muri 貧困者의 無理 Overworking the Poor

P'i saeng mongyurok 皮生夢遊錄 Record of Yangban P'i's Dream
　　Adventure

Pŏdŭnamu sŏn tongni p'unggyŏng 버드나무 선 동리 풍경 Scenes of a
　　Town Surrounded by Willow Trees

Pohan chip 補閑集 Jottings in Idleness

Pohyŏn shipchong wŏnwangsaeng ka 普賢十種願往生歌 Songs of the Ten
　　Vows of Samantabhadra

Pŏphwa kyŏng 法華經 Lotus Sutra

Pori t'ajak norae 보리타작 노래 Song of Threshing Barley

Poŭn kiurok 報恩奇遇錄 Record of Repaying Gratitude

Ppaeatkin tŭl edo pom ŭn onŭnga 빼앗긴 들에도 봄은 오는가 Will Spring
　　Come to My Stolen Field?

Pukch'ŏn ka 北遷歌 Song of an Exile in the North

Pulgwi 不歸 No Return

Pulgŭn chŏgori 붉은 저고리 Red Chŏgori

Pulhyo ch'ŏnbŏl 不孝天罰 Heaven Punishes the Unfilial

P'ungyo 風謠 Ballad

P'yehŏ 廢墟 Ruins

P'yobonshil ŭi ch'ŏnggaeguri 標本室의 靑개구리 A Green Frog in a Science
　　Lab

Saebyŏl 새별 New Stars

Sahach'on 寺下村 A Village before the Temple

Sa miin kok 思美人曲 Song to My Love

Sa mo kok 思母曲 Song of Maternal Love

Samdae 三代 Three Generations

Samdaemok 三代目 The Collection From the Three Kingdoms

Samguk chi 三國志 Tale of the Three Kingdoms

Samguk sagi 三國史記 The History of the Three Kingdoms

Samguk yusa 三國遺事 Memorabilia of the Three Kingdoms

Samsŏlgi 三說記 Samsŏlgi

Samsŏng taewang 三成大王 Song of the Great King Samsŏng

Samsŏn ki 三仙記 Diary of Three Daoist Immortals

Sang ch'un kok 賞春曲 Song to Welcome Spring

Sangdae pyŏlgok 霜臺別曲 Song of the Censor

Sangjŏ ka 相杵歌 Song of Threshing Rice

Sangnoksu 常綠樹 An Evergreen

Sangsa pyŏlgok 想思別曲 Song for My Last Love

Sanhwa kongdŏk ka 散花功德歌 Song of Offering Flowers Before Buddha

Sanjung shingok 山中新曲 New Songs From the Mountains

Sansŏng ilgi 山城日記 Diary from Sansŏng

Sanyuhwa 山有花 Flowers in the Mountains

Sasu mongyurok 泗水夢遊錄 Record of a Dream Visit to Sasu

Segye ilju ka 世界 一周歌 Song of a Trip Around the World

Sejong shillok chiri chi 世宗實錄 地理志 Veritable Records of King Sejong

Set'ak shinsŏl 洗濯 新設 Opening a Laundry

Shibyŏn 시변 Different Types of Poetry

Shi kyŏng 詩經 The Book of Songs

Shihwa ch'ongnim 詩話叢林 A Comprehensive Collection of Essays on
    Poetry

Shijip sari norae 시집살이 노래 Song of a Newlywed

Shim Ch'ŏng chŏn 沈淸傳 Tale of Shim Ch'ŏng

Shimunhak 詩文學 Poetic Literature

Shin arirang 신아리랑 New Arirang

Shindo ka 新都歌 Song of the New Capital

Shinjip 新集 Shinjip

Shin ŭigwan ch'angŭi ka 申議官倡義歌 Song to Soothe Officer Shin

Ship kyemyŏng ka 十誡命歌 Song of the Ten Commandments

Shiyong hyangakpo 時用鄉樂譜 Musical Scores for Songs and Poems

Sonyŏn 少年 Youth

So 소 The Water Buffalo

Sŏ Taeju chŏn 鼠大州傳 Tale of Sŏ Taeju, the Rat

So Taesŏng chŏn 蘇大成傳 Tale of So Taesŏng

Sŏ Tongji chŏn 鼠同知傳 Tale of Sŏ Tongji, the Rat

Sŏbang ka 西方歌 Song of the Western Paradise

Sŏbuk hakhoebo 西北學會報 Journal of the Northwest Association

Sŏdong yo 薯童謠 Song of Sŏdong

Sŏgyŏng pyŏlgok 西京別曲 Song of Sŏgyŏng

Sohak 小學 Lesser Learning

Sohwa ship'yŏng 小華詩評 Essays on Korean Poetry in Classical Chinese

Sok miin kok 續美人曲 Second Song to My Love

Sŏkpo sangjŏl 釋譜詳節 The Life of Buddha

Sŏnghwangban 城隍飯 Offering Rice at the Village Altar

Sŏngsan pyŏlgok 星山別曲 Songs of Sŏngsan

Sŏok ki 鼠獄記 Record of a Rat's Trial

Sŏsa kŏngukchi 瑞士建國志 Record of Swiss Independence

Sŏwang ka 西往歌 Song of a Journey West

Sŏyu kyŏnmun 西遊見聞 Things Seen and Heard on a Journey to the West

Ssanghwajŏm 雙花店 A Mandu Shop

Suborok 受寶錄 Upon Receiving This Auspicious Diagram

Sugung ka 水宮歌 Song of the Water Palace

Sugyŏng nangja chŏn 淑英娘子傳 Tale of the Maiden Sugyŏng

Sukhyang chŏn 淑香傳 Tale of Sukhyang

Sushim ka 愁心歌 Song of Melancholy

Susŏng chi 愁城志 Record of Victory Over Worry

Taedong kimun 大東奇聞 Strange Stories From the Great East

Taedong p'ungyo 大東風搖 Collected Poems From the East

Taedong yasŭng 大東野乘 Popular History of the Great East

Taehak 大學 Great Learning

Taegwanjae mongyurok 大關齋夢遊錄 Record of a Dream Visit to Taegwanjae

Taehan chaganghoe wŏlbo 大韓自強會月報 Korean Self-Strengthening Society Monthly

Taehan maeil shinbo 大韓每日新報 The Korea Daily News

T'aegŭk hakpo 太極學報 T'aegŭk Journal

T'aep'yŏng ch'ŏnha 太平天下 Peace Under Heaven

T'aep'yŏng hanhwa kolgye chŏn 太平閑話滑稽傳 Peaceful and Humorous Stories for Leisure

Talch'ŏn mongyurok 達天夢遊錄 Record of a Dream Visit to Talch'ŏn

T'angnyu 濁流 Muddy Waters

Tanjang ka 斷腸歌 Song of a Broken Heart

Todong kok 道東曲 Song of Todong

Toijang ka 悼二將歌 Chant for Two Great Generals

T'okki chŏn 토끼전 Tale of the Tortoise and the Hare

T'omak 土幕 Mud Wall

Tongch'ŏn 동천 Winter Heaven

Tongdong 動動 Tongdong

Tongguk shigye hyŏngmyŏng 東國詩界革命 For a Revolution in Eastern Poetry

Tongguk Yi sangguk chip 東國李相國集 Collected Works of Minister Yi of Korea

Tongguk yŏji sŭngnam　東國輿地勝覽　An Augmented Survey of the
　　Geography of Korea
Tongin shihwa　東人詩話　Essays on Poetry by Easterners
Tongmong sŏnsŭp　童蒙先習　Readings for Children
Tongmun sŏn　東文選　Eastern Literary Anthology
Tongmyŏng wang p'yŏn　東明王篇　The Lay of King Tongmyŏng
Tongnak p'algok　獨樂八曲　Songs of Lonely Pleasure
Tongnip ka　獨立歌　Song to Independence
Tongnip shinmun　獨立新聞　The Independent
Tongya hwijip　東野彙集　A Collection of Yadam From the Eastern Field
Tosan shibi kokpal　陶山十二曲跋　Postscript to the Twelve Songs of Tosan
Tosan shibi kok　陶山十二曲　Twelve Songs of Tosan
Tosol ka 兜率歌　Song of Tuṣita Heaven
Tosu sa　道修辭　Song of Perfecting Buddha's Way
Tushi ŏnhae　杜詩諺解　Annotated Poems of Du Fu
Tyot'yŏn nok　됴텬록　A Record of an Official Visit to China
Ubu ka　愚夫歌　Song of Three Foolish Men
Ŭiyudang ilgi　意幽堂日記　Diary of Ŭiyudang
Ujung haengin　雨中行人　A Wanderer in the Rain
Ŭndae chip　銀臺集　A Collection From the Silver Pavilion
Unmyŏng　運命　Fate
Ŭnsegye　銀世界　Silver World
Unsu choŭn nal 운수 좋은 날 A Lucky Day
Wang o ch'ŏnch'ukkuk chŏn　往五天竺國傳　Record of a Journey to Five
　　Indian Kingdoms
Wŏngak kyŏng　圓覺經　Màhāvaipulya-pūrnabuddha-sūtra-prasannārtha-sūtra
Wŏn ka　怨歌　Song of Regret
Wŏn saeng mongyurok　元生夢遊錄　Record of Yangban Wŏn's Dream
　　Adventure
Wŏnwang saeng ka　願往生歌　Prayer to Amitābha
Wŏrin ch'ŏngang chi kok　月印千江之曲　Songs of the Moon Reflecting a
　　Thousand Rivers
Yakhanja ŭi sŭlpŭm　弱한者의 슬픔　Sadness of a Weak Woman
Yangban chŏn　兩班傳　Tale of Yangban Ho
Yangshin hwadap ka　良辰和答歌　Song for My Lucky Day
Yi Ch'unp'ung chŏn　李春風傳　Tale of Yi Ch'unp'ung
Yijo hanmun tanp'yŏn chip　李朝漢文短篇集　Anthology of Short Stories in
　　Classical Chinese of the Chosŏn Period

Yiŏn   俚諺   Songs From Everyday Life
Yiŏn in   俚諺引   Introductory Essays on Songs From Everyday Life
Yŏgong p'aesŏl   櫟翁稗說   Tales of Yŏgong
Yŏlha ilgi   熱河日記   Rehe Diary
Yŏn haeng ka   燕行歌   Song of a Journey to Yanjing
Yŏn hyŏngje kok   宴兄弟曲   Song of a Banquet for My Brothers
Yongbi ŏch'ŏn ka   龍飛御天歌   Songs of Flying Dragons
Yongbu ka   庸婦歌   Song of a Foolish Wife
Yongdam yusa   龍潭遺詞   Song of the Dragon's Lotus Pond
Yonggung puyŏn nok   龍宮赴宴錄   Record of a Banquet in the Dragon Palace
Yu Ch'ungnyŏl chŏn   劉忠烈傳   Tale of Yu Ch'ungnyŏl
Yugi   留記   Yugi
Yukchabaegi   육자배기   Yukchabaegi
Yukhyŏlp'o kangdo   六穴砲強盜   Armed Robbery
Yuŏn   遺言   A Dying Wish
Yuk hyŏn ka   六賢歌   Song of Six Sages
Yusan ka   遊山歌   Song of Making Merry in the Mountains

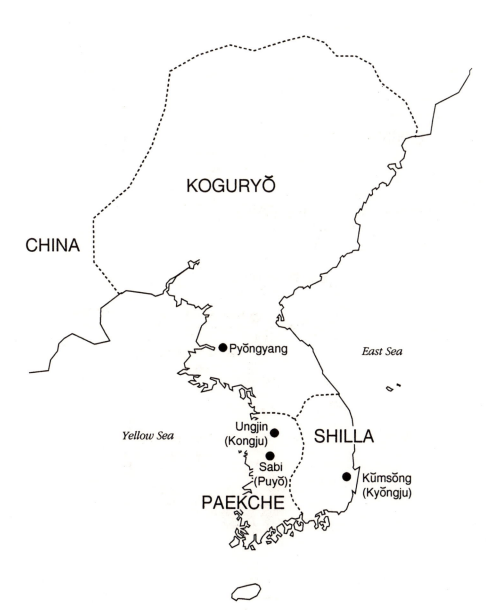

The Three Kingdoms in the fifth century A.D.

CHINA

KORYŎ

● Sŏgyŏng
(Pyŏngyang)

● Kaegyŏng
(Kaesŏng)

East Sea

● Namgyŏng
(Seoul)

Yellow Sea

Tonggyŏng ●
(Kyŏngju)

The Koryŏ Dynasty: 918–1392

CHINA

CHOSŎN

East Sea

● Hansŏng
(Seoul)

Yellow Sea

The Chosŏn Dynasty: 1392–1910

CHINA

NORTH
KOREA

● Pyŏngyang

Demilitarized Zone

East Sea

Yellow Sea

● Seoul

SOUTH
KOREA

Contemporary Korea since 1953

Select Bibliography

The original Korean edition of *Understanding Korean Literature* (Hanguk munhak ŭi ihae) contains a lengthy bibliography of works in Korean for further reference, which Professor Kim limited to books and noted articles relating to topics covered in that text, and which was intended to direct readers to more detailed works on specific areas of interest.

The following bibliography lists important works on, and translations of, Korean literature in Western languages and is an abridged version of the original Korean bibliography, both of which provided valuable background information to the translator. Like Professor Kim's original bibliography, the one provided here is designed to lead readers to important works in which they may find more detailed information. A considerable number of translations of modern Korean literature are available in Western languages, but only collections that relate to the contents of *Understanding Korean Literature* appear here. important periodicals, bibliographies, and works on Korea that contain references to Korean literature have been included to direct readers to additional sources.

Books and Articles in Western Languages

Bouchez, Daniel. "Les peregrinations de Dame Xie dan le Sud: Étude sur un roman coréen." Doctoral diss., Université de Paris 7, 1975.

Ch'ae Man-Sik. *Peace Under Heaven: A Modern Korean Novel.* Translated by Chun Kyung-Ja. Armonk, N.Y.: M.E. Sharpe, 1993.

Cho, Oh-kon, comp. and trans. *Traditional Korean Theater.* Berkeley: Asian Humanities Press, 1988.

Choe, Ikhwan. "Form and Correspondence in the Sijo and the Sasŏl Sijo." *Korean Studies* 15 (1991): 67–82.

Chung, Chong-Hwa, ed. *Korean Classical Literature: An Anthology.* London: Kegan Paul International, 1989.

Eckardt, Andre. *Geschichte der Koreanischen Literatur.* Stuttgart: W. Kohlhammer, 1968.

Fulton, Bruce, and Ju-chan Fulton, comps. and trans. *Words of Farewell: Stories by Korean Women Writers.* Seattle: Seal Press, 1989.

Haboush, Jahyun, trans. *The Memoirs of Lady Hyegyŏng.* Berkeley: University of California Press, 1996.

Howard, Keith. *Bands, Songs, and Shamanistic Rituals: Folk Music in Korean Society.* Seoul: Royal Asiatic Society, Korea Branch, 1989.

Hwang, Sun-wŏn. *Shadows of a Sound: Stories by Hwang Sun-wŏn.* Translated by Martin J. Holman. San Francisco: Mercury Press: 1990.

―――. *The Descendants of Cain.* Translated by Suh Ji-moon. Armonk, N.Y.: M.E. Sharpe, 1997.

Kim, Donguk. *History of Korean Literature.* East Asian Cultural Series 20. Translated by Leon Hurvitz. Tokyo: Centre for East Asian Cultural Studies, Tokyo University, 1980.

Kim, Han-Kyo, ed. *Studies on Korea: A Scholar's Guide.* Honolulu: University of Hawaii Press, 1980.

Kim, Jaihuin, comp. and trans. *Contemporary Korean Poetry.* Oakville, Ontario: Mosaic Press, 1994.

Kim, Kichung. *An Introduction to Classical Korean Literature: From Hyangga to P'ansori.* Armonk, N.Y.: M.E. Sharpe, 1996.

Kim, So-un. *The Story Bag.* Tokyo: Tuttle, 1967.

Ko, Won, comp. and trans. *Contemporary Korean Poetry.* Iowa City: University of Iowa Press, 1970.

Konishi, Jin'ichi. *A History of Japanese Literature.* Vols. 1–3. Translated by Aileen Gatten, Mark Harbinson, and Nicholas Teele; edited by Earl Miner. Princeton: Princeton University Press, 1984–1991.

Korean Culture and Arts Foundation. *Who's Who in Korean Literature.* Elizabeth, N.J.: Hollym International, 1996.

Korean National Commission for UNESCO. *Synopses of Korean Novels: Reader's Guide to Korean Literature.* Seoul: Korean National Commission for UNESCO, 1972.

―――, ed. *Modern Korean Short Stories.* 10 vols. Seoul: The Si-sa-yong-o-sa Publishing Company, 1983.

―――. *Korea Journal: Index 1961–1991.* Seoul: Korean National Commission for UNESCO, 1991.

Kuh, K.S., ed. *Koreanische Literatur: Ausgewhälte Erzählungen.* 2 vols. Bonn: Bouvier, 1986.

Ledyard, Gari. "The Korean Language Reform of 1446: The Origin, Background, and Early History of the Korean Alphabet." Ph.D. diss., University of California, Berkeley, 1966.

Lee, Ann. "Yi Kwangsu and Korean Literature: The Novel Mujŏng (1917)." *Journal of Korean Studies* 8 (1992): 81–137.

Lee, Ki-baik. *A History of Korea.* Translated by Edward W. Wagner with Edward J. Shultz. Cambridge: Harvard University Press, 1984.

Lee, Peter, H. *Kranich am Meer: Koreanische Gedichte.* Munich: Carl Hanser, 1959.

―――. *Studies in the Saenaennorae: Old Korean Poetry.* Rome: Istituto Italiano per il Medio ed Estremo Oriente, 1959.

―――. *Korean Literature: Topics and Themes.* Tucson: University of Arizona Press, 1965.

————. *Lives of Eminent Korean Monks.* Cambridge, Mass.: Harvard University Press, 1969.

————. *Songs of Flying Dragons: A Critical Reading.* Cambridge, Mass.: Harvard University Press, 1975.

————. *Celebration of Continuity: Themes in Classic East Asian Poetry.* Cambridge, Mass.: Harvard University Press, 1979.

————, ed. *The Silence of Love: Twentieth Century Korean Poetry.* Honolulu: University of Hawaii Press, 1980.

————, comp. and trans. *Anthology of Korean Literature: From Early Times to the Nineteenth Century.* Honolulu: University of Hawaii Press, 1981.

————, trans. *A Korean Storyteller's Miscellany: The P'aegwan Chapki of O Sukkwŏn.* Princeton: Princeton University Press, 1989.

————, ed. *Modern Korean Literature: An Anthology.* Honolulu: University of Hawaii Press, 1990.

————, trans. *Pine River and Lone Peak: An Anthology of Three Chosŏn Dynasty Poets.* Honolulu: University of Hawaii Press, 1991.

————, ed. *Sourcebook of Korean Civilization.* 2 vols. New York: Columbia University Press, 1993–1996.

Maurus, Partrick. "Nationalismes et modernité: La mutation de la poésie coréene moderne, 1894–1908–1927." Doctoral diss., Université de Paris 7, 1994.

McCann, David R. *Form and Freedom in Korean Poetry.* Leiden: E.J. Brill, 1988.

Myers, Brian. *Han Sorya and North Korean Literature: The Failure of Socialist Realism in the DPKR.* Ithaca, N.Y.: East Asia Program, Cornell University, 1994.

National Academy of Arts, Republic of Korea. *Survey of Korean Arts: Literature.* Seoul: 1970.

————. *Survey of Korean Arts: Folk Arts.* Seoul: 1974.

O'Rourke, Kevin, trans. *A Washed-out Dream.* Larchmont, NY: Larchwood Publications, 1980.

————, trans. *The Cutting Edge: A Selection of Korean Poetry, Ancient and Modern.* Seoul: Yonsei University Press, 1982.

————, trans. *Singing Like a Cricket, Hooting Like an Owl: Selected Poems of Yi Kyu-bo.* Ithaca, N.Y.: Cornell East Asia Program, Cornell University, 1995.

Orange, Marc, and Su-chung Kim, trans. *Histoire de Dame Pak, Histoire de Sukhyang.* Paris: l'Asiathèque, 1982.

Park, On-Za. *A Bibliography of Korean Literature in English or Translated into English.* Seoul: Hanshin Publishing Co., 1993.

Pihl, Marshall R. "Engineers of the Human Soul: North Korean Literature Today." *Korean Studies* 1 (1977): 63–110.

————. *The Korean Singer of Tales.* Cambridge, Mass.: Council of East Asian Studies, Harvard University and the Harvard-Yenching Institute, 1994.

Pihl, Marshall, Bruce Fulton, and Ju-chan Fulton, comps. and trans. *Land of Exile: Contemporary Korean Fiction.* Armonk, N.Y.: M.E. Sharpe, 1993.

Rutt, Richard. *The Bamboo Grove: An Introduction to Sijo.* Berkeley: University of California Press, 1971.

————. "Traditional Korean Poetry Criticism." *Transactions of the Korea Branch of the Royal Asiatic Society* 47 (1972): 105–143.

Rutt, Richard, and Chong-un Kim, trans. *Virtuous Women: Three Masterpieces of*

Traditional Korean Fiction. Seoul: Korean National Commission for UN-ESCO, 1974.

Skillend, W. E. *Kodae Sosŏl: A Survey of Traditional Korean Style Popular Novels.* London: School of Oriental and African Studies, University of London, 1968.

So Chong Ju. *Midang: The Early Lyrics of So Chong Ju.* Translated by Brother Anthony of Taize. London: Forest Books, 1993.

Solberg, Sammy Edward. "The Nim-ui Chimmuk (Your Silence) of Han Young-un: A Korean Poet." Ph.D. diss., University of Washington, 1971.

Suh, Ji-moon, comp. and trans. *The Rainy Spell and Other Korean Stories*, revised and expanded ed. Armonk, N.Y.: M.E. Sharpe, 1997.

Sym, Myung-ho. *The Making of Early Modern Korean Poetry.* Seoul: Seoul National University Press, 1982.

Walraven, Boudewijn. *Songs of the Shaman: The Ritual Chants of the Korean Mudang.* London: Kegan Paul International, 1994.

Yu, Beongcheon. *Han Yong-Un and Yi Kwang-Su: Two Pioneers of Modern Korean Literature.* Detroit: Wayne State University Press, 1992.

Zong, In-sob. *Folk Tales from Korea.* London: Routledge and Kegal Paul, 1952.

Periodicals in English

The following magazines and journals often run articles on and translations of traditional and contemporary Korean literature:

Journal of Asian Studies, Journal of Korean Studies, Korea Journal, Koreana, Korean Culture, Korean Studies, Manoa, Muae, Transactions of the Korea Branch, of the Royal Asiatic Society.

Books in Korean

Ch'oe Tongsŏk. *Hyŏndae shi ŭi chŏngshin sa* [History of Ideas in Modern Korean Poetry]. Seoul: Yŏrŭmsa, 1985.

Ch'oe Tongwŏn. *Koshijo yŏngu* [A Study of Shijo]. Seoul: Hyŏngsŏl ch'ulp'ansa, 1977.

Chŏng Chaeho. *Hanguk kasa munhak sa ron* [Theories of the History of Korean Kasa Literature]. Seoul: Chimmundang, 1982.

Chŏng Pyŏnguk. *Hanguk kojŏn shiga ron* [Theories of Traditional Korean Poetry]. Seoul: Shingu munhwasa, 1977.

Chang Tŏksun. *Hanguk sŏlhwa munhak yŏngu* [A Study of Korean Myths]. Seoul: Seoul National University Press, 1970.

——. *Hanguk sup'il munhak sa* [History of Korean Essay Literature]. Seoul: Saemunsa, 1983.

Chang Tŏksun, et al. *Hanguk munhak sa ŭi chaengjŏm* [Controversies in Korean Literary History]. Seoul: Chimmundang, 1986.

Chang Yangwan. *Chosŏn hugi hanshi yŏngu* [A Study of Late Chosŏn Period Poetry in Classical Chinese]. Ch'unch'ŏn: Sŏngshim Women's University Press, 1983.

Cho Kyusŏl and Pak Ch'ŏlhŭi, eds. Shijo ron [Theories of Shijo]. Seoul: Iljogak, 1978.

Cho Tongil. *Hanguk sosŏl ŭi iron* [Theories of the Korean Novel]. Seoul: Chishik sanŏpsa, 1971.

——. *T'alch'um ŭi yŏksa wa wŏlli* [Mask Dance: History and Principles]. Seoul: Hongsŏngsa, 1978.

——. *Hanguk munhak sasang sa shiron* [Theoretical Views of Traditional Korean Literary Thought]. Seoul: Chishik sanŏpsa, 1979.

——. *Hanguk munhak t'ongsa* [Comprehensive History of Korean Literature], 3rd ed. 5 vols. Seoul: Chishik sanŏpsa, 1994.

Cho Yunje. *Hanguk shiga sagang* [A Historical Overview of Korean Poetry]. Seoul: Ŭlsŏ munhwasa, 1954.

——. *Hanguk munhak sa* [History of Korean Literature]. Seoul: Tongguk munhwasa, 1965.

Hwang P'aegang, Kim Yongjik, Cho Tongil, and Yi Tonghwan, eds. *Hanguk munhak yŏngu immun* [An Introduction to the Study of Korean Literature]. Seoul: Chishik sanŏpsa, 1982.

Im Tonggwŏn. *Hanguk minyo yŏngu* [A Study of Korean Folk Songs]. Seoul: Sŏnmyŏng munhwasa, 1974.

In Kwŏnhwan. *Koryŏ shidae ŭi pulgyoshi yŏngu* [Research on Koryŏ-Period Buddhist Poetry]. Seoul: Minjok munhwa yŏnguso, Korea University, 1983.

Kang Hanyŏng. *P'ansori* [P'ansori]. Seoul: Sejong taewang kinyŏm saŏphoe, 1977.

Kim Hŭnggyu, *Munhak kwa yŏksajŏk ingan* [Literature and People in History]. Seoul: Ch'angjak kwa pip'yŏngsa, 1980.

Kim Haktong. *Hanguk kaehwagi shiga yŏngu* [A Study on Late Nineteenth Century Poetry]. Seoul: Shimunhaksa, 1981.

Kim Inhwan. *Sangsangnyŏk kwa wŏngŭnbŏp* [Imagination and Perspective]. Seoul: Munhak kwa chisŏngsa, 1993.

Kim Kwangsun. *Ch'ŏngun sosŏl yŏngu* [A Study of Classic Heroic Novels]. Seoul: Hyŏngsŏl ch'ulp'ansa, 1980.

Kim Mungi. *Sŏmin kasa yŏngu* [A Study of Kasa by Commoners]. Seoul: Hyŏngsŏl ch'ulp'ansa, 1983.

Kim Yunshik. *Hanguk kŭndae munye pip'yŏngsa yŏngu* [A Study of the History of Modern Korean Literary Criticism]. Seoul: Hanyŏl mungo, 1973.

Kim Yunshik and Kim Hyŏn. *Hanguk munhak sa* [A History of Korean Literature]. Seoul: Minŭmsa, 1973.

Kwŏn Yŏngch'ŏl. *Kyubang kasa yŏngu* [A Study of Kyubang Kasa]. Seoul: Yiu ch'ulp'ansa, 1980.

Minjok Munhak Sa Yŏnguso, ed. *Minjok munhak sa kangjwa* [Lectures on the History of Nationalistic Korean Literature]. 2 vols. Seoul: Ch'angjak kwa pip'yŏngsa, 1995.

Ōtani, Morishige, *Chosŏn hugi sosŏl tŏkcha yŏngu* [A Study on the Readership for Novels in the Late Chosŏn Period]. Seoul: Minjok munhwa yŏnguso, Korea University, 1985.

Pak Ŭlsu. *Hanguk shijo munhak taesajŏn* [Comprehensive Dictionary of Korean Shijo Literature]. Seoul: Asaea munhwasa, 1992.

Pak Nojun. *Shilla kayo ŭi yŏngu* [A Study of Shilla Kayo]. Seoul: Yŏlhwadang, 1982.

——. *Koryŏ kayo ŭi yŏngu* [A Study of Koryŏ Songs]. Seoul: Saemunsa, 1990.

Sŏ Taesŏk. *Hanguk muga ŭi yŏngu* [A Study of Korean Shaman Chants]. Seoul: Munhak sasangsa, 1980.

———. *Kundam sosŏl ŭi kujo wa paegyŏng* [Classic War Novels: Background and Structure]. Seoul: Ewha Women's University Press, 1985.

Sŏ Yŏnho. *Hanguk kŭndae hŭigŭk sa yŏngu* [A Study of the History of Modern Korean Drama]. Seoul: Minjok munhwa yŏnguso, Korea University, 1982.

Song, Minho. *Hanguk kaehwagi sosŏl ŭi sajŏk yŏngu* [A Historical Study of the Korean Novel in the Late Nineteenth Century]. Seoul: Iljisa, 1975.

Yi Chaeho. *Hanguk hyŏndae sosŏl sa* [History of the Modern Korean Novel]. Seoul: Hongsŏngsa, 1979.

Yi Kawŏn. *Hanguk hanmunhak sa* [History of Korean Literature in Classical Chinese]. Seoul: Minjung sŏgwan, 1961.

Yi Usŏng and Im Yŏngt'aek, eds. *Yijo hanmun tanp'yŏnjip* [Anthology of Short Stories in Classical Chinese of the Chosŏn Period]. 3 vols. Seoul: Iljogak, 1973.

Index

Kim Hunggyu is professor of Korean literature at Korea University and is currently serving as director of The Korean Cultural Research Center at Korea University. He holds a Ph.D in Korean literature from Korea University. He is a specialist in traditional Korean poetry, particularly *shijo*, and is the author of a number of books and articles on traditional and modern Korean poetry.

Robert J. Fouser is a Ph.D candidate in applied linguistics at Trinity College, Dublin and associate professor at Kumamoto Gakuen University in Kumamoto, Japan. After completing a B.A. in Japanese language and literature at the University of Michigan, he studied Korean intensively at Seoul National University and lived in Korea for many years. He has written numerous articles on Korean art and culture.